MAN & WATER

L. Douglas James, *Editor*

MAN &
WATER

*The Social Sciences
in Management
of Water Resources*

THE UNIVERSITY PRESS OF KENTUCKY

This book is dedicated
to Howard W. Beers

A publication of the Center for Developmental Change
and the Kentucky Water Resources Institute
University of Kentucky

ISBN: 0-8131-1292-3

Library of Congress Catalog Card Number: 73-77253

Copyright © 1974 by The University Press of Kentucky

A statewide cooperative scholarly publishing agency
serving Berea College, Centre College of Kentucky,
Eastern Kentucky University, Georgetown College,
Kentucky Historical Society, Kentucky State University,
Morehead State University, Murray State University,
Northern Kentucky State College, Transylvania University,
University of Kentucky, University of Louisville, and
Western Kentucky University.

Editorial and Sales Offices: Lexington, Kentucky 40506

CONTENTS

1 The Challenge to the Social Sciences

L. Douglas James

From the dawn of history, people have felt a sense of helplessness as they observed the ravages of a flash flood or the slow, quiet death of prolonged drought. Some have been motivated by such experiences to try to do something, but very few have been able to use information gained from their observations to implement change. Many ideas failed (dry wells, breached levees, saline fields, and others), but some succeeded. Those who were successful were better able to withstand subsequent storms or droughts.

Thus through a series of failures and successes, people have gained an understanding of nature. They have painstakingly accumulated the technical ability to design, construct, and operate physical facilities to serve their desired ends. In the example that is the focus of this book, man has made water a *resource* he can use, and water resources development has enhanced his life.

New design technology increases the number of approaches man has available to accomplish any desired task (provide water to a city for example), but all his alternatives are not equally desirable. Certainly, the planner must make sure that his selection will physically accomplish the task (delivery of the water), but he must also *justify* the task as worth doing (does the city really need more water?). If the task is justified, he must determine the optimum design. He seeks a given performance at minimum sacrifice or maximum performance from a given sacrifice. For justification and optimization studies, estimates of both the sacrifices required to do the job and the values gained through performance of the completed job need to reflect direct effects on people as well as indirect effects on them through environmental change.

The job of learning how to use resources wisely in this broader sense requires the same trial-and-error experimentation as has the more familiar job of learning to design for physical performance. Hopefully, undesirable consequences can be detected before they become disasters, but experimentation cannot be avoided entirely. As his trials suggest better ways to sift through available alternatives to achieve social goals in the context of uncertain consequences and conflicting viewpoints, man will be able to transform water resources development for physical performance into water resources management for social performance.

Theoretical constructs and empirical information compiled by the social sciences can reduce reliance on prototype experimentation and thereby improve water resources management, but this expertise is not being used to anywhere near its potential. This book is dedicated to helping social scientists become more effective in contributing their expertise to formulating management policy so that resources management failures may be fewer and successes may be more frequent.

PURPOSES FOR WATER DEVELOPMENT

Water development is achieved by operation on some process within the hydrologic cycle. The facility used to modify a process in the hydrologic cycle is a project. Until recent years, most projects were built to meet a single need, or purpose. A brief review of the purposes of project construction as understood by engineers will introduce the social scientist to the vocabulary.

Disposal of Excess Water

A flood is "an overflow of lands which, although they are adjacent to water, are not normally covered by it, and hence are used (or usable) in the same way that other lands are used."[1] Interference with human activity as well as the destruction of property is considered flood damage. Flood control is the effort to reduce these damages in magnitude or frequency.[2] Drainage is the effort to reduce the damage or inconvenience associated with events which because of their long duration, localized character, or frequent occurrence cannot be considered floods.[3] Projects to reduce the ponding of water on highways or in urban areas or to lower field water tables to enhance plant growth are common examples of drainage projects.

Provision of Supplemental Water

Water is not always available where or when people want it. Water supply is the effort 1) to divert water from locations where it is readily available to other locations where it could be used more profitably or 2) to store water when it is plentiful for use in times of short supply. Irrigation is water supply for crops. Urban (or municipal and industrial) water is supplied to households, industries, commercial establishments, or public facilities.[4]

Use of Water in Streams

Water flowing in streams (or stored in reservoirs) has five distinct uses. Navigation is its use as a roadway for transport of freight or passengers.[5] Hydroelectric power plants convert the energy of moving water into electrical energy for transmission to widely dispersed areas.[6] Water is used to dispose of unwanted foreign substances so that they can degrade (convert by natural processes into harmless forms) in the stream or be discharged into the sea. Water quality control is the effort to confine the use of water as a waste carrier within socially acceptable bounds.[7] Recreation is the use of water to provide physical, mental, and emotional diversion through one or more of a range of activities that may be either active or passive, in the water or just nearby.[8] The fifth use relates to values from the flora and fauna in or along the stream. Such values range from commercial fishing profit to the esthetics of the stream environment. Fish and wildlife measures protect desirable species.[9] Other measures, such as insect control, eliminate undesirable ones. Projects such as channelization for navigation and reservoirs for low flow augmentation may serve up to five uses.

Conflicts and Complementarities

A project designed for one purpose invariably affects other uses of streams. If two uses enhance each other, the two are complementary. For example, surcharge storage on a water supply reservoir reduces flood peaks. If one use detracts from another (swamp drainage destroys wildlife habitats), the two are in conflict. Good planning seeks to take advantage of complementarities and to compromise conflicts. A multipurpose project is one planned, constructed, and operated to serve two or more purposes. A multiproject system is a group of projects planned, constructed, and operated in coordination.

OBJECTIVES OF WATER DEVELOPMENT

Ends Behind the Purposes

The purposes expressed for water resources development are means to more fundamental objectives. This fact has been officially recognized in the United States through congressional directives to water resources planners. The Flood Control Act of 1936 (U. S. Statutes 1570) established the policy of not building a project unless "benefits to whomsoever they may accrue are in excess of the estimated cost" and the "lives and social security of people" are enhanced.

Three aspects of this policy deserve special note. Benefits and costs must express the desirable and undesirable effects of a project in commensurable (monetary) units. Otherwise, numerical comparison is no index of whether or not a project should be built. The discipline of engineering economy originated from the need for more rational route selection in the railroad building era of the late 1800s and has developed a widely accepted set of procedures for comparing diverse effects occurring at different times.[10] Benefits (consequences is a more precise term) conventionally include the algebraic sum of all project effects whether they be positive or negative. Costs conventionally include all expenses of project construction and operation.

The second aspect is that "whomsoever" is meant to convey the best interest of humanity as a whole (or at least of all the people of the United States). This general viewpoint conforms to a fundamental criterion of welfare economics stated by Pareto. "Any change which harms no one and which makes some people better off (in their own estimation) must be considered to be an improvement."[11] The point here is to note the injection of individual sovereignty through the words *in their own estimation* and not to become sidetracked on how to resolve conflict situations in which some are harmed and others are helped (a matter discussed at length in the literature).[12] Not only are the objective aspects of the effect on each person (the cost of replacing damaged property) to be considered, but the individual's subjective feelings are to be considered too (sentimental attachment to irreplaceable property).

Thirdly, the impossibility of expressing all values in commensurable units is recognized. *Social security* encompasses all that affects the way a person perceives the quality of his life. The term transcends effects that can be assigned a monetary value to incorporate values traditionally called intangibles or irreducibles in engineering economy studies.

Even though the goal expressed in the 1936 legislation states the objective of water resources development to be to promote social gain in the broadest sense, the benefit-cost ratio based on dollar values of reducible effects has been the primary index of project merit over the last thirty-five years. Economists have made a major contribution in refining a methodology for reducing diverse effects, but many people feel that it still does not properly recognize important considerations.[13] After a six-year study (1965-1971), a Special Task Force of the United States Water Resources Council[14] recommended that the traditional procedure of estimating economic effects and accompanying the estimates with a side display describing the intangibles be replaced by estimates of effects in terms of an accounting based on four separate, but not necessarily equal, objectives.[15] The concept is for the planning agency to assess positive as well as negative consequences with respect to each objective in separate accounting ledgers and summarize ledger contents in a manner that will allow political decision makers to examine tradeoffs among objectives. The four accounts attempt to capture explicitly the full scope of social performance as the underlying purpose of resource development.

Substance of the Four Accounts

1) *National Economic Development:* The economic development objective is to maximize the dollar value of project benefits net of costs in order to maximize national income through economic efficiency and thus ensure that every dollar invested yields the greatest number of dollars in return.[16] Benefits converted into monetary units include "the value to users of increased outputs of goods and services," values gained through external economies, and values gained through the use of unemployed resources. Costs include the value of resources used to implement the plan, values lost through external diseconomies, and values lost as resources are displaced and subsequently become unemployed.[17] The adjective *national* expresses the concept that effects should be counted no matter where in the nation they occur and does not imply any preference for projects for which either costs or benefits are widely distributed throughout the country. The distinctiveness of this objective is that it includes all project effects that can be expressed in monetary units.

2) *Environmental Quality:* The environmental quality objective is to restore, conserve, or improve the quality of natural and cultural resources and ecological systems in ways beyond those that can be expressed in monetary units. Specific items include changes to areas of natural beauty (open and green space, wild and scenic rivers, mountain or wilderness areas, and estuaries, for example) and to especially valuable archeological, historical, biological, and geological resources. Effects on environmental pollution (water, land, and air) are also included. Special stress is given to

the importance of avoiding irreversible effects.[18] The archeological and historical resources are likely to be of the greatest professional interest to social scientists.

In measuring progress toward national economic development, once all values are expressed in monetary units, no ambiguity exists either in comparing magnitudes or in *distinguishing desirable from undesirable effects.* Environmental effects, however, are expressed in terms of a variety of "relevant physical or ecological criteria or dimensions, including the appropriate qualitative dimensions."[19] Examples include trees, fish, or river miles. Since diverse units cannot be aggregated, project desirability with respect to this account cannot be expressed in a single index. The tradeoffs among gains and losses have to be made by politically chosen decision makers or through some public participation process. Of special interest to social scientists is the problem of decision making when one individual perceives environmental loss from the same change another perceives as environmental gain. Some way is needed to associate perceptions of desirability with physical measurement of environmental change and to reconcile differences among individuals and interest groups in their attitudes toward various kinds of environmental change.

3) *Social Well-Being:* The social well-being objective is to enhance the lives of people in ways that cannot be adequately expressed in monetary units or through quantitative measurement of environmental change. Relevant effects include changes in population patterns, security from hazards to health and safety, national economic stability, educational and cultural opportunities, national security, and in distribution of gains and losses between rural and urban areas or among socioeconomic groups.[20] One way to measure progress toward the objective is to categorize and describe all the ways in which the lives of people are effected by a certain project and to estimate the number of people affected in each category. Social scientists can potentially contribute a great deal toward systematic measurement and analysis of these effects and toward the development of methods for reconciling interpersonal differences in viewpoint on the desirability of any given change.

4) *Regional Development:* The regional development objective is to distribute fairly the benefits from achieving the first three objectives over the total geographical area of the country. Regional development is measured through the magnitude of each cash flow (monetary value received or sacrificed), each environmental change, and each effect on social well-being specified by 173 defined trade areas.[21] It is more difficult to measure progress toward regional development than toward the other objectives because most project effects can be predicted in total

magnitude more easily than they can be designated by location. Some people doubt whether more equitable distribution of effects by trade areas is really as legitimate a national goal as more equitable distribution between rich and poor, farm and city, and the other class distinctions contained in the social welfare concept. The practical problems of measuring welfare by trade area and of reconciling conflicting viewpoints among areas are of interest to social scientists.

Procedure for Applying the Four Accounts

The procedure for applying the four accounts to water resources management decisions is far from settled. The official recommendations, as of the end of 1971, were not to use social well-being as a separate objective and to use regional development only if specifically authorized for depressed areas.[22] Environmental quality was recommended as an objective. Environmental effects thus moved from the status of being a side display of intangibles (given qualitative and often secondary consideration when decision makers compared alternatives for economic merit) to the status of a joint indicator of merit along with economics.[23] The changes required in procedures for gathering information for management decisions are under study, and it is still premature to predict how the overall direction of water resources management will be affected.

The question of how best to present information on social effects to decision makers is still open and is rightfully a topic of interest to social scientists on its own. There can be little doubt that the need to consider social well-being is generally recognized. The influence of social well-being on congressional decisions is seen in an empirical study by Haveman who found that "a substantial number of the projects which failed to satisfy the benefit-cost criterion when maximum national income or economic efficiency was the sole objective do, in fact, satisfy it when the objective is multidimensional."[24]

Means for Ends

The traditional water development purposes are only a few of many possible physical means (for example, education, health services, police protection) for furthering basic objectives set forth in this section. Comprehensive program development in the spirit of the four accounts will reveal cases where water resources development for one or more purposes is in order. It will reveal other cases where it is more appropriate to change the mode of operating existing facilities than to build new ones. In still other cases, capital expenditures for purposes other than water development will be found more appropriate. In fact, the most appropriate alternative is sometimes for people to adjust to their environment rather than try to change it.

A Philosophy of Water Management

The above methodology provides a scientific approach to water resources management but does little to portray the emotional commitment often found among those who have viewed the wastelands of earth, dreamed of making them into gardens, and built civilizations on their accomplishments. The Dutch diked out the sea, drained swamps with windmills, and (through a spirit captured in the story of the small boy who held his hand in the dike through the long, cold night) built their country into a world power with the most distinctive culture of Europe. The American frontier moved westward as men built dams to hold the water from melting snows to irrigate summer crops. The frontier spirit that made the deserts blossom is still a strong force in American culture. In the mid-twentieth century, Jews from around the world have fulfilled the words of their ancient prophets by returning to the long barren land of their ancestors and restoring its agriculture and forests. Other examples of how man has used water as a key factor in his economic and cultural development range from the terraced rice paddies of Luzon to the farmlands along the Nile.

Man has ingeniously used water as a resource to upgrade the quality of his life. Pipes have brought water into the home and ended the walk to the well. Aqueducts have brought water to cities and made possible a growth that could provide employment and the amenities of urban living. Drainage systems have almost eliminated mire and mud in city streets. Sanitary systems have carried away piles of garbage and human waste and protected against the spread of waterborne disease. Irrigation has provided fresh fruit and vegetables throughout the year. The convenience of sure and instantaneous power has reduced daily drudgery and the oppressiveness of summer heat. Inland lakes have opened new vistas for outdoor recreation to those who never had such opportunities before.

All this is not to deny that these benefits have had their price. Tremendous personal sacrifices were forced on people who did not want to make them. Whole civilizations collapsed when water systems failed during drought or were destroyed by enemies. The environment has been scarred, and many see a grave threat to the environmental base essential to man's physical and mental health.

Many say the threat is so grave that water resources development should stop. If it is stopped, the message is clear to those who still carry their water in a jug from a distant well, who live by subsistence agriculture, who shiver in the cold and swelter in the heat, who bury their own waste and see their children die from typhus when their neighbor does not, who seldom eat a green vegetable and cannot study under an electric light. They have no hope for anything better. The threat is also clear to those who have the necessities of life but dream of new ways to upgrade their lives. Every change in life style changes the demands on water resources. Water resources development cannot be stopped. It is the formulation of new ways to upgrade life that captures the true spirit of resource management.

PROCESSES IN WATER DEVELOPMENT

Process Classification

When man sees an opportunity to further his objectives by some change to his water resources management program, he needs to proceed on two levels. For optimization, he needs to go into the detail required to specify an exact design for possible implementation. For justification, he needs to view the proposal from a perspective that will permit him to decide whether the idea is worthwhile or not. Good planning on both levels depends on an ability to forecast future performance, and that ability comes through an understanding of the processes or causative sequences of events connected by linkages through which the character of a preceding event influences the character of a subsequent one.

Good planning is thus founded on a perceptive understanding of relevant linkages that need to be classified for orderly analysis. One type of classification is by the governing laws. Some linkages follow laws in the physical sciences (the quantity of power generated by a given flow through a power plant) while others follow laws in the social sciences (the number of visitors attracted to a recreational lake) or in the biological sciences (the number of fish that can live in a reservoir).

Linkages can also be classified by their strength. Some events become the sole cause of subsequent events (building a dam forms a lake). Other events depend on interactions among a number of causes (industrial development requires labor, transportation, water, and so forth). An event may lead to one outcome in one context of related interacting events and another outcome in another context (a project may unify a people in the common desire to upgrade their lives or become a point of continual controversy between opposing camps). Few processes can be fully explained through simple cause-and-effect linkages; interacting causes are the normal situation. Microlinkages are on a small scale and are more likely to represent simple cause and effect (a field yielding twice as much corn with supplemental irrigation). Macrolinkages are on a large scale and

almost always highly interactive (the effect of water resources development as one aspect of modern technology in changing the character of the
economy and the environment of the country).

A third way to classify linkages is by order. A first-order linkage (or
consequence) occurs when one event is the direct cause of a following
event (supplemental water increases a farmer's income by increasing his
crop yield). A second-order linkage occurs when one event causes a second
event and the second event causes a third event (cotton mills have more
cotton to process because farmers use water to grow more cotton). Chains
of third- and higher-order linkages can be outlined. Relationships of higher
order are very interactive and difficult to estimate in a quantitative way,
but they are likely to determine important macroeffects, relating to
technological, environmental, and economic change.

The social processes are of particular interest in this book. Since social
linkages are not understood as well as physical linkages, an appropriate
way to expand the base of social knowledge is by examining the pathway
others have already followed in expanding the base of technological
knowledge.

Physical Processes

The stages of growth in sophistication of man's understanding of physical
processes is illustrated by the steps through which he has learned to
understand the hydrologic cycle. In an excellent treatise, Kazmann traces
from antiquity man's growth in ability to explain events within the
hydrologic cycle.[25] The early mythology of whimsical supernatural
powers was followed by logic reasoned by the Greek philosophers from
what they perceived to be fundamental principles (ca. 350 B.C.). However,
these principles were found to contain major errors when the curious
began to measure actual rainfall and streamflow events (ca. 1650). Hydrology thereafter turned to controlled experiments to express in mathematical formulas the relationship among the interacting variables in individual
linkages. Recently (ca. 1965) mathematical models, combining formulas
representing individual linkages, have been developed to duplicate
observed event sequences (simulate streamflow from rainfall, for example)
from information on the events that caused them. The formulas have been
derived from scientific experiments where possible, but hydrologists are
still required by necessity to use empiricisms to explain key linkages.

Man's desire to manage water to further his objectives, however, has not
waited for hydrology to develop a truly comprehensive forecasting model.
Engineered design based on false principles led to failures, but the successful designs led to empirical rules that made the next design better. Some,

such as sizing a culvert from the time required to ride around a watershed on horseback, were very crude, but they filled a need when research lagged.

Man has learned, through his research and its applications, that physical processes are not unexplainable but rather are governed by a relatively few basic forces acting on physical matter. Gravity causes rain to fall and water to run downhill. Solar radiation provides the energy that causes water to evaporate and to rise into the atmosphere, only to cool, condense, and fall again. These forces act on a relatively few basic materials. The examples of air, soil, and water stand out in the hydrologic cycle. The aim of research is to understand how materials respond to forces in different contexts.

As man has expanded his understanding of these physical processes, the forces behind them, and the materials on which they act, he has developed a technology able to adjust physical process patterns for his own purposes. The technology of water resources development has established widely accepted procedures for use in engineering design and has trained a multitude of engineers how to apply them.[26] Their effort has made possible the construction of increasingly large and more complex systems of dams, power plants, and conduits.

Biological Processes

The physical facilities constructed for resource development directly disrupt plant and animal life and produce effects through higher-ordered linkages by causing environmental changes around them and in the areas they serve. For example, because species are linked through food chains, changes in the population of one species have repercussions throughout the system. An understanding of causal relationships among living organisms is important to many water resources management policy decisions. Of special interest to the social sciences are relationships involving interactions between living things and nonliving habitats as studied under the heading of ecology. From the days of Hippocrates, physicians have recognized interactions between physical and mental health and the environment.[27] The recent literature has emphasized the need for man to develop a "generally acceptable and beneficial environmental ethic."[28]

Biological linkages definitely need to be considered by social scientists as they devise criteria and procedures for better water resources management. Biologists, on the other hand, are going to be required to develop quantitative means of tying environmental disturbances to effects on various life forms. Some biologists argue that resource development should wait until they learn which environmental disturbances will be disastrous. This argument loses its credibility unless biologists are making a concentrated effort to forecast more accurately. The same imperative to add constructiveness to criticism applies to social scientists.

Design Processes

The role of design is to devise a physical facility or a management program capable of performing a designated function. The designer must begin with the need expressed by his client and develop a way to deal with it. He must specify his end product in all the detail that implementation personnel require to produce a working prototype. For example, where the need for a firm water supply is best met by a reservoir, the dam's size and location must be figured to the nearest inch. A workable combination of spillways and outlet works must be detailed. Suitable materials must be chosen and fabricated in a manner that will withstand whatever forces the dam may encounter over time. Construction methods must be chosen, and even the day to begin must be selected.[29]

Many questions may be resolved by using the principles of engineering economy to determine the design that can handle anticipated physical events at least cost.[30] If the physical processes causing those events are poorly understood, a factor of safety is added and a larger or more durable design is specified. As research or experience produces a better understanding of key linkages, design economy can be achieved because less money is spent for precautions made necessary by uncertainty.

The physical sciences have given man the ability to forecast future extremes of physical forces and event sequences and specify designs that function to provide the desired outputs under a wide range of physical conditions. The complexity of the design process, however, is greatly increased by opening it to consideration of what functions should be served. These issues can only be resolved by predicting how the alternatives affect people and by comparing the desirability of the predicted effects. Man had to develop an understanding of physical processes in order to be able to act at all; he must improve his understanding of social processes in order to be able to act wisely.

Social Processes

Social linkages explain the way people react to one another and to their environment. A given linkage involves a perception of an outside event, the formation of an attitude toward that event, and a subsequent pattern of behavior modified by that attitude.[31] Man's understanding of how people perceive and react is being expanded through research in the social sciences that is going through much the same phases as described previously for hydrology. However, the inability of social institutions to keep pace with, let alone direct, technological advance is a major social problem. In a study unrelated to water resources, Mesthene notes that "we have not made very much progress . . . in tracing the cause-effect relationships, by which technological innovation leads to changes in society."[32]

The physical scientist has long felt a responsibility to develop the understanding required to design for physical performance. He has responded to demands for technological improvement with answers (or guesses) and sometimes made mistakes. The social scientist is just beginning to experience a pressure to contribute to social improvement. He still shows much more reluctance toward constructing the models of social processes required to predict consequences and then choose wisely among alternatives than he does toward advocating pet social programs. As Forrester has appropriately asked, "What justification can there be for the apparent assumption that we do not know enough to construct models but believe we do know enough to directly design new social systems by passing laws and starting new social programs?"[33]

All this is not to imply that social scientists are not making progress toward a better understanding of how man responds to the physical, biological, and social forces touching his life. Even though man as a research subject is infinitely more difficult to experiment with and to understand than are the materials studied by physical scientists, social scientists are beginning to collect substantial empirical data and to derive many useful constructs. The state of the art is still far short of the general response models found in hydrology, but social science data can make substantial contributions to better resource management.

The range of social processes relevant to water resources management is best seen by visualizing the job required to plan in the manner recommended by the Water Resources Council.[34] Social effects occur on the microlevel and on the macrolevel, from sole causes and through complex interactions, and from first-order contact through multiorder chains of events. More specific illustrations are found by considering a large dam and reservoir as an example.

To begin with, social processes operate within agencies responsible for planning the project. As stated by Wiener, it is a mistake to consider a plan as an "impersonal product of a planning methodology"; it is rather "the very personal intellectual fruit of an individual."[35] This individual works with a group of professional colleagues and is subject to constraints imposed by the policies of his employing agency and a wide range of influences from his private life. The constraints and biases these interacting factors impart to planning need to be better understood.

Some social processes are set in motion because land areas are required for project construction. People learn they will lose their homes, feel a grave personal loss, experience a series of emotional negotiations over price, collect their money, and find their social relationships and possibly their economic status altered after they move. Others feel the loss of their neighbors or part of their property but also perceive opportunities to gain from the project. Still others may live some distance from the project but feel a loss when they learn natural or cultural features are to be inundated. Social scientists can contribute a great deal toward a better understanding of the attachments people have to their homes, their community, and natural areas; of how individuals interact to establish a group consensus and influence public opinion; and of how to minimize the social harm as people suffer adverse consequences from plan implementation.

Many social processes are set in motion by project implementation and performance. Individuals who work on construction may increase their income and gain training through job experience that may upgrade their lives and guide their children toward still better lives. Individuals less exposed to devastating floods may be freed from a burden that once drained their incentive to improve themselves. The whole social and economic framework of a community may change as a project entices new employment opportunities. Other communities may suffer when jobs move elsewhere (for example, losses to Southeastern cotton farming with shifts to irrigated cotton in the Southwest). The culture of a community near a reservoir may change from an agricultural to a recreational orientation. The structure of a local government may be changed as property is removed from the tax roles and as induced migrations into and out of the area change the composition of the population and the views of the old-timers. The confrontations and compromises made in the political exchanges culminating in the decision for construction may affect compromises on many other political issues.

Some social processes are set in motion by the financial arrangements used to pay for the project. Funds diverted from other programs in the public sector affect people who formerly benefitted from those programs. Funds collected in taxes from the private sector reduce the funds the taxpayer has left for investment and consumption and may affect his motivation to work for self-improvement. Funds collected in financing a project through user charges reduce the use of project output (water, navigable waterways, recreation beaches, for example) and dampen the enthusiasm for project construction of those who do not receive free service but must pay for what they get. Social scientists can contribute to a better understanding of the perceptions and compromises that go into working out the financial arrangements and of the consequences given arrangements have on people.

A constructed project must be operated. Comprehensive operation goes beyond day-to-day execution of established rules. Sometimes the optimum management practice is to change these rules (as to the division between flood control and recreation storage in a reservoir, for example), but the commitments made during project planning usually make such rule changes institutionally difficult to implement. Often, flexibility is severely constrained by statutory law, administrative policy, and the contracts signed for project financing. Prolonged inflexibility, however, leads to alienation created by outdated policies and has important consequences for social stability.

Some very important social processes involve large-scale linkages. Each new project brings a further change in the balances between public and private investment, between the natural and the man-made in the environment, between the rural and the urban sectors of the economy, and between beneficiaries and society at large. The accumulative effects of many projects may set processes in motion that no one project can individually.

Obviously, our present understanding of these many social linkages is inadequate to predict the differences in consequences among alternatives in more than a vague, qualitative way. Methods for forecasting how resource development will affect people need to be improved in order to develop better designs; better design is becoming increasingly critical as expanding population and technology intensify the consequences of error.

Choice Processes

A choice process is the procedure used to define options, gather information on differences in their effects, and reach a decision. Choices may be classified by whether they are made by individuals or by groups. The options may be classified by whether they are structural options for changing the physical system or nonstructural options for changing human adjustment to a fixed system. The four possibilities may be illustrated by examples from the alternatives for dealing with flood hazard. A decision by the owner of a building to make it watertight so that floods will not damage the contents (commonly called flood-proofing) is an example of a structural option executed by individual choice. A structural option executed by group choice is exemplified by a decision of a community to build a levee along the river bank so that water cannot enter the town. A nonstructural option executed by individual choice is illustrated by a decision to sell one's floodplain home and move to higher ground. An example of a nonstructural option executed by group choice is a decision to zone a floodplain as a hazard area not to be developed for urban use.

The practice is to emphasize group choices in formulating water resources management policy; however, a sound policy requires a thorough understanding of the forces influencing decisions at all levels. People react to structural measures and legal requirements to conform to nonstructural policy in ways determined by their attitudes, their perceptions of the policy, and the way the policy was communicated to them. Group non-structural management approaches will succeed best if they can be communicated to individuals in ways that will make them want to con-form rather than feel they are being required to conform. For the flood control example, zoning has not been found to be effective in keeping people from building houses on floodplains that are widely perceived as attractive homesites. The more factors that planners use (poor access, unattractive appearance, undesirable neighboring land use) to make people perceive floodplains as undesirable residential locations, the more effective zoning will be. Social scientists can contribute a great deal to the under-standing needed in order to make nonstructural measures effective.

The ideal information on which to base a choice is 1) a clear definition of all the alternatives, 2) precise statements of the consequences of each alternative as obtained by examining each physical, social, and biological process that would be set in motion, and 3) a consolidation of the information showing major differences among alternatives.[36] Special care should be used to display tradeoffs between pairs of alternatives.[37] The ideal choice process is to review the information in an objective manner and then decide from the national or "to whomsoever" viewpoint.

Real choices are made from limited information. Individuals seldom spend much time at information gathering, and corporations and public agencies formalize the process for relatively few decisions. On the whole, more information is gathered for making group choices than for making individual ones; and more information is gathered for making choices on structural than on nonstructural options. The best informed choices are thus on group structural measures, and yet the large water resources development projects resulting from these choices seem to be the choices that have come under the most extensive criticism. Worse resource man-agement mistakes are probably being made through the other three cate-gories of choices, but the information base is often insufficient to detect that something is wrong, let alone correct it.

Real choices are also often made from a narrow or biased viewpoint. Individual choices emphasize the personal viewpoint of the chooser, though everyone has some concern for the welfare of others. Group choices emphasize a public viewpoint, but political and jurisdictional differences as well as bias or even graft prevent this ideal from being achieved. Choices are frequently made on both levels by people who can't or don't take the time to comprehend the information they have. Often conscious choices are avoided, and the state of *nondecision* causes choices by the less cautious to govern. At all levels, the specific points that swing decisions are poorly understood. The color of the folder has been known to make the difference.

History provides many examples of how people have used their land and water resources in ways they later regretted. Some of the most devastating abuses have been the aggregate consequence of thoughtless actions on the individual level (littering, carelessly causing fires, using environmentally harmful products, and others) by people who gain little personal advantage but are too busy or too unconcerned to care. Other environmental abuses have resulted from people pursuing economic gain or some other specific (and worthy) benefit. Sometimes they overlook or choose to ignore the broader viewpoint. At other times hindsight proves a calculated risk not to have been worthwhile. Communities have enticed industry because they wanted the jobs and then objected to the price of polluted air and water.

Some of the most complicated social choice issues involve externalities, situations where choices by one individual affect others who are neither obligated to pay for the good they receive nor able to collect for the harm.[38] The external diseconomies of pollution are of particular concern. Increased populations and levels of output are increasing the production of waste products, and natural sinks, where wastes can be harmlessly dissipated into the environment, are being exhausted.[39] In essence, the desire of society to limit the ill effects of the external diseconomies caused by individuals acting in self-interest and the desire to take advantage of opportunities to realize external economies are key factors justifying group decisions in a democratic society.

Role of the Social Scientist

Physical, biological, design, social, and choice processes may be portrayed as sequences in which each event is an effect of what comes before and a contributory cause of what follows. Building a better understanding of these cause-and-effect linkages for physical and biological processes is primarily the concern of other disciplines, but understanding design, social, and choice processes is of interest to social scientists. The social sciences have the expertise and with it the responsibility to improve man's understanding of how differences in the physical world vary in their effects on people, of what can be done to encourage people to react differently to their physical surroundings, and of how choices are made. Better understanding of which alternatives are socially feasible and of how decisions are made provides a better basis for designing alternatives so that future decisions will be more effective.

THE CHALLENGE

The Source of the Imperative

The technology that has multiplied man's capability to change his physical world has simultaneously increased his responsibility to develop mechanisms for using this technical capability wisely. The job will certainly require a major effort on the part of social scientists to develop the models required to predict differences in effects among alternatives. The models will not meet the needs of decision makers, however, unless better procedures are developed for using available information wisely. Before going on to explore the needed modeling capability in greater detail, two critical aspects of decision making require more discussion. The first is the need for better coordination between individual and group choices. The second is the need to remain flexible enough to change past choices that prove wrong. As to coordination, group choices must be widely accepted to be successful. A public awareness of group choices must be created or countless individual choices may completely negate the best conceived policy. A sense of public participation is often needed if individuals are to feel they have contributed to the decision making in a way that gives them incentive to make the group choice work.

As to flexibility, the long term general welfare requires that even the best policies be regularly reviewed. Human goals are time variant. The effects of an implemented alternative can only be known with certainty by trial. The viewpoint that society has to "muddle through" because people cannot really know if they want something without experiencing it contains a lot of truth.[40] In a thoughtful study of what biological change can tell us about social change, Dunn notes how "we must come to understand how social systems behave as learning systems."[41] The design of responsive and socially acceptable feedback mechanisms for monitoring social change and redirecting it to promote social objectives presents many major challenges to social scientists.

Theoretical and Practical Needs

If they are to provide the better understanding of key processes required to reach informed resource management decisions, social scientists must 1) develop more comprehensive theories for explaining key linkages and 2) communicate their theories to those who must resolve day-to-day management questions. Many social scientists have felt the need for better resources management but have been unable to relate their expertise to the need. A major objective of this book is to help the social scientist focus on situations in which current resource management policy is doing the poorest job of achieving social objectives.

The challenge of the social scientist oriented toward theory is to develop better constructs for explaining how people react in given situations. The explanation needs to be quantitative, but most constructs will have to be expressed in a probabilistic manner. For example, a typical construct would predict that type-of-person A in the context of the set-of-events B would have probability X of choosing C and probability Y of choosing D. Such constructs can be used to provide the linkages in a simulation model, the most powerful tool for formulating water resources management policy.[42] Limited understanding of causal linkages in sequences of social events has been a major factor limiting the development of useful models.

The challenge to the social scientist oriented toward applied problems is to help those responsible for resource management to apply available theoretical constructs in ways that will lead to better choices in day-to-day decision making. For better group decisions, a great deal of care is needed in documenting and presenting models so that planners can apply them and properly interpret the results. Also required are empirical approximations for predicting consequences in situations where theory is too fragmentary to be helpful. Sometimes, these approximations must be just as crude as those of the old-time hydrologist who sized a culvert by riding around the watershed.

Better individual decisions require mechanisms for increasing the frequency with which people perceive that their own best interest is served by working with, rather than against, group decisions and the common welfare. For example, charges levied on polluters may provide an economic incentive for reducing pollution if regulatory measures are not doing the job.[43] Another mechanism is to reinforce perceptions that encourage people to conform to public policy. Techniques for making a floodplain appear undesirable for residence have been mentioned previously.

The physical sciences relating to water resources management once went through much the same conflict between the theoretical and the applied currently found in the social sciences. Kline traces the conflict in fluid mechanics between hydraulics based on applying empirical data to

practical designs and hydrodynamics based on mathematics and idealiz-
ations about fluid flow.[44] He quotes the nineteenth century hydraulicians
as calling the hydrodynamicists "a collection of wooly-minded theorists,
who would not know a practical problem if it bit them," while the
hydrodynamicists referred to the hydraulicians as "slightly educated
plumbers." The late nineteenth century was an era when both groups were
developing relatively sophisticated methods for analyzing fluid flow at the
same time debate raged in the United States government on whether
streamflow measurement was really needed for irrigation project design.[45]
Eighty years later, social scientists are debating theory while government
planners overlook some of the most elementary principles for meeting
social needs.

Models of Social Processes

A model represents a process in a way that can be used to take information on causes (forces) and the materials (people) those causes affect and
to abstract from that information a prediction of how the process will
operate into the future. The quality of the model depends on how closely
and how consistently it yields predictions that in retrospect prove to have
matched prototype performance. Traditionally, water resources engineers
have gathered empirical information on measurable physical phenomena,
analyzed their data in the framework of known physical laws, and con-
densed their findings into formulas, tables, or monographs for use in
design. Traditionally, social scientists have collected empirical information
on human *response,* analyzed their data to develop improved constructs of
human interactions, and presented their findings in scholarly journals. The
task of the model builder is to construct from theory and empirical data a
formulation of the process and the information needed to model it.

The model builder must define the total process, subdivide the whole
into its subprocesses or linkages, and diagram the relationships among
these linkages. The task of capturing the essence of a complicated process
(for example, the movement of people onto a floodplain where they
experience floods and respond to damage) involves the art of deciding
which linkages have a significant effect on the outcome, finding adequate
expressions of the cause-and-effect relationships operating within each
linkage, and expressing information on these linkages in a manner commensurate with the model as a whole.

Some understanding of a process may be gained from qualitative
descriptions of its linkages. Mathematical representation in a form suitable
for computerization is necessary, however, for more complex and more
realistic models. Some linkages can be adequately represented by deter-

ministic constructs that portray what will happen in a given situation as something that can be known with certainty. Deterministic constructs adequately represent the trajectory of a cannon ball, but most social processes are better represented by probabilistic constructs that list all the possible outcomes to a given situation and use empirical data to assign probabilities to each such linkage from a situation to an outcome. Once the linkage to an outcome is known, that outcome becomes the situation for the next stage of possible outcomes with empirically assigned probabilities. By using Monte Carlo methods and random numbers, one can start with the initial situation and pick the linkages that define one possible route through the total process. This simulation process can be repeated many times to define the distribution of possible outcomes for use in decision making.[46]

Predictive models built from deterministic linkage constructs can contribute to many water management decisions. For example, an input-output model uses economic linkages to predict the consequences of production changes in one industry on other sectors of the economy.[47] Input-output models can also be used to forecast the effects of production changes on air and water pollution.[48] Predictive models built from probabilistic linkages are available for simulating other aspects of human behavior.[49]

The list of processes for which new predictive models could contribute to better management is long. Possibilities include models of people moving onto floodplain land, reacting to stream pollution or power shortages, or voting on referendums or bond issues. A model beginning with the perceptions and attitudes that lead people to litter public areas could contribute to better maintenance of recreation facilities as well as to new approaches for reducing land pollution.

Predictive models, however, don't get to the heart of social processes. Social systems have been aptly characterized by Forrester as multiloop nonlinear feedback systems.[50] They are feedback systems because the choices that determine future events depend on perceptions of past events. A single decision maker acting on a single process perceives the state or output of the process, acts to improve it, observes the change, and acts again. The sequences of observation and adjustment are called loops. Chances are that at the same time someone else will also be observing the same process and exerting his influence to accomplish other changes. Thus, multiloop systems are involved. The nonlinearity comes from the fact that the outcome of any action is not directly proportional to the effort put into it. Feedback loops must be built into any model that is truly going to simulate the dynamic behavior of social systems. For example, feedback models have provided many useful insights into a better understanding of urban systems.[51] Well-constructed feedback models would make a major contribution to better water resources management.

Prototype Feedback Systems

The primary importance of the feedback concept, however, is not in building more realistic models. Prototype feedback systems monitor social states, report information to decision makers, and result in actions to change the state for the better. Social scientists can do a great deal to make each step more effective. The monitoring requires 1) the development of social indicators indexing the current situation in terms of the social objectives and 2) procedures for routinely gathering the data needed to know current values for these indicators.[52] A number of indicators are available for measuring progress toward national economic development (gross national product, unemployment, personal incomes, and others), but data on environmental quality and social well-being are fragmentary at best. Bauer has well noted that "for many of the important topics on which social critics blithely pass judgment, and on which policies are made, there are no yardsticks by which to know if things are getting better or worse."[53] The recent work by the Water Resources Council in defining water resources management objectives needs to be followed by the regular collection of information on social (and environmental and regional) indicators if planners are to know whether or not the multiple objectives are being achieved.

The primary imperative for better social monitoring is that no matter how sophisticated choice processes become, mistakes will be made. Some mistakes can have very severe consequences, and these can only be minimized by employing both monitoring procedures that can detect when something is just starting to go wrong, and decision-making procedures that can rapidly correct for error.[54] The monitoring must be able to detect the consequences of aggregations of individual decisions. The corrective procedure must be able to overcome the inertia inherent in reversing group decisions and must quickly induce change in decisions by individuals.

Specific Management Needs

Social scientists can 1) contribute conceptual order to man's understanding of social processes and 2) use the understanding they gain to provide practical advice on specific resource management policy decisions. Contributions at both levels relate to five specific management needs.

1) The alternatives need to be more specifically defined. Social

scientists must take the leadership in defining viable nonstructural alternatives (land-use control, population control, life-style adjustments). The engineer has developed the expertise needed to advise decision makers if structural designs will not work for technical reasons or to recommend design changes for more efficient performance from those that do work. The social scientist needs to develop and apply this kind of expertise with respect to the nonstructural approaches if such approaches are ever going to become truly viable alternatives. Social scientists can also contribute by developing ways for expanding the awareness of all design options into all choice processes.

2) The consequences of alternatives need to be more accurately predicted. Social scientists need to develop better models for forecasting the effects of the alternatives on people and for anticipating how people will react to changes in resource availability or in the environment.

3) Social objectives need to be more precisely stated. The fourfold objectives recommended by the Water Resources Council are clearly not the last word.[55] The goals individuals strive for from life and society's concept of what constitutes a fair compromise of goal conflicts among individuals are continually changing. Social scientists can contribute more precise goal statements, better ways to maintain goal statements as current expressions of what people want, and more equitable means for resolving goal conflicts.

4) Policy decisions need to be more expeditiously implemented. Each implementation (from a dam to a zoning ordinance) causes social change and encounters inertia if not hostility. Social scientists first need to develop a better understanding of how people react to change and then need to advise on how to implement policies so as to minimize adverse reactions. Special effort is needed to develop more effective ways to implement nonstructural alternatives.

5) The consequences of current policy (implemented choices) need to be more conscientiously monitored.

Breadth of the Challenge

The challenge specified at these five levels in the context of water resources management relates to the desire of the "new" social scientist to make vital inputs into public policy in fields such as transportation systems, urban renewal, poverty programs, national defense, and pollution control. Water resources management provides a convenient context for discussing the obstacles to better teamwork among social scientists, technical experts, and politically chosen decision makers.

In every area of modern life an expanded understanding of physical processes opens the door to more sophisticated designs. Each technological advance opens the door to new abuse of man's environment or upset in social relationships. The most ardent conservationist must admit that severe water shortages or devastating floods create serious social problems. The strongest advocate of industrial expansion must recognize the threat of unconstrained pollution. The challenge is to create a strategy for selecting the best ways to apply technology, for implementing the strategy in a manner least likely to set off adverse social shock waves, and for monitoring the implementation to make sure it continues to work effectively.

Many of those who review the progress of mankind see a process of unbalanced growth.[56] A society moves far ahead in one area only to find its neglect of another area has created a bottleneck to further advancement. Only by a concentrated effort to overcome this restriction is further progress possible. Our society may well be approaching a bottleneck to improvement of the general welfare as technological solutions meet increasing resistance. One can see the beginnings of a concentrated effort to break up this bottleneck evolving within the Federal Council for Science and Technology and the Office of Water Resources Research.[57] These organizations desire to support research in the social sciences which will develop a better strategy for resource management.

THE DISCIPLINES

Some idea of the effort being made within the social science disciplines to contribute to more effective water resources management can be obtained from the number of active researchers supported by the U.S. Office of Water Resources Research by discipline as noted in the accompanying table. The effort in the social sciences is shown to lag far behind that in the physical and the biological sciences and their engineering applications; moreover, the research effort within the social sciences relative to these other disciplines has not been changing much. Within the social sciences, economics has consistently accounted for nearly two-thirds of the total effort, but participation in anthropology and sociology has been growing most rapidly.

Between 1967 and 1969, the Committee on Science and Public Policy of the National Academy of Sciences and the Problems and Policy Committee of the Social Science Research Council assembled a panel of scholars from a number of disciplines, including each of these five, and had each panel define, review, and appraise its field of knowledge. These statements provide a point of departure for those familiar with water

Scientific Disciplines of Professional Investigators
of Office of Water Resources Research Title I Projects

	1966	1967	1968	1969	1970	1971	1972
Social Sciences	63	107	123	151	152	146	169
Anthropology	0	1	1	4	5	9	4
Economics	45	72	88	100	95	86	116
Geography	9	14	13	13	16	11	15
Political Science	5	13	13	16	21	17	18
Sociology	4	7	8	18	15	23	16
(% of Total)	(10)	(13)	(13)	(13)	(13)	(12)	(13)
Agriculture & Forestry	46	58	62	85	79	68	78
(% of Total)	(8)	(7)	(6)	(7)	(6)	(5)	(6)
Biological Sciences	105	146	189	221	221	264	290
(% of Total)	(17)	(17)	(20)	(18)	(18)	(21)	(22)
Engineering Sciences	259	347	356	451	452	511	519
(% of Total)	(41)	(41)	(37)	(38)	(37)	(41)	(39)
Physical Sciences	115	124	145	174	226	195	199
(% of Total)	(18)	(14)	(15)	(15)	(19)	(15)	(15)
Planning and Management	21	43	30	48	63	47	41
(% of Total)	(3)	(5)	(3)	(4)	(5)	(4)	(3)
Other*	20	30	60	64	26	21	26
(% of Total)	(3)	(3)	(6)	(5)	(2)	(2)	(2)
TOTAL	629	855	965	1194	1219	1253	1322

*Includes history, home economics, pharmacology, radiology, seismology, textiles, toxicology, veterinary science, and various conservation and applied mathematics programs.

Source: Office of Water Resources Research, U. S. Department of the Interior, 1972 Annual Report, p. 39.

resources management problems, but unfamiliar with current research interests in the social sciences. The statements can be used to assess the contribution each discipline can make.

Anthropology

In the words of the anthropology panel, "anthropology deals with the origin, development, and nature of man and his culture."[58] Its distinctiveness is in its comparative searches through cultures of the past and present for "the common denominators of human existence and the forces that condition persistence or change in customs or whole cultures."[59] The subfield of ethnology is interested in interpersonal relations and social groups as well as in customs, traditions, and values. Archeology is interested in past societies and cultures. More so than members of the other four disciplines, the research anthropologist looks for answers by personally questioning the people involved and getting to know them.[60] A warning note in terms of the purposes of this book is the panel's statement that "an anthropologist is judged by his peers not according to what an administrator thinks of his work and *not because he contributes to social improvement programs*, but because of the cumulative evaluation by anthropological colleagues of his scientific performance, *mainly his publications*."[61] The italics have been added to emphasize statements relevant to getting social scientists involved in water resources management policy.

Economics

The economics panel defined their discipline as seeking to "explain the behavior of the economic system as an interactive mechanism . . . by which resources are allocated, prices determined, income distributed, and economic growth takes place."[62] Special concern is noted by the discipline for "the development of mechanisms for reallocating resources to meet social needs."[63] According to Gaffney, "economics, contrary to common usage, begins with the postulate that man is the measure of all things. Direct damage to human health and happiness is more directly 'economic,' therefore, than damage to property, which is simply an intermediate means to health and happiness. Neither do economists regard 'economic' as a synonym for 'pecuniary.' Rather, money is but one of the means to ends, as well as a useful measure of value."[64] The panel of economists noted a specific desire to "encourage research on new methods of operating government programs and of providing incentives to individuals and businesses to conduct their own activities in a manner that will promote public objectives."[65] In a way, the desire answers the challenge presented in this book, but it still suggests a greater emphasis on research than on applications.

Geography

The geography panel noted that traditionally "geography is concerned with giving man an orderly description of his world."[66] The geographer "must not only consider a world of social, economic, and political behavior, but also a world in which such behavior is intertwined with the humane arts and the physical environment of man."[67] Within the discipline, the panel notes a trend to "observation of behavior and analysis of . . . processes."[68] Geographers have studied "the ways in which men structure their views of the external world in their own minds" and thereby help "to explain patterns of decision-making behavior that have hitherto been poorly understood or simply dismissed as irrational."[69]

Political Science

The political science panel defined their discipline to be the "study of government."[70] They are interested in the origin, emergence, integration, transformation, and decline of political communities. They study forms of community organization and the rules and practices communities use to resolve conflicts and make decisions. The recent trend in the discipline has been toward greater interest in the individual and the small group.[71] The concern of the discipline with any specific issue, such as water resources management, depends to a large degree on the importance of that issue in current political discussion, and resource use and environmental issues are obviously on the rise.

Sociology

The sociology panel saw their discipline as the study of "all that is social in human conditions."[72] They study man in his biological and physical environment, as an individual relating to others, and as one of a group acting through collective behavior to establish community structure and culture.[73] The major sociological perspectives are 1) explaining patterns of regularities and variations in population distributions, both structurally and spatially; 2) the social-psychological aspects of human behavior; 3) the collective aspect; 4) the structural relations men and women form within society; and 5) the cultural forms that lend meaning to social behavior and that regulate and legitimize behavior. Sociologists study the interdependencies of all these aspects in both static and dynamic terms. Like the political scientists, the sociologists noted that their research will "be affected by the crisis of our times."[74]

THE STUDY PLAN

Need for Better Rapport

Thoughtful comparison between water resources management needs and the statements by which leading social scientists define their disciplines suggests their potential to make a major contribution. The fact is, however, that their contribution is far short of its potential. There is strong evidence of poor communication between those responsible for water resources managements and social scientists.

Status of Current Accomplishment

The social scientists who have made significant contributions to improve resource management policy are in an especially good position to stimulate greater interest among their colleagues. With this goal in mind, the Water Resources Institute and the Center for Developmental Change at the University of Kentucky sponsored a series of colloquia between October 1969, and February 1970. Five distinguished social scientists, who have achieved international reputations as leaders in the contributions their disciplines have made to water resources research, were invited on separate dates. Each person was invited to address three questions:

1) WHAT HAVE BEEN THE CONTRIBUTIONS MADE BY SOCIAL SCIENTISTS IN YOUR DISCIPLINE TO WATER RESOURCES DEVELOPMENT? The question seeks to explore the nature, extent, and quality of the research reported by social scientists in the discipline, the audiences to which these studies have been directed (other social scientists, policy makers), and the evidence that policy makers are aware of the reported research and are influenced by it.

2) WHAT ARE THE MAJOR WATER RESOURCES DEVELOPMENT PROBLEMS WHICH MIGHT MOVE TOWARDS SOLUTION WITH ASSISTANCE FROM SOCIAL SCIENTISTS IN YOUR DISCIPLINE? The question seeks an evaluation of the opportunity for contributions by social scientists by discipline.

3) WHAT ARE THE PROFESSIONAL INCENTIVES AND REWARDS FOR AN INCREASED INVOLVEMENT OF SOCIAL SCIENTISTS IN YOUR DISCIPLINE IN WATER-RELATED RESEARCH? The question seeks an evaluation of the sensitive question of "payoff," especially in the form of recognition by colleagues. Will water-related research contribute to the theoretical and empirical concerns of the discipline, as well as to the solution of pressing resource management problems? If it appears that such research will be only a peripheral concern of the discipline, how is this situation accounted for?

It was hoped that 1) by describing the theoretical and applied problems social scientists have already tackled and how specific research findings have improved water resources management practice, 2) by pinpointing specific problems by discipline wherein social scientists can contribute to resolve pressing resource management problems, and 3) by demonstrating through example to the academic social scientists that resource-management-oriented research can provide a professionally rewarding experience while meeting a critical social need, more productive research effort would be stimulated in the social sciences.

Assessment of the Situation

In order to assess the situation with the goal of making recommendations on how the efforts of the two groups might be brought closer together, the five discipline papers were sent to two groups of reviewers for comment. One objective was to strengthen the content of the papers, but a second objective was to examine the comments for specific issues that need to be resolved in order to bring the two groups closer together. Representatives of the five disciplines were asked to critique the original papers from their discipline and add whatever general comments they felt appropriate. The thirteen critiques were used by the authors in revising their papers. They also gave a discipline by discipline reading on interest in the resource management problem.

Scholarly representatives of various groups active in influencing water management practice were also approached. Each was provided all five discipline papers and asked to review the total manuscript from his perspective of the need for better management. These reviewers were requested to answer such questions as: Do the papers serve a useful purpose from your viewpoint? For which practical problems do you believe help from the social sciences is most urgently needed? How might the difficulties you have experienced in trying to apply the research findings of social scientists to practical problems be reduced? Responses were obtained from people in 1) the federal agencies responsible for water resources development, 2) the federal hierarchy for coordinating policy and procedures among agencies, 3) water resources management on the state level, 4) water resources engineering, 5) conservation, 6) agriculture, and 7) law.

The goal of the final part of this book is to highlight the key points made in the various reviews and discuss their implications for better resource management. The hope is to suggest ways to achieve more effective interaction between social scientists and responsible decision makers.

SUMMARY

Water resources management suffers as alternatives are overlooked, consequences are unforeseen, the wishes of the people are misunderstood, formulated policy is ineffectively implemented, or the consequences of installed projects are not recognized. Social scientists need to determine how to do a better job of defining alternatives, predicting consequences, remaining responsive to current objectives, implementing policy, and monitoring effects of implemented policy. They need to express their findings in a manner that effectively communicates with practicing planners and to train working technicians to make the day-to-day applications. The planners need to digest the findings, abstract the implications to their work, and change policy as appropriate.

The need to improve water resources management relates to the more general issues of how conscious social choice can or should be used to direct the development and adoption of technological innovation and of how to improve the probability that the social choices will turn out to be truly in the best long-run interest of mankind. Blending the contributions of technology and the social sciences and incorporating sound theories into practical applications will be required, but the most difficult task of all may be getting people from diverse backgrounds to work together. No exercise such as this can hope to do more than provide a pause to reflect and then a little help for doing a few things better.

1. U.S. Code (Washington, D.C.: Government Printing Office, 1940), p. 2964.

2. For a discussion of the procedures used in planning flood-control projects, see L. Douglas James and Robert R. Lee, *Economics of Water Resources Planning* (New York: McGraw-Hill Book Company, 1971), pp. 229-65.

3. For a discussion of drainage project planning, see Ibid., pp. 267-82.

4. For a discussion of water supply planning, see Ibid., pp. 285-321.

5. For a discussion of navigation planning, see Ibid., pp. 353-69.

6. For a discussion of hydroelectric project planning, see Ibid., pp. 325-50.

7. For a discussion of water quality control planning, see Ibid., pp. 373-92.

8. For a discussion of recreation planning, see Ibid., pp. 399-418.

9. For a discussion of planning fish and wildlife enhancement measures, see Ibid., pp. 421-32.

10. For standard texts, see Eugene L. Grant and Grant Ireson, *Principles of Engineering Economy*, 5th ed. (New York: The Ronald Press Co., 1970) and E. P. DeGarmo, *Engineering Economy*, 4th ed. (New York: The Macmillan Co., 1967).

11. As quoted in William J. Baumol, *Economic Theory and Operations Analysis* (Englewood Cliffs, N.J.: Prentice-Hall, Inc., 1961), p. 267.

12. See Abram Bergson, *Essays in Normative Economics* (Cambridge, Mass.: Harvard University Press, Belknap Press, 1966).

13. A later chapter discusses this in detail.

14. The task force includes the Secretaries of Interior; Agriculture; Army; Health, Education and Welfare; and Transportation plus the Chairman of the Federal Power Commission and thus represents all the water planning agencies in the federal establishment.

15. U.S. Senate Committee on Public Works, "Procedures for Evaluation of Water and Related Land Resource Projects: Findings and Recommendations of the Special Task Force of the United States Water Resources Council" (Washington, D.C.: Government Printing Office, 1971), serial no. 92-20. Subsequent political compromises are modifying the details of the approach and even the group of stated objectives, but the concept of multiple objective planning is becoming more firmly established.

16. For a description of the computational procedure, see James and Lee, *Economics of Water Resources Planning*, pp. 32-33. For a description of economic efficiency, see John V. Krutilla and Otto Eckstein, *Multiple Purpose River Development: Studies in Applied Economic Analysis* (Baltimore: Johns Hopkins Press, 1958), pp. 15-51.

17. U.S. Senate Committee on Public Works, "Procedures for Evaluation," p. 8.

18. Ibid. Section III-D contains twenty-five pages describing specific environmental items to be considered.

19. Ibid., p. III-D-2.

20. Ibid., Section III-E contains ten pages on measurement.

21. Ibid., pp. VI-6 to VI-8 are maps showing the counties in the United States in each trade area.

22. *Federal Register*, vol. 36, no. 245, 21 December 1971, pp. 24144-94.

23. See the Guidelines for Federal Agencies under the National Environmental Policy Act Issued by the Council on Environmental Quality, 23 April 1971 *(Environmental Reporter* 71:0301).

24. Robert H. Haveman, *Water Resource Investment and the Public Interest* (Nashville, Tenn.: Vanderbilt University Press, 1965), p. 148.

25. Raphael G. Kazmann, *Modern Hydrology* (New York: Harper and Row Publishers, 1965), pp. 5-20.

26. A standard text is Ray K. Linsley and Joseph B. Franzini, *Water-Resources Engineering*, 2d ed. (New York: McGraw-Hill Book Co., 1972).

27. The title to Hippocrates' basic work is translated *Airs, Waters, Places.* The threads of environmental concern are traced through history in Clarence J. Glacken, *Traces on the Rhodian Shore* (Berkeley: University of California Press, 1967).

28. Lynton K. Caldwell, *Environment: A Challenge to Modern Society* (New York: Natural History Press, 1970), p. 234.

29. The basic principles used in dam design are outlined in the United States Bureau of Reclamation, *Design of Small Dams* (Washington, D.C.: Government Printing Office, 1960).

30. For details, see Grant and Ireson, *Principles of Engineering Economy*.

31. See Myra R. Schiff, "Some Theoretical Aspects of Attitudes and Perception," (Toronto: University of Toronto, Department of Geography, Natural Hazard Research, Working Paper no. 15, 1970).

32. Emmanuel G. Mesthene, *Technological Change: Its Impact on Man and Society* (Cambridge, Mass.: Harvard University Press, 1970), pp. vi-vii.

33. Jay W. Forrester, "Counter Intuitive Behavior of Social Systems," *Technology Review* 73 (January 1971): 2.

34. U. S. Senate Committee on Public Works, "Procedures for Evaluation."

35. Aaron Wiener, *The Role of Water in Development: An Analysis of Principles of Comprehensive Planning* (New York: McGraw-Hill Book Co., 1972), p. 52. Wiener explores this issue in some detail.

36. Eugene L. Grant, "Concepts and Applications of Engineering Economy,"

Special Report 56, Economic Analysis in Highway Programming, Location, and Design (Washington, D.C.: Highway Research Board, 1960), pp. 8-14.

37. U.S. Senate Committee on Public Works, "Procedures for Evaluation," p. 20.

38. James and Lee, *Economics of Water Resource Planning,* pp. 107-10 contains an introduction to the literature and a brief categorization of kinds of externalities.

39. This problem is the theme of Allen V. Kneese, Robert V. Ayers, and Ralph C. d'Arge, *Economics and the Environment: A Materials Balance Approach* (Baltimore: Johns Hopkins Press, 1970).

40. C. E. Lindblom, "The Science of Muddling Through," *Public Administration Review* 19 (Spring 1959): 79-88.

41. Edgar S. Dunn, Jr., "Economic and Social Development: A Process of Social Learning" (Baltimore: Johns Hopkins Press, 1971), p. 21.

42. James and Lee, *Economics of Water Resource Planning,* pp. 463-88 outlines the state of the art of water resources simulation.

43. Allen V. Kneese, "Protecting Our Environment and Natural Resources in the 1970s" (Washington, D.C.: Resources for the Future Reprint no. 88, 1970) presents this argument very forcefully.

44. Stephen J. Kline, "Research and Planning in Fluid Mechanics," *Journal of the Hydraulics Division* (ASCE) 98 (May 1972): 765-73.

45. Arthur H. Frazier and Wilbur Heckler, *Embudo, New Mexico, Birthplace of Systematic Stream Gaging* (Washington, D.C.: U.S. Geological Survey Professional Paper 778, 1972).

46. For more extensive discussion of the technique, see Myron B. Fiering and Barbara B. Jackson, *Synthetic Streamflows* (Washington, D.C.: American Geophysical Union, 1971).

47. William H. Miernyk, *The Elements of Input-Output Analysis* (New York: Random House, Inc., 1966).

48. James C. Hite and Eugene A. Laurent, "Empirical Study of Economic-Ecologic Linkages in a Coastal Area," *Water Resources Research* 7 (October 1971): 1070-78.

49. John M. Dutton and William H. Starbuck, eds., *Computer Simulation of Human Behavior* (New York: John Wiley and Sons, Inc., 1971).

50. Jay W. Forrester, "Counter Intuitive Behavior of Social Systems," *Technology Review* 73 (January 1971): 1-16.

51. Jay W. Forrester, *Urban Dynamics* (Cambridge, Mass.: The M.I.T. Press, 1969).

52. Raymond A. Bauer, ed., *Social Indicators* (Cambridge, Mass.: The M.I.T. Press, 1966).

53. Ibid., p. 20

54. Raymond A. Bauer, *Second-Order Consequences: A Methodological Essay on the Impact of Technology* (Cambridge, Mass.: The M.I.T. Press, 1969) expounds on the need and the solution.

55. U.S. Senate Committee on Public Works, "Procedures for Evaluation."

56. Albert O. Hirschman, *The Strategy of Economic Development* (New Haven: Yale University Press, 1958).

57. Federal Council for Science and Technology: Committee on Water Resources Research, "A Ten Year Program for Federal Water Resources Research" (Washington, D.C.: Government Printing Office, 1966), pp. 9-29; Office of Water Resources Research, "Cooperative Water Resources Research and Training, 1969 Annual Report," pp. XV-XIX.

58. Allan H. Smith and John L. Fischer, eds., *Anthropology* (Englewood Cliffs, N.J.: Prentice-Hall, Inc., 1970), p. 5.

59. Ibid.

60. Ibid., p. 85.

61. Ibid., p. 88.

62. Nancy D. Ruggles, ed., *Economics* (Englewood Cliffs, N.J.: Prentice-Hall, Inc., 1970), p. 3.

63. Ibid., p. 4.

64. Mason Gaffney, "Applying Economic Controls," *Bulletin of the Atomic Scientists* (June 1965).

65. Ruggles, *Economics*, p. 121.

66. Edward J. Taaffe, ed., *Geography* (Englewood Cliffs, N.J.: Prentice-Hall, Inc., 1970), p. 5.

67. Ibid.

68. Ibid., pp. 7-8.

69. Ibid., p. 90.

70. Heinz Eulav and James G. March, eds., *Political Science* (Englewood Cliffs, N.J.: Prentice-Hall, Inc., 1970), p. 5.

71. Ibid., p. 6.

72. Neil J. Smelser and James A. Davis, eds., *Sociology* (Englewood Cliffs, N.J.: Prentice-Hall, Inc., 1970), p. 6.

73. Ibid., p. 30.

74. Ibid., p. 70.

2 Anthropological Contributions to the Cultural Ecology and Management of Water Resources

John W. Bennett

On the whole, anthropologists have studied water resources as a by-product of their research on cultural history and human subsistence, and not as a substantive topic in its own right.[1] In surveying this literature, we have tried to feature those types of information most commonly occurring, and to suggest some unifying themes from the field of cultural ecology. The subjects to be treated in this essay are as follows: 1) water resource development in prehistoric cultures, particularly the ancient civilizations of the Middle East and Middle America; 2) the theoretical concept of "hydraulic society" or "irrigation civilization"; 3) the ecological and cultural consequences of modern, large-scale water development projects in the tropics; 4) ethnological and applied-anthropological work on the use of water in modern tribal and peasant societies; 5) problems of water management, with special reference to economic maximization and competitive-cooperative interactions; and 6) some cultural implications of water resource development and conservation in North America.

The review of the literature has impressed the writer with the great potential contribution anthropological research has to practical applications in resource management and development. In a time of environmental crisis, anthropological studies of resource management contain considerable data with direct relevance to problems of conservation and environmental quality. The frequent failure to use such data on the part of planners and decision makers is part of the general failure of our society to develop a sense of values about environment. On his side, the anthropologist has an impressive opportunity for relevant research now that public awareness of the problem has become acute.

The contributions of anthropology to water resource management, however, are not limited to the ecology of living groups. Some of the most useful studies have been produced by archeologists, with their special historical and technical perspective. Much can be learned about the long-range implications of resources development schemes from the studies of ancient water systems by prehistorians working in arid and semiarid lands in Asia and North and South America. In addition, the level of technical analysis provided in these publications is often superior to that displayed by socio-cultural and applied anthropologists, who are usually more concerned with features of human behavior than with the economic and technological feasibility of resource arrangements. Still, there is much of value in the materials from cultural anthropology, and contributions from the discipline need to be studied by those responsible for water resource management. The University of Kentucky is to be commended for making possible this modest beginning.

CONTRIBUTIONS FROM ARCHEOLOGY

River Basin Archeology

Archeological studies of areas inundated by large reservoirs have played an important role in the development of the discipline and have made a number of marginal contributions to the study of man's use of riverine resources and topography. The pioneer work in the field was directed by William S. Webb of the University of Kentucky in the 1930s and 1940s, in connection with the construction of the TVA dams. Webb's survey volumes of the Norris Basin and others on the Tennessee constitute the first publications in river basin salvage archeology.[2]

This survey work was required because the inundation of portions of large river valleys by man-made lakes has destroyed countless archeological sites—a fact which says something about the location of prehistoric settlements with respect to water. Incipient food producers and their successors, village agriculturalists, were usually attracted to rivers, lakes, and seashores, and their remains are characteristically stratified with respect to distance from the water source. For river basins distinctive economies, often varying systematically by historical period, will be found occupying the upper terraces, the lower terraces, and the alluvial valley. Remains of purely hunting economies are usually dispersed across these loci, without regard for riverine or lacustrine resources per se. Thus, prehistoric populations might emphasize the collection of fish and shellfish, water for irrigation, the river as a transportation artery, or all of these together.

Man-made reservoirs can flood up to and including tertiary terraces on large streams, thus covering successive cultural horizons and subsistence styles. When funds can be obtained—they have been relatively abundant for this purpose in the United States—archeological crews can salvage specimens before the lake fills. The most spectacular example was the work set in motion by the Aswan Dam, which endangered thousands of Nubian archeological sites ranging from Paleolithic to early Christian. Sponsored by UNESCO, American and European archeological teams surveyed and dug numbers of these sites, and the relocation and restoration at higher location of some thirty-two temples was begun.[3]

In the United States, the most intensive work was done on the Tennessee River during the TVA construction period, and currently on the Missouri and Arkansas rivers, in connection with the Corps of Engineers dam-building programs.[4] As in Nubia, the sites explored in these American programs have ranged from preagricultural through incipient urban settlements of later cultures.[5]

River basin salvage archeology has contributed valuable ecological and geological data. In efforts to date sites, reconstruct primitive economies, and better understand cultural stratification with reference to basin topography, archeological and natural-science teams have made studies of the paleobotany and palynology of the valleys, the sequence of terraces and their dates, and human interventions with possible topographic significance.[6] The work of James Ford in the bayou region of Louisiana in the 1950s enabled geologists to date certain terraces and water levels of the Mississippi.[7] Photographic methods developed by archeologists have been used to trace premodern systems of dams, fishing technology, and other riverine usages.[8]

Archeological Studies of Prehistoric Waterworks

Of greater significance for water resources management are studies on the water utilization and development schemes of prehistoric and protohistoric peoples. Archeological studies of water shortage systems in Bronze and Iron Age times in the Negev and Sinai peninsula have been used as models for modern agrarian development schemes in Israel and elsewhere. In some instances, the old systems of terraces, check dams, and directed runoff have simply been restored.[9] Archeologists thus can provide considerable information relating to the long-run practicality of alternative designs. Robert McCormick Adams, in describing studies in the Khuzistan region, stresses the lessons archeological data on irrigation may provide for planners: "How do the current plans and promises compare, we may ask, with earlier achievements in the same area?"[10]

The sheer variety of structures created for obtaining and better utilizing water in prehistoric and early historic societies deserves more attention than it has received from contemporary hydraulic engineers. Such societies developed suitable water control systems for every precipitation pattern in climates ranging from desert aridity to variable humidity, and the technical functions of many of these structures were misunderstood for generations. In a well-known case, Sir Aurel Stein misidentified the *gabarband* walled terraces in Baluchistan as dams; and since runoff in Baluchistan is not sufficient to fill the supposed pools, he concluded that the climate had undergone progressive desication. The conclusion has since been modified by Robert Raikes,[11] who also is aware of the studies by Israeli archeologists and engineers on ancient water conservation schemes in the Negev.[12] The Israeli work has convincingly shown that Negev desert lands were fertile in ancient times because of well-engineered devices to extract maximum use from all available water and not because of a more humid climate.[13]

The waterworks constructed by low-energy agricultural societies fall into twelve classes: 1) diversions of running streams into nearby fields; 2) ponds to hold water for later use; 3) catchment basins for rainfall; 4) slope development to increase aquifer recharge by holding water in silted terraces behind ramparts; 5) dams for diverting streamflow into ditches for domestic and agricultural use; 6) large canal and distribution systems to carry river water to cultivated areas; 7) large reservoirs for long-term storage; 8) devices to tap groundwater at water-table levels, including the famous *qanats* of the Middle East and Africa; 9) artificial islands used for agriculture in permanent shallow lakes (the *chinampas* of Mexico); 10) aqueducts and tunnels transporting water for domestic supply; 11) a large variety of wheels, levers, and bucket systems used to lift water to higher elevations; and 12) a variety of schemes for draining excessively moist soils.[14]

Some of these devices deserve special comment. The *qanats* have been given considerable attention due to their long persistence and impressive simplicity and efficiency. They can be used wherever water-table elevations under a hillside are higher than the land surface of an adjacent valley. The *qanats* are constructed by digging a series of vertical "wells" on the hillside down to the water table and then tunneling horizontally from the bottoms of the shafts out to the base of the slope, where the water is channeled fanwise onto fields. Iran is often viewed as the home of the *qanat* since the devices are numerous there,[15] but similar systems have been reported over the Middle East and western Sahara,[16] the coastal Peruvian civilizations,[17] and the Tehuacan Valley of Mexico.[18] The essential simplicity of the system as a means of increasing flows from natural seepages or springs often found at the base of scarps favored the independent development of *qanats* in many regions with water shortages and the requisite geology.

A considerable variety of prehistoric irrigation systems have been found in Meso-American civilizations. The arid Pacific Coast of South America has a particularly large assortment,[19] and Paul Kosok has compiled a photographic album showing aerial views of many of these systems, as well as a study of the Lambayeque multiple-valley stream.[20] Prehistoric peoples of the region also employed subirrigation by excavating fields to lower the zone of cultivation close to the water table. The sunken gardens of the Peruvian coast have been traced through the Spanish colonial period, when they apparently were used more extensively than in prehistoric times.[21] The *chinampas* of Mexico were plots floated on permanent lakes. Elsewhere along the Peruvian coast, the *mahama* consisted of walled fields situated along river terraces subject to flooding.[22] In Bolivia, the ridged fields, called *camellones* by the Spanish, were essentially raised plots for elevating crop land above poorly drained areas.[23] The *riego a brazo* or "pot irrigation" technique practiced by the Zapotec in the Oaxaca area of southern Mexico involves the digging of wells in the cornfield, down to the water table. Water is drawn up in ceramic jars and poured on the crop when needed.[24]

John Rowe informs me that in the Ica Valley, Peru, dry slopes were watered for cultivation by moisture precipitated from dense fog impounded behind small terraces. In central Mexico, dry valley slopes were terraced to receive flood waters and eventually build up deep deposits of arable silt.[25] In a detailed study of the *chinampas*, Armillas makes clear that the plots of saturated land as used by the Aztecs, were the culminating product of several centuries of usage of the swamplands of the valley, including permanent towns erected on hummocks, completely surrounded by water, and connected by causeways.[26] These raised gardens (ridges of land protruding above the shallow water, not the floating gardens of legend) thus signify one of the most extensive and intensive uses of permanent wetlands in human history. As archeological work uncovers a greater variety and intensity of water-control systems, few opportunities appear to have been missed by prehistoric peoples.

The variety of these schemes, relying on delicate small-scale adjustments to local conditions, contrasts with a modern philosophy, which emphasizes large-scale projects of stereotypic design. The difference is a result of the objective of maximization: to produce the largest possible amount of water in order to serve the largest number of people. The premodern systems were often ecosystemically related to low population levels, and were substantively efficient in supporting the small population willing to devote much labor to the task. However, the more elaborate schemes involving extensive canals and reservoirs, like those of Ceylon and Southeast Asia, or Southwest Asia in preclassical times, were capable of supporting large and dense populations. On the other hand, the brittleness of the large, complex projects in the face of technical breakdown and marauding invaders resulted in periodic collapse and depopulation.

The existence of structural flood-control systems in early civilizations has been difficult to demonstrate. The case of Mohenjodaro provides evidence that flood-proofing was used.[27] Works included ramparts, high platforms for houses, and drains in the settlement itself. However, I have not found evidence that this Bronze Age Indus River Valley civilization attempted to divert or control floodwaters upstream, and in any case, repeated flooding of the city may have resulted in its eventual decline and abandonment. The Romans built several large dams in Italy and created diversion works to guard against flash floods in the Nabatean-Roman metropolis of Petra.[28] There are other instances of this kind though insufficiently researched.[29] The use of lowlands along the Nile for annual agricultural irrigation became a means of flood control by land use adjustment since over time settlements and monument sites were located above the highest flood levels. There is also evidence of careful channeling to direct floodwaters into the cultivated areas at the right time. Many of these systems also protected against erosion.[30]

The work by Robert McC. Adams in Southwest Asia has served as a model for a series of investigations seeking to describe the development of irrigation systems through time and evolving cultural horizons, with typical interruptions or stimuli furnished by invasions and conquest.[31] Particularly for Syria, Iraq, and Iran, archeologists have attempted reconstructions of technical and social history from earliest prehistoric times to the contemporary era.[32] The guiding approach of these studies has been cultural ecology, and the focus has been on the effects of particular technoeconomic adaptations on settlement patterns and social organization. As data on the last factor is hard to obtain, reconstructions of social structure probably will remain ambiguous.

From a purely technological standpoint, water usage systems can be classified on a simple-to-complex basis, beginning with complete reliance on rainfall, through various local diversions for irrigation, and culminating in the extensive canal systems of the city-states and urban-based civilizations. The actual chronological history of the various technical adaptations and the relationship of these schemes to the development of plant and animal domestication, settlement patterns, and sociopolitical structures, however, are less clear, and theories of the linkage of these factors have changed as data accumulates. An earlier and well-known position associated with the name of Robert Braidwood held that hunting-gathering peoples in the highlands, where the wild ancestors of seed grains and some domestic animals are particularly abundant, learned to cultivate these species and then moved down to the arid river valleys, developing irrigation in the process.[33] Eventually population pressure in the lowlands led to nucleated settlements, large-scale irrigation, and political centralization.

Binford and Flannery have proposed an alternative to the Braidwood thesis.[34] They suggest that the upland areas were homes of hunting-gathering peoples who prospered on the abundant wild food supply, developing a "broad spectrum" subsistence base, and thereby experiencing population increase. In the classic manner of such developed, "Mesolithic" food-collecting groups, daughter populations would move out of the optimal region toward the margins where water and natural foods would be less abundant or less easily available. Plant domestication and cultivation began as the food collectors brought the seeds of the wild species with which they were familiar to the dryer lowlands. In arid climates, this necessitated the development of irrigation and crop management in the marginal areas. Eventually, farming moved back into the optimal zones.

Some prehistorians, like K. V. Flannery, as in the reference cited above, have seen the development of irrigation as the emergence of a new niche in natural ecology. The alteration of humidity had its impact on flora, with many new plants becoming established through weed growth and deliberate cultivation. The increase in human population on formerly resource-deficient habitats permanently transformed these regions, requiring continuous management and experimentation to the present day.

As food production permitted the growth of village populations in the dry lowlands and river valleys, irrigation would spread, linking villages by canals. The evolution of such an early village irrigation system, based on a lake and canal system and continuing through its subsequent decline due to ecological change, has been described by Helbaek.[35] Increasingly extensive irrigation permitted the emergence of urban civilization. Truly large-scale irrigation would then be created by these emergent city-states, a thesis particularly emphasized by Robert McC. Adams.[36] "Civilization" could thus be founded on essentially village-type irrigation works, and irrigation would not be the cause of the centralization necessary for the state-empire and its complex technology and military force.[37]

The essential element in this new approach is that environmental deficiencies, not abundances, explain the development of irrigation technology—a point of view reminiscent of Toynbee's notion of "challenge and response," but quite possibly borne out by the accumulating evidence of village sites in oases on arid plains and in river valleys older than the earliest food-producing communities in the well-watered and grassy uplands.[38]

Later resource development is associated with the city-states in the large river valleys.[39] If Adams is correct, the urbanized state simply enlarged the older systems. Main trunk canals took water from major rivers, and a complex network of smaller canals distributed it throughout the entire valley. The acceleration in system development is noteworthy: whereas the development of rainfall-plus-small-scale-irrigation systems occupied three or more millenia in Southwest Asia, the development of the canal systems in the valleys seems to have taken an average of three to four centuries.

The major social implications of such development are articulated by Adams as follows: "In a way which had no parallel in earlier periods, vast efforts were devoted to comprehensive programs of irrigation extending over virtually the entire arable surface. This entailed bold and imaginative planning and administration, a whole series of technical innovations, and above all, the investment of state funds on what must have been an unprecedented scale."[40] Thus, a sociopolitical entity of a new type emerged: the *state*. This entity extended its rule and control of resources over many towns and villages under an administrative system with centrally controlled taxation to provide the funds for the waterworks. One remarkable aspect of this stage of development is the extension of canals into zones where under modern conditions agriculture is unprofitable even with a reasonable water supply. This evidence suggests an efficient irrigation system and also a driving need to use the system as a force for political unification and control—or the other side of the coin, the needs for political control generated by the system.

Another noteworthy aspect of these massive schemes, according to Adams, was the utilization of increased agricultural productivity for investment in new craft industries. The development of a luxury textile industry, use of irrigated areas as loci for settlement of war prisoners, and for fruit, sugarcane, rice, and other trade crops are all noted. Commercial activities began to replace subsistence agriculture. Trade to obtain exotic raw materials and seed and root stock became important.

A third major accompaniment of large-scale irrigation was the development of an advanced engineering technology for designing dams, weirs, pumping devices, canals, tunnels, conduits, siphons, and earth moving equipment. The ingenuity, scope, and scale of the works produced are comparable to the water systems of western North America before the series of multipurpose projects beginning with Hoover Dam. However, under ancient conditions, waterworks were labor-intensive; thus water resource development represented a very large increase in "social capital." This situation proved dangerous when for some reason the labor could no longer be supplied.

While the system was capable of supporting true cities, villages remained the mainstay of the agrarian economy. The society thus displayed a complex pattern of settlement in which population was dispersed in nucleated centers of all sizes, the size of a community reflecting its position in a complex statewide division of economic function, rather than the subsistence value of its agricultural production. Gordon Childe saw the Southwest Asian rivers as inducing such growth as a result of human response to their distinctive ecological properties.[41]

There seems little doubt that the period of urban and agricultural expansion that came with the development of centralized irrigation systems in Southwest Asia represented the most complex indigenous culture ever enjoyed in the region. Much the same can be said for parts of Meso-America, and perhaps Southeast Asia as well. These generalized assessments carry implications for contemporary development programs: the key to success is to be found in the sociopolitical organization that makes possible determined economic and engineering efforts. The remarkable fact about the origins of advanced agricultural economy and urban civilization in the ancient world was its location in regions limited in water supply.

However, the later decline of these systems points to the fundamental precariousness of development in arid regions. These early urbanized civilizations, based on water resource development, were susceptible to determined military depredation, and their engineering capabilities, while remarkable, did not prevent inevitable silting and salinization. Social decline and depopulation was extraordinarily rapid once the network of canals and impoundments no longer functioned. There is no reason to assume that the situation is any different today. We are witnessing the potential fragility of comparable schemes in the Israeli-Arab conflict. Clearly, large-scale water resource development in moisture-deficient situations contains both the seeds of effective social and economic development, and also of its opposite: sociopolitical disintegration and depopulation.

The ever-present danger of overdevelopment has led a number of specialists to suggest greater reliance on local schemes less easily disrupted and producing at a lower level for a smaller and more stable population. In fact, the most enduring water development schemes in arid lands support small populations dispersed in town and village nuclei, with a dominant subsistence basis. The *qanats* of Iran have endured through the extensive depredations of conquerors and destroyers of the larger canal and dam systems, and the regions served by them have retained a basic economic and demographic stability through the centuries, at the price of a static economy.[42]

Ancient irrigation systems can be assumed to have suffered from the ills afflicting contemporary schemes: ponding due to poor land leveling and consequent waterlogging and salinization; inadequate drainage to export water with excessive mineral content; weed growth and leakage in canals and ditches; silting; soil exhaustion; and so on. It is possible that subsequent invasions were encouraged by the signs of agrarian decline in coveted regions.[43]

However, the ecological efficiency and duration of ancient water systems are extremely difficult to assess with archeological methods since analysis of phase outs of production requires very precise measurements over small intervals of time. A major paper on problems of silting and salinization of the great Sassanian-period schemes in the Diyala Valley of Iraq traces the ecological deterioration in contrast to the efficiency of the earlier and and simpler systems.[44] Hans Helbaek has utilized techniques which permit observations on the ecological consequences of irrigation schemes based on the fact that changes in the remains of cultivated plants are indicative of water shortages or of the presence of minerals in damaging quantities.[45] There is a strong suggestion in Adams's work that the constant shifting of centers of power in Mesopotamian ancient history may have been associated with degradation of irrigation systems as well as with the unstable military and economic situation.

Investigations of the degradational effects on soils and crops might well be made in the Fayum, where in the twelfth dynasty an enormous impoundment of Nile waters was created by embankments, opening up about 27,000 acres for intense cultivation. Reservoir operation required careful watch of the Nile flow in the south, at the Second Cataract, with information on the rise sent rapidly northward to the water masters. The arrangement also provides a good example of the sophisticated central organization and control required for large-scale irrigation.[46]

The problem of ecological decline suggests the need for a more complex theory of the rise and fall of irrigation-based civilizations. Let us assume that as irrigation systems increase in extent or gross production, they also begin to decrease in efficiency or marginal productivity. As the irrigation system makes it possible for population to increase and political organization to expand, it also begins to develop serious ecological problems. The costs of repairing canals, plugging leaks in dikes, and proper leveling of land may increase until society is unwilling to bear them. An improperly maintained system may function well enough to sustain a considerable population but still be rapidly degrading. Even today, a great many irrigation systems do not invest sufficient capital at the beginning to avoid these destructive cycles. Many systems, ancient and modern, are not able to sustain an adequate maintenance program because of ineffective organization or labor supply.[47]

Thus the ecological and technical problems of ambitious water resource developments relate to fundamental issues of both civilization's decline and its growth. Both scholars studying the past, and planners of modern large-scale projects have placed the emphasis on growth, but it is perhaps time to study the causes of decline and collapse. Historically, these phenomena have been as apparent as their opposites.

HYDRAULIC SOCIETIES

"Hydraulic societies" is a phrase referring to a particular version of the problem of irrigation and the development of civilization, and is in addition a major theoretical issue in anthropology and history. The issues involved received their first major public airing in a symposium edited by Julian Steward where the concept of *irrigation civilizations* was offered as a case of cross-cultural regularity.[48] Karl Wittfogel, whose book *Oriental Despotism* was the next major public statement, had introduced the term *hydraulic society* in his contribution to Steward's symposium.[49]

In keeping with other theses proposed by Marx and Engels, the type of society they called "Asiatic" features centralized bureaucratic controls and despotic power. While this concept was later revised by Marx and in the twentieth century was further modified by the Stalinists, Wittfogel wishes to return to the early Marx-Engels concept. Their Asiatic type of society he calls *Oriental despotism*. As a historian of China, Wittfogel uses China as the archetype of Asiatic society, and stresses the importance of large-scale irrigation in consolidating centralized bureaucratic power. These bureaucratic elites could further entrench themselves through associations with religious hierarchies and through the development of centralized economies with redistributive features.[50] Wittfogel proceeds to identify true and quasi-Oriental despotisms or hydraulic societies around the world, developing a ramified typology. However, the notion of centralization stemming from the control of water and waterworks pervades the classification and thus translates it into a general theory of sociopolitical development.

At the most minute level, this approach has produced some useful studies of cultural parallelisms in village peoples. An example is Beardsley's field study of parallels in Japanese and Spanish rice-growing communities.[51]

At the most general level, Wittfogel's theory suggests a single sweeping explanation of complex historical events spanning considerable time. Such intellectual constructions often contain generalized truth set in a matrix of empirical error. In the Wittfogel case, the truth lies in the plausible connection between large-scale water projects and the sociopolitical forms necessary to initiate or operate them. Even Robert McC. Adams, probably Wittfogel's most Olympian critic, armed with detailed empirical knowledge of water systems in ancient Southwest Asia and Mexico, presents evidence to show the need for central political organization and nucleated population in societies with such systems.[52] It is reasonable that the larger and more geographically coherent the irrigation system, the more centralized the political control over the relevant territory is likely to become.

Millon, on the basis of a comparative survey of seven societies of varying population magnitudes, concluded "that there is no simple tendency for centralization of authority over water allocation to increase with the size of the system or the numbers of people involved."[53] While the conclusion is reasonable, Millon's survey should not be taken as definitive, due to its limited sample and to the complexity of the issue. (Note the phrase *no simple tendency*.) The tendency does exist; manifestations of specific relationships depend on other factors.

In one of the most revealing papers on the Wittfogel thesis, Edmund Leach pointed out that Wittfogel in his discussion of China ignored a second major type of Asian hydraulic society, the Indian system.[54] This approach to large-scale development, as exemplified by Leach with data from ancient Sinhalese civilization (Anuradapura-Pollanarua), contains many village-scale irrigation works which are sustained by cooperative labor, and, at the other extreme, grandiose waterworks constructed by the kings, primarily for irrigating ornamental gardens rather than agricultural plants. The king granted land with water rights to local magnates and religious bodies, and the huge waterworks were built slowly over centuries. They were not the instant creations of tyrants and did not require enormous levies of forced labor. Leach might have added that later the Sinhalese system declined, and that one reason for this decline might have been the inadequacy of a feudal system in providing the labor needed for maintenance. However this may be, Leach acknowledges that because of the lack of good historical data on the sociopolitical structure of ancient societies, his own reconstruction, like Wittfogel's, can only be tentative.

Other critics have noted that use of the concept of hydraulic control to identify the cooperative discipline characteristic of such village peoples as the Hopi with the military statism of Mesopotamia is simply to ignore the diverse causation of social organization. The key to the social systems of rice-growing villagers is to be found in kinship and functional groupings of neighbors, not in political institutions associated with military and ritual elites. In such local societies, cooperative interaction over water allocations is as likely to emerge as despotic control. Others have held that the approach ignores the interaction of many factors in social systems and attributes to a particular technological configuration a massive and uniform causal influence.[55]

Richard Beardsley's comparison of Spanish and Japanese rice-growing villages (cited earlier) observed that the cooperative tasks of water management introduced a "solidarity" or "vigor" in irrigation-oriented communities which other agricultural village peoples did not have.[56] While the strength of the social organization was manifest in a certain centralization of management and thus superficially resembles the Wittfogel concept (though Beardsley does not engage in a discussion of Wittfogel), the solidarity and centralization of these rice-growing communities is not a case of despotism but of its alternative, voluntary allocation of authority among equals.

The Leach thesis may also relate to the situation in Egypt where during the sixth dynasty central political authority collapsed as local magnates asserted their independence.[57] While this development cannot be clearly attributed to resource factors, it appears that irrigation facilities reached a peak of development during the sixth dynasty. With the localities becoming increasingly strong and independent, the increasing water resource development could have contributed to the breakdown of central power. While Wittfogel could argue that despotism was simply being transferred to local hands, a more subtle interpretation of his thesis would acknowledge the importance of the particular locus of despotism, or the size of the units under examination. Peter Kunstadter found that in Thailand hill tribes the introduction of irrigation resulted in *decreases* in communal and centralized social and religious functions and *increases* in individualistic management and localization of governing functions.[58]

In another sense, the Wittfogel approach is part of a line of inquiry stemming from recognition of the persistent fact that in Egypt, Southwest Asia, and China, urban civilization emerged in riverine environments, arid or semiarid regions through which permanent streams flow. There is no question that the constellation of factors which influenced population to cluster in oasislike centers serving a variety of social and economic needs lies at the basis of Southwest Asian and Oriental civilizations. These particular conditions placed an emphasis on strong political organization and its military-political controls.

In the New World, the pattern was more diverse and water was more diffusely distributed and abundant.[59] Only on the dry Pacific coast of South America is there evidence for population nucleation and political centralizations around extensive waterworks. The Lower Colorado River, in spite of its similarity to Southwest Asian conditions, did not become a focal point for the growth of a civilization, and extensive irrigation, as among the Hohokam peoples in the fifteenth century, emerged on the tributaries and not along the major river. High civilization in the valley of Mexico was based on lakes, not rivers.

Along European rivers, the temperate-humid environment did not force population nucleation, and urban civilization appeared very late and then was largely derivative.[60] These variant patterns for the New World and Europe suggest that water deficiency, or more generally, the quantity available, may be paramount in determining the sociopolitical consequences of water resource development.[61] The important empirical relationship between water controls and sociopolitical organization definitely remains a significant arena for inquiry and comparative research. It is also an area having potential application to planning modern water development schemes.

TROPICAL RIVER DEVELOPMENT:
HUMAN ECOLOGY OF DAMS AND MAN-MADE LAKES

During the past two decades a series of large river-control projects have been initiated in Africa, Southeast Asia, and Latin America.[62] Since these projects have been planned mainly by American and European developers, planning concepts were based on the large dams of the temperate regions of North America and Europe. These temperate-region dams customarily have been defended as multipurpose water-control schemes, but most of them were conceived in response to specific needs for power or flood control. In Africa as well, the dams and lakes have been planned largely for major development purposes, although recreation, fisheries, and other secondary objectives have been widely advertised.

The basic planning issue is the suitability in tropical regions of large reservoirs designed for a temperate ecology.[63] For none of these tropical reservoirs were the ecological aspects of creating large bodies of relatively still water in high-temperature climates intensively investigated. In fairness to the planners and engineers, the assessment of ecological and social impacts in such unprecedented circumstances, and in an atmosphere of powerful nationalistic advocacy, was realistically impractical and often beyond the capacity of the agencies. Each of the major dams has a history of complex political and financial negotiation which often prevented adequate or properly timed feasibility surveys.

There is, of course, a more general issue here. Inherent in the nature of large-scale resource development and utilization schemes is the fact that a certain element of trial-and-error experience is hard to avoid. Famous examples that come to mind are the homesteading settlements on the United States and Canadian frontiers in the nineteenth and twentieth centuries. While knowledge of ecological conditions in the West was sufficient to have avoided some of the subsequent depopulation and agricultural failure, the political situation required immediate settlement, and the approach was simply to fill the place with people and let Nature take its course. The authorities were aware that a human cost would be involved but guessed that the cost could be borne, given the economic potential of North America and the ready possibility of migration. While it is debatable as to whether the example is entirely applicable to the modern dams, the pressures leading toward rapid development have been similar. Nevertheless, as technology and a capability for adequate evaluation of consequences improve, the trial-and-error argument, and the whole policy of "instant development" under political imperatives, becomes harder to defend. Despite the extent to which experience with error in the cases of the Kariba and Volta dams demonstrated need for prefunding feasibility surveys in depth, the Koffu Dam in the Ivory Coast was constructed with no ecological studies and a social impact survey was made *after* construction.

As of 1970, only one important series of papers has been published on the human consequences of dam and lake building in the tropics. These papers include a series of anthropological studies initiated by the Rhodes-Livingstone Institute, originally directed by Elizabeth Colson and carried on by her and Thayer Scudder. Less comprehensive studies by other anthropologists on the Mekong River development program are also at hand.[64] Studies of medical aspects of tropical water impoundments, agronomic studies, and animal and plant ecology research have contributed other materials with varying significance for the human context.

Scudder's cultural ecology research has been focused on the Kariba Dam on the Zambezi River in a deeply entrenched reach between Zambia and Southern Rhodesia. Construction was undertaken for the purpose of providing power for industrial development in regions far from the dam site. The dam and lake area was the home of about 60,000 Gwembe Tonga who were not consulted, and who had to be resettled in two major groups, one on the new lake, the other farther downstream. If the Volta River dam in Ghana, the Kainji Lake Basin scheme in Nigeria, and the Aswan project in Egypt are added to the record, a total of 275,000 Africans have had to be relocated and readapted to new environments.[65] Although there are differences from case to case, in no case did planning for human impact, relocation, or rehabilitation equal the need.

A related need is for surveys which explore the possible consequences of a wide range of alternatives. For example, the preconstruction planning studies of agricultural rehabilitation after resettlement in the Volta dam project in Ghana assumed simply that the existing regimes would be perpetuated and reconstituted. However, President Nkrumah decided to ignore these proposals in favor of a "big step": to develop a completely new irrigated and mechanized agriculture which would replace all existing systems, a policy which has subsequently proven to be a failure.[66] If the disadvantages had been researched earlier, the decision might not have been made.

The Kariba Dam project is a complex and continuously evolving case, but several things appear to be clear: 1) the Tonga had a ninety percent subsistence economy which was destroyed by the relocation; 2) while the Tonga by the late 1960s had made considerable progress in developing a new agricultural regime, this progress occurred at the cost of greater dependence on government help and outside markets; 3) preplanning for the new agricultural program was nonexistent, and assistance in developing a new regime was minimal. The tentative conclusion is that the dam and lake have not resulted in any overall improvement in Gwembe agriculture or its productivity and returns, and readaptation has largely been a Tonga accomplishment.

Scudder describes the Tonga pre-dam agricultural program as fluctuating with the rather erratic pattern of natural flow and flooding of the river. Crops were spaced between the annual flood and the rainy season, providing for two crop seasons each year. Erratic flooding, and soil exhaustion, had induced the Tonga to begin cultivation of dry, upland terrace soils by the 1950s, and some believe that resettlement of some of the Tonga would have been necessary even without the dam and lake, due to increasing difficulties in the agricultural program. However, the dam forced the resettlement issue and virtually wiped out the two-crop seasonal system, requiring the Tonga to adopt a single rainy-season crop program. Cultivation along the shores of the lake has been difficult due to the extensive drawdown associated with power uses of the dam water. The Tonga have turned to livestock as a major supplement, but this has its difficulties due to the tsetse fly and capital shortages. Extensive irrigated agriculture could be developed downstream with the enhanced water flow, but this requires much capital assistance from government.

Scudder notes that agriculture has been the least satisfactory aspect of these tropical water development programs, since the methods of production worked out by the indigenous population are usually the most productive and ecologically suitable for a region with difficult or specialized resources.[67] Movement to less suitable environments usually means the need for agricultural intensification which requires capital and technology beyond the capacity of the local people, and/or their governments to provide or sustain.

The rise and fall of the Kariba reservoir level, a phenomenon always associated with large dams used for power production or downstream irrigation, has created further difficulties. The fluctuating of water surface levels in response to demands for power output, made yields of crops dependent on marginal flooding unpredictable by the local farmers. While increased water supplies available for irrigation might confer greater predictability to downstream agriculture, this does not apply in situations such as the Kariba lake area, where natural flooding is the only socially feasible irrigation method. The effect on largely subsistence agricultural regimes is thus very serious, and development is forced into intensifying patterns with their increased capital requirements.

One secondary justification given for large dams in tropical regions has been the value of fisheries programs. At Kariba, predictions of upwards of 20,000 tons of fish annually were made before construction. With the lake full, the fish population increased rapidly, as nutrients supplied by decaying underwater ground vegetation were added to the diet. This increase in the fish population fell off rapidly, however, due to eutrophication of the lake waters caused by the nutrient conditions mentioned earlier, and a diminishing phytoplankton supply, the prime food of most of the fish species. While the initial supply of fish created a vigorous fishing industry, functioning as a cushion against deprivation caused by the disorganized agricultural regime, this industry declined as the conditions changed. As of 1970, the fish population was once more moving upwards as a new ecological cycle in the huge lake began to emerge. It will require careful study to determine the characteristic patterns in tropical fishery situations and the possibilities for development of a stable fishing economy.

P. B. N. Jackson found that the cost of making fisheries economically viable in the African reservoirs always exceeds the original estimates.[68] The principal factor in the Kariba and Volta cases was that the clearing of the bush from the lake area, though extensive, was not adequate to avoid the altered nutrient conditions mentioned previously. More recent observations, however, suggest that the cost of bush clearing can be greatly reduced by simply clearing "bush lanes" to permit access channels, and leaving the rest of the bush in place. The cycles of increase and decrease can then be endured, and eventually the bush areas will provide feeding and breeding grounds for fish populations. As the fish cross from one patch to another, men fishing in the cleared lanes can catch them.

Jackson calls for better training programs for fisherman, the construction of adequate docking and harbor facilities for fishing fleets, and outlet works to permit deoxygenated water to escape from lower levels of the lake and to reoxygenate it before it moves into the stream channel. Compromises will have to be made with irrigation and power usages in order to minimize drawdown, which is as damaging to the marginal spawning and incubation grounds as it is to alluvial agriculture. Fisheries, in their role of supports for local populations affected by the projects, can return benefits as substantial in their own way as the more imposing power and irrigation objectives.

The medical aspects of these dams and lakes have also been studied. An unfortunate by-product of the fisheries operation at Kariba lake was the rapid spread of trypanosomiasis (sleeping sickness) through the spread of the tsetse fly as fish traders moved from village to village in the resettlement area. The disease was more serious in its bovine form than in the human form, but by 1966 the outbreak was reduced by about half, using standard control measures.[69] Malaria is often associated with the concentration of a large labor force at the dam site; Waddy notes that a special term, *the malaria of tropical aggregations of labor* has come to be used for this syndrome.[70] One of the most publicized cases was the de Lesseps attempt at the Panama Canal, where over 52,000 men out of 87,000 employed were treated for malaria, with 6,000 deaths. Webster found that the medical expenditure for the de Lesseps venture was 0.5 percent of the total cost;[71] the medical expenditure percentage on the Kariba dam project was the same.

Two debilitating diseases have been especially associated with the aquatic conditions created by large dam construction: schistosomiasis and onchocerciasis.[72] Schistosomiasis has been particularly prevalent in the Aswan High Dam project. "Egypt 10," a schistosomiasis research and control project sponsored by the World Health Organization, suggests that many of the irrigation advantages of the dam may be negated by the health debits.[73]

Schistosomiasis is a generic name for a series of illnesses caused by related organisms (liver flukes), which start their complex life cycle with man. The eggs deposited in human tissues hatch into larvae which leave the human body and enter water snails. In the final larval stage, the organism re-enters the human body by burrowing into exposed skin in the water and causes a serious disease very difficult to treat. Propagation of the disease is enhanced as large numbers of people are exposed to a large body of sluggishly moving water in which snails can breed—a condition created behind any large dam. Infection rates were high at Aswan in both the laboring population and the indigenous villages along the Nile. The disease, spread by villagers coming into contact with the infected snails in the newly irrigated land, is becoming a major cost factor in Nile irrigation. The wearing of rubber boots, which has been urged as a protective device, has not been done effectively due to Islamic practices of ablution. Control might be effected by chemical eradication of the snail host, but this is extremely costly and beyond the financial capacity of most African countries.

Onchocerciasis is a less debilitating disease, although the occurrence of blindness in the terminal phase has made it a threat to local people. The filarial worm which causes the disease is spread by black flies, one of the world's worst insect pests in their own right. The Owen Falls damsite in East Africa was hit by a black fly invasion, leading to the flight of the entire worker population for several weeks. Actually, large reservoirs tend to control the disease because the worm breeds best in running, oxygenated water, and the slower stream velocities behind dams inhibit breeding. However, flow in irrigation canals and increased population density encourage the disease.

In general, the period of dam construction is one of the most dangerous for the human population. Building these structures takes five or six years, and during this period a population of around 25,000 may aggregate in the vicinity, including workers, their families, and others attracted by commercial possibilities. The local village which becomes the community center is usually lacking in modern sanitary facilities and services. The contractor may or may not have prepared for temporary sanitation. Intestinal diseases are unavoidable. Malaria is common but controllable, but the other diseases mentioned previously are harder to handle. No really effective means have yet been found for deliberate control or eradication.

Scudder collected vital statistics on the relocated Tonga population.[74] After the dam began to fill in 1958, 7,600 Tonga were moved from the reservoir area and resettled, some at considerable distances from their villages. Of the 1,600 moved in 1958, forty-one children died during the first three months of 1959; and of the 6,000 moved later, 100 people, mostly children, died within four months after relocation. Fifty-three adults died the following year. These constitute high death rates, but Scudder is careful to point out that these mortality figures concern the transition period immediately after relocation, and should not be taken as permanent condition.

During the transition period before the Tonga reconstituted their agricultural regime, they were subsisting largely on famine-relief food provided by the Zambian government on the condition that the food would be paid for by cash from the compensation funds allotted the Tonga. The idea was to stimulate adaptive behavior on the part of the Tonga. However, the cash was given to the household heads, who, in accordance with Tonga customs, found other ways to spend the money, withholding much of it from food purchase. Consequently, the Tonga fell back on the collecting of wild vegetable foods, as they had been accustomed to doing during drought periods, and since they were unfamiliar with the flora in their new home, they collected and consumed a poisonous root which caused a number of deaths and much sickness.

Scudder also notes that the high death rate following resettlement was associated with a general homesickness and despair possibly leading to reduced vitality among the youngest and oldest segments of the population (an effect noted by students of urban renewal projects in the United States). This effect seems to have been particularly acute for the 6,000 who were moved 100 miles from their original home to a sparsely populated area inhabited by tribesmen speaking a different language and practicing different customs. Homesickness was probably aggravated by the failure of the government to provide full information on the need for resettlement since the relocated groups lived at considerable distance from the dam and did not comprehend the full extent of the new lake. More extreme reactions were encountered in the Sudan from the Aswan relocation program, where riots and chronic civil disturbance accompanied the relocation.[75]

Obviously, more time needs to be devoted to planning mass relocation programs. These large tropical water development projects are based on exhaustive technical feasibility studies but provide inadequate, last-minute programs for the human and social problems of relocation and give insufficient attention to ecological consequences of the altered biosphere. Planners have generally shown only a dim awareness of the complexities of native subsistence economies and their problems of adaptation to a new habitat. The post hoc, trial-and-error approach to such problems contrasts sharply with the detailed technical planning for the engineered construction; needed is "a more sophisticated approach to population resettlement."[76]

In a paper published with Scudder's paper on man-made lakes, R. Jackson illustrates how the complex political and economic factors involved in these big schemes make it virtually impossible to achieve continuity in planning.[77] After the initial Preparatory Commission Report of 1956, a five-year interval ensued while funds were sought internationally for the Volta project. The *economic* justification used for the project was that power generated by the dam would be used for the production of aluminum to be sold on the world market. The *public* justification of the project was to lessen the reliance of Ghana on a single crop, cocoa. Fluctuations and uncertainties in the aluminum market delayed financing and construction until 1961, and Jackson remarks, "during this hiatus the scientific problems got into the background."[78] He also notes that ten years of work went into planning resettlement, but a "crash program became inevitable" because of the hiatus and outmoding of the previous plans. The clearing of the lake for fishery development involved enormous costs which could not be financed from the expected returns from the aluminum sales. Such experiences illustrate the extent to which the people affected by these large-scale projects become pawns of international policy and processes. Better planning is desirable, but where consequences are unforeseeable, even with more research, it is doubtful if planning contains all the answers.[79] We need a sense of values which recognizes that a slower, experimental approach to resource development, with many pre-construction surveys, can avoid much of the ecological and social damage which is a product of the crash, big-solution approach.

Even where reasonable preparation is made to receive the settlers in their new locality, mistakes are made in basic accommodations due to the failure to study the cultural habits of the people. The Egyptian government constructed villages for relocated Nubians in ways violating their kinship and neighbor settlement pattern and thereby contributed to disorder and resistance on the part of the settlers and a long period of delay in economic establishment. In other cases, unreliable water supplies or communities located too close or too far from agricultural resources have forced unnecessary social changes. Resettlement can never be done without human or cultural costs, but certainly some improvements are in order. Project planners must recognize that dam building changes society; it is not simply a technical or economic affair. This factor is particularly important where the populations affected by the projects are largely on a subsistence economy.

Some examples of specific cultural effects from Scudder's work are useful. The relocated Tonga had formerly lived in villages spaced across the landscape with minute attention to the distribution of shared resources. The annual agricultural procedures were controlled by a ritual leader who signaled the times for planting, cultivating, and harvesting and controlled the amounts of land used in various ways. Over time, these patterns had contributed to a homeostatic balance of the size of the local population, its spatial dispersion, and its use of resources. After relocation disrupted the entire cultural-ecological regime, the ritual leadership role ceased to acquire players. This was caused not only by the absence of detailed knowledge of the locality and resources, but also because the Tonga ceremonial specialists felt that their gods did not accompany them to the new location. This belief delayed the reestablishment of effective agricultural routines and was a contributing cause to the need for food relief.

The Tonga funeral ceremony includes lengthy drumming. The indigenous inhabitants of the areas to which the Tonga were brought lacked this custom. When the Tonga began to drum, the local people asked them to stop, lest their own spirits be offended. Hunting shrines, magical routines, and many other security-conferring rituals of Tonga culture associated with life crises and economic activities could not be established for similar reasons. For several years after resettlement, Tonga culture was disorganized.

The Tonga required up to four years to innovate new strategic patterns of decision and task-performance.[80] One of the first adaptations was to use the old Tonga institution of "instrumental friendships" to establish a better relationship with the Goba people with whom they now had to live and share land. The incentive was to obtain the right to use additional agricultural land, badly needed by the Tonga, from the half-utilized Goba fields. Cattle and money were given in exchange. A number of other symbiotic arrangements between Tonga and Goba have gradually emerged.

Another adaptation concerned the emergence of spirit mediums (*mangelo*) who claimed they could cure a number of anxiety-produced or accentuated illnesses. While these functionaries had always existed in Tonga society, the need for their services increased because of the desire of the people to contact the new spirits of Goba territory and reassure them that the Tonga would not harm or offend them. As the *mangelo* went into action, the death rate dropped, the Tonga farmers came to have more confidence in local resources, funeral drumming resumed, and the society became more stable.

Papers on the Mekong River development program provide a comparative perspective on tropical river development, although most of the studies concern future possibilities since the program was in its early stages as of 1970. The Mekong project involves the Lao, Thai, Khmer, and Vietnamese peoples since the basin is in all four countries; its very inception constitutes an historic change in mainland Southeast Asian politics because all four have been hereditary enemies. Ingersoll notes that the cultural picture of the Mekong basin contains three dimensions of contrast: 1) the detailed cultural differences represented by the many languages spoken by national majorities, minority enclaves, and tribal hills people; 2) the "horizontal" cultural differences among the religious patterns of Buddhist-Brahmanic, Taoist, Confucianist, and related sects, differences between rural and urban cultures, and differences among the wet-rice, floating-rice, and upland farming styles; 3) a basic "vertical" culture contrast between the peoples of the plains and the hills.[81] Plains people are settled agrarian populations with long-established techniques of dealing with national and urban institutions. The hills people are largely tribals, more or less independent of the larger sociopolitical entities, and with indigenous cultures.

The many levels of heterogeneity among basin peoples need to be thoroughly evaluated in basin planning, and yet Sewell and White voice the familiar criticism of the lack of social evaluation in contrast to the excellent technical feasibility work.[82] The magnitude of the investments required to ensure efficient operation of the big dams without excessive social and ecological costs can be gathered by reading some of the duplicated or semi-published documents prepared by various advisory groups. For example, Jasper Ingersoll, in a duplicated report on the social feasibility of the huge Pa Mong dam and reservoir in Laos, noted that irrigation relates to physical, economic, and social systems and that feasibility studies are needed for all three if economic "profitability" and social "usability" are to be attained.[83] His lists of requirements and conditions that should be present "if the Pa Mong project is actually undertaken" include: adequate and predictable water supply; control of diseases; accessible markets for new products; no land speculation; fair and just land compensation; small service areas for irrigation districts; prevention of "corruption" that affects irrigation efficiency; a "vast increase in credit facilities for farmers"; effective education to utilize irrigation properly; fully technologized preparation of irrigated lands; provision for domestic water systems; promotion of participation by local people in all Mekong irrigation schemes; and coordinated environmental and social research.[84] The report does not examine the probability of such measures being carried out. They would be equally relevant, perhaps even utopian, for a project in wealthy North America.

This oblique approach is visible also in a published paper by Ingersoll.[85] He describes the consequences of the Mekong project in favorable terms and notes that "the development of a people in a river basin is essentially a process of growth in their capacity to use and produce wealth."[86] He sees "psychological shifts," described in generalized terms, "from forming identity in inherited positions and traditional groups, toward forming identity in personal and professional achievements."[87] Ingersoll forecasts the political outcome of the Mekong project as a "shift from a single, general power center, toward distribution of power among various effective, specialized centers of decision-making."[88] However, anyone familiar with the political history of Southeast Asia knows that it is equally probable that an increase in wealth will result in increased centralization of power and subsequent exploitation—a conclusion made at least historically plausible by the review of the medieval Khmer centralized water control systems in a paper by Solheim and Hackenberg.[89]

Another series of papers by ecologists, resource analysts, and anthropologists offers a more critical picture of the Mekong program.[90] In these, the potential ecological consequences of the Pa Mong mainstream dam in Laos are considered to be as serious as the African cases, with dangers from the usual tropical diseases, fertilizer pollution, fishery troubles, changes in human nutrition, and needs for resettlement of several hundred-thousand persons. Some of these specialists have advocated a series of small dams on the Mekong tributaries in place of the big mainstream impoundments. A number of such dams have already been built. However, Joel Halpern (personal communication) reports that the big dams have by no means been abandoned, because of their electric power potential. Thailand needs power for industry, and poor Laos would be happy to export it from the mainstream dams. Even the Pathet Lao have acceded to the big-dam approach, by simply not harassing the Japanese team in charge of construction of the Nam Ngum dam (although an American technician on the site was attacked). But the papers also question the inevitability of economic gains to Laos. The increased urbanization and difficulties of financing social services, the disruption of an adapted agriculture, migration from rural to urban areas— all usual consequences of this type of development—would increase the potential for social conflict many times and also the amount of dependence on outside resources.

ETHNOLOGICAL AND APPLIED ANTHROPOLOGICAL STUDIES

Anthropological studies of small-scale water development systems associated with contemporary tribal and peasant societies is the most frequently occurring research by professional anthropologists on water. The materials are published in standard ethnological monographs of communities and particular culture groups and in applied anthropology studies made in conjunction with development programs.

Water and Culture

The descriptive ethnological literature dealing with water usage among tribal and peasant peoples is considerable and deserves treatment in its own right. The resources utilization patterns of tribal peoples often reflect a generalized pattern of evolutionary development associated with their general subsistence base. A convenient guide is C. Daryll Forde's classic text, *Habitat, Economy, and Society*.[91] Forde reported on tribal groups arranged in three grand classes: Food Gatherers, Cultivators, and Pastoral Nomads. From Gatherers to Cultivators, one moves from nomadic to sedentary life. The change presumably increases the amount of human energy available for more complex activities. Pastoralism has been viewed as an offshoot from Gathering, its practitioners often attaining the cultural complexity of Cultivators but with nomadism often imposing limitations on cultural development.

The assumption of increasing cultural complexity as one moves toward cultivation applies best to long spans of time and to many societies. For smaller or shorter units of observation, one finds more exceptions. Forde designed his text to show this combination of general tendency and local variation, and the groups he describes ethnographically were chosen with this idea in view. For example, one of his Gatherer groups is the Paiute of the Great Basin, who roamed the desert in search of vegetable food and small animals, but who also occasionally used snowmelt water to grow patches of desirable wild plants on mountain slopes, a form of irrigation one might expect in more settled peoples.

The use of water resources by tribal peoples is basically dependent upon the nature of the supply. Thus, Forde's Cultivator groups range from oceanic-rainfall yam growers and sea fishermen, through intensive-irrigation rice growers of south Asia, to the Hopi of the American desert, who water their corn by hand from natural springs in their arid land. As Forde made clear in his theory chapters, the key to the pattern in a particular society lies in the constellation of resources in its particular locality—rather than in evolutionary laws. If generalizations can be made across the many variable adaptations rooted in usable resources, they would issue from factors such as food supply, energy, time, and population base, which confer greater or lesser stability and exploitative capability depending upon their frequencies and combinations.

Another facet of the ethnological literature concerns attitudes and values associated with water, including its use in rituals from simple bathing to elaborate purification ceremonies. The frequent use of water for these purposes, and the elaborate attitudes often associated with them, is a symbolic recognition of the transcendent importance of water to life. Often, however, the elaboration in ritual use does not correlate with the amount of water available. In both India and Japan water is an important ingredient in religious symbolization, but in India potable water is often scarce, and in Japan it has always been abundant. Clearly, the role of water in myth and ritual can develop out of nonutility factors.

The cultural position of water has an ecological and physiological underpinning one does not find, for example, for air or soil. Air is *too* pervasive, and soil is used too indirectly. Water, on the other hand, exerts a constant pressure in the form of thirst, one of the basic biological drives underlying human responses.[92] Obviously, no human activity that persistently thwarts satisfaction of the drive for water can endure very long. This truism, however, does not explain the many persisting human activities that interrupt the thirst-satisfaction drive for relatively long periods, such as the search for visions and the feeling of mastery over bodily pangs. At the same time, prolonged water shortages caused by natural conditions generate anxiety and fear, and thirst will condition acceptance of new water systems opposed on ritual or social grounds.[93]

Since water resources project planners often assume universality for certain attitudes in their own cultures, it is useful to comment on some variations found by ethnologists. Taste or flavor is a factor in water preferences in many village cultures, where water from a particular source of supply has been used for generations. Lebanese Arabs had come to like stagnant pool water, offensive to the development team, and rejected a new fresh water supply on the grounds that the iron pipe would ruin the flavor.[94] Indian villagers preferred mud-tasting river water to water from a new well, which was perceived as hot and saline.[95]

While taste varies, most people prefer clear water. Applied anthropologists have noted the influence of the preference for clear water in conditioning acceptance of new wells. Murkiness in water seems to suggest dirt, injurious substances, and a fear of the unknown. The preference for clear water can, however, work both ways. I recall an incident in an archeological field camp when the crew persisted in drinking sparkling clear water from a well known to be contaminated with microorganisms and rejected brown, gritty, iron-tasting water from a clean well. Persistent cases of the "trots" forced a change.

The use of water for cleanliness, and its gradual merging into ritual, has similar contradictory dimensions. Indians bathe in contaminated water supplies. The Japanese proclivity for hot baths has been analyzed as a part of the Japanese emotional surrogate for sexual pleasure, but medical researchers have known that the hot public bath is a source of various parasitic diseases.[96] In a Peruvian village, the residents scrupulously boil their drinking water, not because they know about germs, but because since illness is culturally defined as a "hot" entity, they believe it can be countered with another "hot" substance: boiled water.

Applied Anthropological Studies

The anthropologist is often the person most informed concerning microenvironments and microcultural features affecting natural resource usage. He is in an excellent position to advise planners on the geographic, technological, and sociocultural feasibility of their proposed changes—from putting wells in villages to building big dams. The mistakes already noted as stemming from inadequate ecological and social feasibility studies for large projects also apply to many small water development schemes introduced by development officers around the world over the past generation. Much applied anthropological literature is devoted to analyses of these mistakes.[97]

Several important factors contribute to the frequent omission of an anthropologist from project planning teams. These include the ethnocentric assumption that behavioral response patterns are alike the world over; the length of time required for detailed cultural feasibility studies; a willingness to sacrifice microsocial entities for large schemes or to accept a certain percentage of error and failure; and the scarcity of well-trained anthropologists. Moreover, the anthropology profession often awards greater prestige to research topics remote from these practical concerns, and some of the more able people in the field cannot be induced to participate in resource management decision making.

Another difficulty with applying richly detailed but highly localized research findings concerns the inevitability of trial-and-error experimentation in development work as suggested by many of the technological failures of water systems in tribal enclaves. Tom Sasaki studied a reservoir on the Navajo reservation constructed in the early 1940s.[98] By the late 1950s the reservoir no longer held significant amounts of water and had become the site of agricultural fields. The scheme failed because the lack of rainfall in dry years led to drawdowns so severe as to eliminate irrigation, and winds filled the ditches and plots with sand. Navajo technology was insufficiently capitalized to permit a massive attack to overcome these difficulties. Since this reservoir was planned with insufficient knowledge of local weather conditions, the project can be reckoned as one of the trial-and-error experiments in arid-land water development forced by political pressures before adequate research could be done. The lag in communication between the project planners and the anthropologists who do the post-hoc studies is a major unsolved problem.

Another factor evident in the Navajo reservoir example is the need to take into account *extreme* as well as average climatic conditions in planning. Studies of resource and climatic fluctuations and the consequent cultural adaptation have received less attention than they deserve because it is difficult to keep records in precise localities over long periods of time. For over four generations on the semiarid northern Great Plains, farmers tried a variety of measures designed to cope with marginal and fluctuating moisture, experienced repeated failure, and only recently have developed techniques of diversification. Various governmental measures designed to cushion income fluctuation due to climatic variability also have helped.

Many anthropological studies pertain to cultural factors not usually in the sphere of awareness of the planners and engineers. To typify the situation, we shall assume that a government development team is sent to a village to install a new water system, consisting of wells, pumps, and facilities for washing clothes as well as water for irrigation and consumption. The team talks to one or two people in the community who indicate that the facilities should be located as near to the village as possible, for the sake of convenience. Often this plan works; if it works twice for the same team, they are reinforced in their conviction that they have discovered a generally applicable rule: locate water where it is most convenient to the greatest number.

However, unanticipated factors often invalidate conclusions of this type. A particular ritual taboo in another community may make water facilities located too close to the center of the village a source of considerable tension. In still another community, a daily journey by the women from several villages to a common point to exchange necessary social information may be required to maintain the smooth functioning of the social system. Wells located outside of the community may provide this place of exchange. Convenience has to be defined more broadly than by sheer physical distance or location. It depends on cultural factors and social arrangements.[99]

New water facilities often receive too little use because of the failure of planners to budget funds for training in the operation of the equipment involved. Old habits and preferences may inhibit learning, a problem endemic in new irrigation systems in North America as well as in the emerging countries. In a study in the state of Bihar, India, D. P. Sinha (personal correspondence) found two tribal communities in which new wells for stock watering had been installed by Block Development teams. In one village, the wells doubled livestock production; in the other, the wells fell into disuse. The successful case was due entirely to the presence in the village of a veteran of the Indian Army who had received training in the skills required to operate the facilities correctly. A trained person introduced into the other village for a period of only a month or two could have trained the villagers. Allen describes how a resident technician in Iranian villages was able to train the villagers to operate a rather complex irrigation system based on cistern storage of water. Without this training, the systems would have deteriorated.[100]

In theory, I believe that much human action is motivated by needs to accomplish particular tasks of an adaptive nature. These tasks must be performed in such a way as to permit goals to be accomplished with available resources, and also to deal with circumstances created by previous adaptive responses. Much behavior is therefore responsive to *situations*. However, in the absence of adequate cues or obvious rewards, behavior is often guided by past precedents, equivalent to what have been called cultural patterns or traditions. Thus anthropologists, though unfortunately not always clearly distinguishing among the relevant sectors of behavior, have contributed a great deal to our knowledge of the pragmatic motives for problem solution, and to repetitive, stylized behavior that emerges as "unanticipated" response to resource development projects.

Dobyns has shown in his studies of the Papago irrigation project that a critical factor in the failure of the Indians to accept the system offered them by the Indian Service to enhance subsistence agriculture was their desire to realize a higher standard of living through wage labor.[101] During a previous historical period, the Papago had made a significant adaptation to the consumption standards provided by a cash wage economy. The Indian Service built a reservoir in the belief that the Indians really wanted to return to subsistence agriculture. The critical mistake was the assumption by a bureaucracy that it knew what people wanted. Because the people themselves often don't know what they want, there is no simple generalization or solution to the ambiguity.

A more elaborately analyzed case of this type is presented by Allen Holmberg for the Viru Valley in Peru.[102] The introduction of tube well irrigation into the valley, at the request of the farmers, triggered a series of difficulties. The government team carried out a model survey, and requested the help of local people in drilling wells. However, resistance quickly mounted. The project was stopped after sinking only one well because the team consistently ignored local people with knowledge of the local water supply, including one with considerable experience with tube wells. In addition, the wells were drilled on private instead of public land. This act accentuated a series of status differences and hostilities, as well as a clash between rich and poor.

Another common problem in government-planned water schemes for tribal people arises over the prevalence of extended kinship networks in societies with subsistence agriculture. In such cases, individual ownership of natural resources is a rare thing. Ownership is usually vested in the kinship networks and often emphasizes usufruct patterns rather than clear title. In spite of this, development teams have persistently constructed water systems as if private property concepts governed use of the water. While this paper has stressed the difficulties in anticipating the cultural adaptations that so often inhibit acceptance or management of water systems, in the last analysis it must place considerable blame on the planning specialists. Many knowledgeable people are available to advise on possible consequences. The use of social scientists early in planning is fundamental, and clearly many mistakes could be avoided if this procedure were followed.

COMPETITION AND COOPERATION IN WATER DEVELOPMENT

Certain ecological problems of water recur in all societies at all levels of technology. Water as a resource moves; it is a transient substance. This means that whenever people wish to utilize water in one place, they must capture and store the water when and where it is available. Since water that *flows past* is not captured, and may be used by another person downstream, water use for agriculture or human consumption automatically imposes problems of sharing, and generally, of water as a form of property.

Because of its unique fluid characteristics, it is not particularly surprising to find parallels in the social organization of rice irrigators in Japan and Spain, or to note that the technical adaptations made by the Nabataeans in the Negev are comprehensible to Israeli hydraulic engineers.[103] Moreover, the technical uniformity of particular types of waterworks sometimes makes it possible to deduce the generalized patterns of social organization required to maintain them, although this may be more difficult than some scholars have believed.

Therefore, while it is correct to emphasize social and technical parallels due to water's transient nature, one must also be aware of possible differences. Local communities vary considerably in the forms of land tenure, social organization, and decision-making mechanisms useful in solving problems of transiency and limited supply. These differences exemplify one of the more difficult issues in the anthropological study of local societies, and one that poses problems as to the applicability of the anthropological approach to evaluation of large-scale water development programs. For a large-scale program to be studied scientifically, a number of variables need to be known exactly. If anthropologists insist on managing *all* the variables to be sure of their recommendations, many questions could never be answered.

Sharing of a fluid resource requires cooperative relationships. However, in most cases, the specific forms of sharing will depend on pre-existing legal rules, social relations, and cultural styles. Thus, the cooperation displayed by water users in Thailand may be intervillage and kinship-based while the cooperative mechanisms of ranchers in the American West involve ordered competition for water through an individual water-right system administered by courts. Functionally the two patterns may be identical; organizationally they are disparate, since they are based on differing conceptions of property rights. This simple example shows that attempts to encourage cooperation over the use and management of water must take into account existing social, economic, and legal institutions and not proceed on the basis of hazy notions of the innate cooperativeness or inherent competitiveness of human nature,[104] or the assumption that all people conceive of water as individually owned.

The argument may be illustrated by data from a particular region of western Canada, where variant patterns of institutional reinforcement resulted in varying forms of cooperative and competitive interactions concerning water resources.[105] In this region water projects include: 1) small, private schemes developing government-assigned, appropriative water rights by means of ditches dug from creeks to fields that are used to produce forage crops; 2) "small waters" partially financed by government and consisting of stock watering dams, dugouts, and other small reservoirs; 3) large-scale community irrigation programs involving dams and large reservoirs with the impounded water used to irrigate plots of land supervised by the government and rented out to farmers and ranchers, with small charges for the water as well as land rentals.

This system encouraged cooperation in the use of water on the following bases: 1) The water-right system gave people a right to a fixed number of acre-feet during the designated spring flood period. The amounts were adjusted so everyone would obtain his share, and therefore, cooperation was based on a guarantee inherent in the legal regulations governing water rights. 2) The "small waters" system was controlled by the government so that a man applying for a dam would have his permit studied with reference to his neighbor's need for the same water. The review often suggested the desirability of cooperative schemes to the users. Here, again, cooperation was encouraged by third-party (government) adjudication. 3) Informal neighborly assistance and labor exchange existed among plot-renters on the community irrigation tracts. 4) A Water Users' Association emerged to manage and partly to finance community watershed schemes. Here cooperation was partly voluntary and emergent within the social system and partly fostered by a government anxious to get out of the business.

Competitive mechanisms were encouraged by this system in the following ways: 1) Individual water-right holders could violate the law and take more than their share, indirectly encouraging others to do likewise. A "water fight" might result as water ran short. More commonly, however, excess uses would be stopped after clandestine reports of stealing were made by one neighbor about another to the government water bureau. 2) Competition in the "small waters" program could emerge as enterprising operators endeavored to influence the government bureau to build the installation for their convenience. 3) Competitive relations also existed among the plot-renters in the form of stealing water from each other by digging illegal diversion ditches. 4) Competition also emerged in the form of illegal sprinkler irrigation devices installed clandestinely on the creeks and operated late at night.

All these patterns of cooperation and competition are equally plausible in the mixed system of agriculture found in the semiarid West. Private agrarian entrepreneurs compete for resources which they desire to "own" since they must operate their enterprises individually. However, government-regulated irrigation schemes that require various forms of agreement and sharing in order to receive financial benefits induce cooperative relations. The water users take advantage of the government regulations to enjoy the benefits of cooperation, to secure water, and to allay destructive competition by bureau regulation. One set of institutions—private entrepreneurial ownership and exploitation of resources—interacts with another—government-regulated sharing—to produce a mixed system of cooperative-competitive relations. Most systems of water use may well have this mixed character.[106]

The key factor in this process concerns the issue of tenure or ownership right. Water cannot easily be "owned" in watercourses running through separately owned tracts. This issue is apparently of no great moment in the Orient, where a tradition of individual resource ownership has been much less consistent. However, the issue is extremely important in North America, especially in water-deficient regions. Water-right holders in the West have been notoriously reluctant to acknowledge that they do not "own" the water, and one of the commonest abuses is for a man to take his water *after* the time period allotted, in the firm belief that he had a right to it.

The issue of title was also paramount in the community irrigation plot system in the case reviewed previously. Although the users did not "own" either the plot or the water, the fee required for use of the water encouraged the same competitive abuses noted in the case of the private water-right system. More important, the lack of true title to the plot made the users extremely reluctant to form associations and regulate the schemes themselves. They were content to permit the government to finance and regulate the system. Repeatedly, government has had to force water users to take responsibility by terminating public support. This process can be contrasted with the effective cooperative interaction over irrigation by the Mormons and some other groups with traditions emphasizing collective elements.

While the value systems of North American agriculturalists clearly emphasize individualistic and competitive patterns, they also stress neighborly cooperation and exchange. Values alone do not promote cooperation or competition; one must look at values as they are selected by property institutions and external government regulations operating in particular cases. The same men who could fight bitterly over water could also manifest intimate cooperation over stockraising, if the government assigned them a joint grazing lease! In other words, the same institutions and cultural values can work toward cooperation and/or competition, depending upon the mix of institutions and objectives in particular cases.[107]

The topics covered in this section have been explored by Henry Dobyns from a related point of view. He utilizes the concept of the "commons," defined as "a given quantity of a natural resource available for common use by a particular human population." The term has been popularized by Garrett Hardin's article in *Science* in which he notes that the "tragedy of the commons" emerges when maximization of use of a resource by individuals results in injury to others or exhaustion of the supply.[108] In fact, such phenomena as "Oriental despotism" and "irrigation civilization" also relate to the sociopolitical arrangements adopted to divide a finite supply of a resource.

Cooperation and competition become alternative ways of exploiting the hydraulic commons. The nature of water as a transient resource argues for cooperative sharing because if each user maximizes his use of a finite supply, the supply diminishes and other users are deprived. If this point is reached, either cooperative measures to distribute the scarce goods or a third party with powers to penalize those who violate the rules of sharing will emerge.

Sasaki and Adair provide an example from the Navajo. The federal government provided irrigation for the Indians along the San Juan River near Fruitlands in 1933.[109] Operating on the assumption that the Navajo would respond in terms of democratic images of interfamilial cooperation on the use of water, the Indian Service invited Navajo to settle in the area. The Indians crowded onto the irrigated tract and opened ditches and irrigated whenever they wished. At one point, they responded to urgings to cooperate by simply opening all the ditches at once. The project is reported to be in a continual state of ecological degradation and social confusion because the government failed to follow through with a detailed training program. Individual Navajo families, used to cooperating only with their kin, ignored the need to work together. The settlement was planned without reference to these kin groups by government officials who had too little knowledge of the structure of Navajo society. In the single case where more than one family unit from a kin group were present, cooperative rotational rules were worked out and observed.

Weingrod's study of a *moshav* farming cooperative in Israel shows how collective sanctions may impose the discipline of the commons.[110] The village was comprised of Moroccan immigrants who had considerable difficulty in working out cooperative measures on irrigation. In the first stage, the *moshav* as a cooperative unit paid for the water, which meant that the more intensive cultivators were penalized by having to bear the shares of the less efficient. This created considerable dissension, and many of the better farmers began to sell their produce on the black market, leading to a decline in *moshav* revenue. The second stage involved the creation of an individual payment responsibility, including metering of each farmer's water and locked valves permitting cutoff if monthly payments were not made. This procedure worked, and it provides still another example of how mixed systems will evolve in adaptation to the resource supply and the social institutions.

ANTHROPOLOGICAL IMPLICATIONS FOR WATER DEVELOPMENT IN AMERICAN SOCIETY

Cultural anthropological studies of attitudes toward natural resources and resource development in American culture are an important, but unsatisfied need. The urgency of such an inquiry is indicated by the current concern over environmental quality and resources conservation— one of the three or four major problems of contemporary civilization. The basic issue, as Clarence Glacken indicated, is "anthropocentrism": the value, especially pronounced in North America, placed on man as the measure of all things.[111] This value, as apparent in humanistic positions and in anthropological theory as in engineering technology, is seen as an underlying cause of environmental exploitation without due regard for conservationist values. The need to adopt a more humble position, viewing man as one element in a global ecosystem subject to the limited resources of spaceship earth, is strongly advocated.[112]

The American attitude toward water has contradictory aspects. Those demanding water supplies often destroy the watersheds. Increasing population pressure in California has led to hydrologic disruption and severe soil erosion. We drain wetlands in order to "reclaim" land that becomes too friable and dry for productive agriculture. The attitude toward rivers and floods is equally paradoxical; the public demands adequate flood protection while new building on the floodplains invites recurrent disaster. Engineers often reassure the population that everything possible has been done to protect them. They build more dams, induce a feeling of greater security, and leave settlements exposed to a flood too large to control. Our search for outdoor leisure creates more lakes, with untold ecological consequences.[113]

Raymond Dasmann has cogently characterized the cultural pattern as follows: "Americans are impatient with the slow processes of nature, with the normal events of biotic succession and change. They prefer the simplicity of a machine to the intricacies of a biota. The day-to-day problems of watershed management seem tiresome, whereas a large dam built to stop floods 'for all time' has popular appeal. Even when we preserve nature we like to get the job over with, and by some spectacular act of Congress decree preservation forever."[114]

All humans have these exploitative attitudes in varying degrees. The Japanese, possessing the only major modern civilization with conservationist values built into its traditional culture, are now polluting their rivers and lakes even more rapidly than the Americans. It is not that their values have changed, only that their technology has developed to produce more pollution. Even Neolithic societies, as we saw earlier, are capable of ruining the land, but the time required to do the damage is less for modern societies with superior technology.

Can societies learn to control their use of the "commons?" In a culture with dominant emphasis on individual rights, the first stage is probably always the imposition of controls by an external agency. In the Canadian region that I studied, several thousand acres were salinized because farmers were ignorant of the proper irrigation methods and engineers failed to level the tracts properly. Effective control required a complete rebuilding of the works and fields and imposition by a government agency of strict controls over water use. The second stage is the creation of a local Water Users' Association which will take over maintenance of the system and impose its own penalties and rules. This will be difficult, but it will come, as it has in other regions of North America.[115]

Thus, the anthropologist might find a major role in exploring relationships among values, technology, and the uses of nature. This task is not merely one of refined dilettantism, as anthropology's ventures into contemporary cultural character often become. It is based on a critical need to introduce a new hierarchy of values and procedures into water resources management before the situation becomes irretrievable. One preliminary task is to define the present configuration of values and actions carefully enough to show where the changes need to be made. This is, of course, a multidisciplinary task; the economic system, derivative though it may be, is still the major immediate cause of exploitation. The demographer is an essential member of the team since population increase exerts the pressure on resources. The sociologist can help in defining the status and power relationships which lead men toward destructive competition. All disciplines have important roles to play in this program, and none can do the job by itself. Interdisciplinary efforts need both more encouragement and intelligent planning.

ANTHROPOLOGY AND RESEARCH ON WATER MANAGEMENT

The original assignment for this review of the anthropological literature on water resources featured three questions: 1) What have been the contributions of your discipline to water resources development? 2) What are the major water resources development problems which might be solved with assistance from members of your discipline? 3) What are the professional incentives and rewards for increased activity of your discipline in the field of water-related research? By way of conclusion, we may summarize answers to these questions presented or implied in the paper.

1) The entire paper is a substantive answer to the first question; the contributions reviewed represent, we believe, an adequate sample of the materials from anthropology. The thrust of these contributions is descriptive, and they provide a broad spectrum of the diversity and ingenuity of the technical devices, social customs, and property arrangements centering around water use and management. The emphasis is on low-energy technology societies; this is the result of anthropology's preoccupation with this type of society. Other contributions have been suggested in our interpretations of some of these descriptive findings. One important one is the stability of technologically simple schemes, in comparison to the uncertainties associated with elaborate works. Men tend to overdevelop at any level of technology, but especially in the case of civilized societies.

2) Contemporary problems associated with water development which can be illuminated with anthropological research feature the application of new technology to subsistence economies, illustrated in the examples from tropical dams and village-level development projects. Here the anthropological evidence indicates a need for more awareness of the ecological and human consequences of water development and a need to include measurements of social and biological costs in feasibility studies. There is the suggestion that the concept of feasibility be modified by greater concern for factors of quality—quality of environment and of living.

3) The third question concerns the future of water resource research in the discipline of anthropology. With respect to prehistoric archeology and related subdisciplinary inquiries into cultural origins and man-environment relations, the incentives are clear. The search for origins and the history of development is its own reward, and the topic will continue to receive close attention from paleoanthropologists. In the sphere of living socieities, much more could be done, and new incentives are required. The preoccupation of cultural and economic-ecological anthropologists with intradisciplinary problems centering around social organization, values, and ritual, has often obscured relevant technical and instrumental functions—water is often incidental to these inquiries and not the focus of attack. The concern for small communities has led to a neglect of the study of large cultural systems whose attitudes toward resources are much more significant in terms of consequences. The basic difficulty would

appear to be the reluctance anthropologists have displayed in accepting substantive topics, like natural resource use and development, as valid subjects for theoretically oriented research. Professional rewards are not often given to anthropologists who pursue these topics, or who choose to do their research in contemporary or complex societies, as the current phrase has it.

There are, however, signs of change. As the isolated communal society becomes a rarity, and anthropologists turn their attention to societies and social segments of larger entities involved in change processes and institutions of large scale, it can be expected that water resources will be given closer and more direct attention.

The writer acknowledges the assistance of Miss Nancy Edwards and Dr. Henry Dobyns in assembling the materials examined in this paper. The paper has been read and criticized by a number of professional colleagues, notably Thayer Scudder, John Rowe, Robert McC. Adams, and Patty J. Watson. However, the author retains the entire responsibility. The first complete draft of the paper was submitted in 1970; subsequent revisions have kept the literature citations up to date. Approximate cutoff date was March 1973.

1. *Anthropologists* are defined to include persons identifying themselves as members of this academic discipline, and in some instances, researchers in geography, economics, and the medical-biological sciences. *Anthropology* is viewed as a multidisciplinary field, engaged in studies of cultural contexts of resource development in the past and present. A few professional anthropologists have recently participated in field studies initiated by water resources institutes at land-grant universities, but we have decided to omit mention of this particular body of literature since it is closer to a sociological approach, and since the abundant materials from non-North American contexts deserved detailed consideration.

2. For a history of Kentucky archeology and Webb's role in it, see Douglas W. Schwartz, *Conceptions of Kentucky Prehistory* (Lexington, Ky.: University of Kentucky Press, 1967).

3. William Y. Adams, "Organizational Problems in International Salvage Archeology," *Anthropological Quarterly* 41 (1968): 110-21; George J. Armelagos, H. G. Ewing, and D. L. Greene, "Physical Anthropology and Man-Made Lakes," *Anthropological Quarterly* 41 (1968): 122-46.

4. John M. Corbett, "River Basin Salvage in the United States," *Archeology* 14 (1961): 236-40; Fred Johnson, "Archeology in an Emergency," *Science* 152 (1966): 1592-97.

5. For theory and methods of salvage archeology, see Corbett, "River Basin Salvage"; James J. Hester, "Pioneer Methods in Salvage Anthropology," *Anthropological Quarterly* 41 (1968): 132-46; Johnson, "Archeology in an Emergency"; A. J. Lindsay, "Saving Prehistoric Sites in the Southwest," *Archeology* 14 (1961): 245-49; W. W. Wasley, "Techniques and Tools of Salvage," *Archeology* 14 (1961): 283-86. For salvage archeology on the Volta River in Africa, see O. Davies, "Archeological Salvage in Man-Made Lakes," in *Man-Made Lakes,* ed. R. H. Lowe-McConnell, Institute of Biology Symposia no. 15 (New York: Academic Press, 1966).

6. James Schoenwetter and F. W. Eddy, *Alluvial and Palynological Reconstruction of Environments: Navajo Reservoir District,* Papers in Anthropology no. 13 (Albuquerque: Museum of New Mexico, 1964).

7. James A. Ford and G. I. Quimby, *The Tchefuncte Culture: An Early Occupation of the Lower Mississippi Valley*, Memoirs no. 2 (Menasha, Wis.: Society for American Archeology, 1945).

8. Carl H. Strandberg and R. Tomlinson, "Photoarcheological Analysis of Potomac River Fishtraps," *American Antiquity* 34 (1969): 312-19.

9. Michael Evenari et al, "Ancient Agriculture in the Negev," *Science* 133 (1961): 979-96; Michael Evenari et al, *The Negev: The Challenge of a Desert* (Cambridge, Mass.: Harvard University Press, 1971).

10. Robert McCormick Adams, "Agriculture and Urban Life in Early Southwestern Iran," *Science* 136 (1962): 109; Robert McCormick Adams, "A Synopsis of the Historical Demography and Ecology of the Diyala River Basin, Central Iraq," in *Civilizations in Desert Lands*, ed. Richard B. Woodbury, Anthropological Papers no. 62 (Salt Lake City: University of Utah Press, 1962). See also Robert A. Fernea, "Land Reform and Ecology in Post Revolutionary Iraq," *Economic Development and Cultural Change* 17 (1969): 356-81.

11. Robert Raikes, *Water, Weather and Prehistory* (London: John Baker, 1967), chap. 11.

12. Nelson Glueck, *Rivers in the Desert* (New York: Farrar, Straus and Cudahay, 1959). On the Stein identification, see George F. Dales, Jr., "The Role of Natural Forces in the Ancient Indus Valley and Baluchistan," in *Civilizations in Desert Lands*, ed. Richard B. Woodbury, Anthropological Papers no. 62 (Salt Lake City: University of Utah Press, 1962).

13. See, especially, the photographs and maps of climatic patterns in Evenari, "Ancient Agriculture in the Negev."

14. I have been unable to find any detailed studies of the sociocultural aspects of drainage of swamps and wetlands, but this does not mean there are none. (For a brief note on Hohokam drainage practices see Richard B. Woodbury and John Q. Ressler, "Effects of Environmental and Cultural Limitations upon Hohokam Agriculture, Southern Arizona," in *Civilizations in Desert Lands*.) In any case, such drainage would present unusually difficult problems of archeological recovery, and apparently the practice was not extensive in native states or tribal societies, who more often than not found wetlands economically useful, as in the *chinampa* case: P. Armillas, "Gardens on Swamps," *Science* 174 (1971): 653-61. The extensive use of swampy forestland by Mesolithic peoples in the Baltic area is another instance, according to J. G. D. Clark, *Excavations at Star Carr* (Cambridge, Mass.: Cambridge University Press, 1954). In recent historical periods, the capital inputs for drainage have often exceeded those for water supply; the Netherlands is a case in point. The organization of water and land resources for wet rice production in the swampy Mekong delta also represents a major feat of drainage plus control of a useful supply, but the anthropological studies of wet rice growers have emphasized the existing irrigation facilities and their social implications, as we shall note later in the paper. Throughout the anthropological literature, the emphasis has been placed on water *supply* measures, particularly in water-deficient environments, due to the importance this problem has assumed in certain questions related to the origins of agriculture and complex sociopolitical life.

15. The *qanat* is called, among other things, *foggara* in Algeria, *rethara* in Morocco, and *kariz* in Baluchistan-Turkestan. For a detailed description of *qanats* and their influence on human settlement patterns in Iran, see Anthony Smith, *Blind White Fish in Persia* (London: George Allen and Unwin, 1953), chap. 3. Other descriptions of *qanats* may be found in George B. Cressey, "Qanats, Karez, and Foggaras," *Geographical Review* 48 (1958): 27-44; Paul W. English, *City and Village in Iran* (Madison: University of Wisconsin Press, 1966); H. E. Wulff, "The Qanats of Iran," *Scientific American*, April 1968, pp. 94-105.

16. Lloyd C. Briggs, *Tribes of the Sahara* (Cambridge, Mass.: Harvard University Press, 1960), pp. 8-12.

17. Isaiah Bowman, *Desert Trails of Atacama*, Special Publication no. 5 (Concord and New York: Geographical Society, 1924); Iwao Kobori, *Human Geography of Methods of Irrigation in the Central Andes: The Report of the University of Tokyo Scientific Expedition to the Andes in 1958* (Tokyo: Bijitsu Shuppan Sha, 1960).

18. Donald D. Brand, "Review of C. E. Smith, *Agriculture: Tehuacan Valley*," *American Anthropologist* 70 (1968): 417; Earle C. Smith, "Something Old, Something New: Farm Practices Near Tehuacan, Mexico," *Economic Botany* 17 (1963): 210-11; Earle C. Smith, "Archeological Evidence for Selection of Chupandilla and Cosahuico under Cultivation in Mexico," *Economic Botany* 22 (1968): 140-48.

19. Hans Horkheimer, "Nahrung und Nahrungsgervinnung im vorspanischen Peru," *Veroffentlichungen der Ibero-Amerikanischen Bibliothek zu Berlin*, Band 11 (Berlin: Colloquim Verlag, 1960).

20. Paul Kosok, *Life and Water in Ancient Peru* (New York: Long Island University Press, 1965); Paul Kosok, *El Valle de Lambayeque*, Actos y trabajos del 11 Congreso Nacional de Historia del Peru (epoca pre-hispanica), 1958, vol. 1 (Lima: Congreso Nacional de Historica del Peru, 1959).

21. John H. Rowe, "The Sunken Gardens of the Peruvian Coast," *American Antiquity* 34 (1939): 320-25.

22. M. Edward Moseley, "Assessing the Archeological Significance of Mahamaes," *American Antiquity* 34 (1970): 485-587; Jeffrey R. Parsons, "The Significance of Mahamaes Cultivation on the Coast of Peru," *American Antiquity* 33 (1968): 80-85.

23. William M. Denevan, "The Aboriginal Cultural Geography of the Llanos de Mojos of Bolivia," *Ibero-American*, no. 48 (University of California Press, 1966); J. J. Parsons and William M. Denevan, "Pre-Columbian Ridged Fields," *Scientific American*, July 1967, pp. 92-101. Since the above was written, an indispensable paper on various forms of drainage of agricultural fields in pre-Columbian America with references to comparable phenomena elsewhere, has appeared: William M. Denevan, "Aboriginal Drained-Field Cultivation in the Americas," *Science* 169 (1970): 647-54. The paper is important not only because it clears up some of the confusion in the older literature over *chinampas*, ridged fields, garden beds, *camellones*, and other forms, but also because it calls attention to the very much neglected topic of aboriginal drainage systems. Denevan distinguishes between: 1) soil platforms built up in permanent water bodies; 2) ridged or mounded fields on seasonally flooded or waterlogged land; 3) "lazybeds" or narrow ridges on slopes and flats subject to waterlogging; 4) ditched fields for subsoil drainage; 5) fields on naturally drained land, such as river margins; 6) diked and banked fields; 7) aquatic cultivation. Denevan's accounts of these various systems indicate that such "land reclamation" is associated with increasing populations and the corresponding need for greater agricultural production. Most of these works were given up after European conquest because of the large amounts of labor required to maintain them—a point we make in connection later with reference to large-scale irrigation and water impoundment systems.

24. Jose L. Lorenzo, "Aspectos Fisicos del Valley de Oaxaca," *Revista Mexicana De Estudios Anthropologicos* 16; 49-64; K. V. Flannery, et al., "Farming Systems and Political Growth in Ancient Oaxaca," *Science* 158, no. 3800; (1967) pp. 445-53.

25. The *lama-bordo* system: Ronald Spores, "Settlement, Farming Technology, and Environment in the Nochixtlan Valley," *Science* 166 (1969): 557-69.

26. Armillas, "Gardens on Swamps."

27. Dales, "Natural Forces in the Ancient Indus Valley"; Raikes, *Water, Weather and Prehistory*, p. 182.

28. Norman A. F. Smith, "The Roman Dams of Subiaco," *Technology and Culture* 2 (1970): 58-68.

29. John Rowe, personal correspondence, reports check dams for flood diversion in the Ica Valley, Peru. I am indebted to Douglas James for pointing out that, in general, adequate flood control requires more extensively engineered and costly works than irrigation and other supply devices, which would help explain why floodproofing was more common than true flood control in labor-intensive societies.

30. Raikes, *Water, Weather and Prehistory*, p. 172.

31. R. McCormick Adams, "Agriculture and Urban Life"; Adams, "Diyala River Basin": Adams, *Land Behind Bagdad: A History of Settlement on the Dyala Plains* (Chicago: Aldine Publishing Co., 1966).

32. R. McCormick Adams, "Agriculture and Urban Life"; Adams, "Diyala River Basin"; Adams, *Land Behind Bagdad;* Kent V. Flannery, "Ecology of Early Food Production in Mesopotamia," *Science* 161 (1968): 334-38. Frank Hole, Kent V. Flannery, and J. A. Nealy, *Prehistory and Human Ecology of the Deh Luran Plain,* Memoirs of the Museum of Anthropology, no. 1 (Ann Arbor, Mich.: University of Michigan Press, 1969). For a brief description of the transition to irrigation agriculture in arid lands, see Homer Aschmann, "Evaluations of Dry Land Environments by Societies at Various Levels of Technical Competence," in *Civilizations in Desert Lands*, Woodbury. Some anthropological work on land and water resources in the aridity context is summarized in Richard B. Woodbury, "Role of Social Science in Land and Water Utilization," in *Arid Lands in Transition*, ed. Harold E. Dregne, publication no. 90 (Washington, D.C.: American Association for the Advancement of Science, 1970).

33. Robert C. Braidwood and C. Reed, "The Achievement and Early Consequences of Food Production," *Cold Spring Harbor Symposia on Quantitative Biology* 22 (1957): 19-31.

34. L. R. Binford, "Post Pleistocene Adaptations," in *New Perspectives in Archeology*, eds. L. R. & S. R. Binford (Chicago: Aldine Publishing Co., 1968); Kent V. Flannery, "Origins and Ecological Effects of Early Domestication in Iran and the Near East," in *The Domestication and Exploitation of Plants and Animals*, ed. P. J. Ucko & G. W. Dimbleby (Chicago: Aldine Publishing Co., 1969).

35. Hans Helbaek, "Appendix I," in *Prehistory and Human Ecology of the Deh Luran Plain*, Hole, Flannery, and Nealy. For a New World example (Hohokam), see Woodbury and Ressler, "Effects of Environmental and Cultural Limitations."

36. R. McCormick Adams, *The Evolution of Urban Society.*

37. Suggestive evidence for comparable preclassic irrigation in Mexico is provided by Melvin L. Fowler, *Un Sistema Preclasico de Distribucion de Agua en la Zona Arqueologica de Amaluacan, Pueblo* (Pueblo, Mexico: Instituto Poblano de Antropologia y Historia, 1968).

38. The oasis is a particularly significant element in this picture, since it is a relatively resources-abundant island in the midst of desolation. For a revealing picture of contemporary development of these concentrated resources, see the classic account of the Siwa Oasis by G. E. Simpson, *The Heart of Libya: The Siwa Oasis* (London: Harper and Brothers, 1929).

39. For some appreciations of the rate and circumstances of the onset of urban civilization, see R. McCormick Adams, *The Evolution of Urban Society;* Robert J. Braidwood and G. Willey, *Courses Toward Urban Life*, Viking Fund Publications in Anthropology, no. 32 (New York: Wenner Gren Foundation, 1962); Frank Hole, "Investigating the Origins of Mesopotamian Civilization," *Science* 153 (1966): reprinted in *Man in Adaptation, I*, ed. Yehudi Cohen (Chicago, Aldine Publishing Co., 1968); John A. Wilson, *The Burden of Egypt* (Chicago: University of Chicago Press, 1951); Woodbury, *Civilizations in Desert Lands.*

40. R. McCormick Adams, "Agriculture in Urban Life," p. 116.

41. V. Gordon Childe, *Man Makes Himself* (London: Watts and Co., 1941); *What Happened in History* (London: Harmondsworth, 1942).

42. English, *City and Village in Iran*, chap. 3, p. 38.

43. The generalized theory sketched here is based in part on the discussion of the collapse of civilization in the dry zone of Ceylon in Rhoads Murphey, "The Ruin of Ancient Ceylon," *Journal of Asian Studies* 16 (1957): 181-200. Murphey cites the ever-present dangers of weeds, flash floods, and other disasters associated with the large-scale water impoundments and canal systems, although he does not appear to believe that soil exhaustion, siltation or salinization were significant factors in this case. He throws the weight of the argument on malaria epidemics and social disorder that destroyed the capacity of the regime to muster sufficient labor to maintain the works, and the subsequent advantage taken of the situation by invading Tamils.

44. Thorkild Jacobsen and Robert McCormick Adams, "Salt and Silt in Ancient Mesopotamian Agriculture," *Science* 128 (1958): 1251-58. Also, see especially the references in R. McCormick Adams, "Diyala River Basin."

45. Helbaek, "Appendix I," *Prehistory and Human Ecology*.

46. Wilson, *The Burden of Egypt*, pp. 133-34.

47. On the question of capital costs of irrigation and water development generally, see Bert F. Hoselitz, "Capital Formation, Saving and Credit in Indian Agricultural Society," in *Capital Saving and Credit in Peasant Societies*, eds. Ramond Firth and B. S. Yamey (Chicago: Aldine Publishing Co., 1964); Colin Clark, *The Economics of Irrigation* (New York: Pergamon Press, 1967). The extent of social investments can be gathered in Clifford Geertz, *Peddlers and Princes: Social Development and Economic Change in Two Indonesian Towns* (Chicago: University of Chicago Press, 1963). His chapter, "Economic Development in Tabanan," describes the social forms emergent with wet-rice culture.

48. Julian H. Steward, ed., *Irrigation Civilizations: A Comparative Study: A Symposium on Method and Result in Cross-Cultural Regularities*, Social Science Monographs, no. 1 (Washington, D.C.: Pan American Union, 1955).

49. Karl Wittfogel, *Oriental Despotism: A Comparative Study of Total Power* (New Haven: Yale University Press, 1957).

50. For discussions of redistributive economy—essentially a form in which production is husbanded by the state and doled out to consumers, eliminating true market on any significant scale, see Karl Polanyi, Conrad M. Arensberg, and Harry W. Pearson, eds., *Trade and Market in the Early Empires: Economics in History and Theory* (Glencoe, Ill.: Free Press, 1957).

51. Richard K. Beardsley, "Ecological and Social Parallels Between Rice-Growing Communities of Japan and Spain," in *Symposium on Community Studies in Anthropology*, ed. V. E. Garfield (Seattle: University of Washington; American Ethnological Society, 1964). See also Peter Kunstadter, "Irrigation and Social Structure: Narrow Valleys and Individual Enterprise," (Tokyo: 11th Pacific Science Congress, 1966); Rene Millon, "Variations in Social Responses to the Practice of Irrigation Agriculture," in *Civilizations in Desert Lands*, Woodbury.

52. R. McCormick Adams, *Land Behind Bagdad*. See also Marvin Harris's defense of Wittfogel against Adams's critique in Marvin Harris, *The Rise of Anthropological Theory* (New York: Crowell, 1968). For criticism of Wittfogel, see Clifford Geertz, "Two Types of Ecosystems," in *Environment and Cultural Behavior*, ed. Andrew P. Vayda, American Museum Sourcebooks in Anthropology (Garden City, N.Y.: The Natural History Press, 1969); S. M. Eisenstadt, "The Study of Oriental Despotisms as Systems of Total Power," *Journal of Asian Studies* 17 (1958): 435-46. For a look at some of the Meso-American data with a bearing on the thesis, see Robert F. Heizer, "Agriculture and the Theocratic State in Lowland Southeastern Mexico," *American Antiquity* 26 (1960): 215-22, reprinted in *Man in Adaptation, I*, Cohen; William T. Sanders, "Hydraulic Agriculture, Economic Symbiosis, and the Evolution of States in

Central Mexico," in *Anthropological Archeology in the Americas*, ed. B. J. Meggers (Washington, D.C.: Anthropological Society of Washington, 1968); William T. Sanders, "Cultural Ecology of Nuclear Mesoamerica," *American Anthropologist* 64 (1962): 34-44, reprinted in *Man in Adaptation*, *I*,Cohen. In a larger context, the Wittfogel concept is another in the family of explanations of culture growth based on energy accumulation: William F. Cottrell, *Energy and Society: The Relations of Energy, Social Change, and Economic Development* (New York: McGraw-Hill, 1955).

53. Millon, "Variations in Social Responses," p. 80.

54. E. R. Leach, "Hydraulic Society in Ceylon," *Past and Present* 15 (1959): 2-26.

55. Murphey, "The Ruin of Ancient Ceylon."

56. Beardsley, "Rice-Growing Communities of Japan and Spain."

57. Wilson, *The Burden of Egypt*, chap. 4.

58. Kunstadter, "Irrigation and Social Structure."

59. Sanders, "Hydraulic Agriculture"; Sanders, "Cultural Ecology of Nuclear Mesoamerica"; Woodbury and Ressler, "Hohokam Agriculture."

60. H. T. Waterbolk, "The Lower Rhine Basin," in *Courses Toward Urban Life*, Braidwood and Willey.

61. Grahame Clark, "Ecological Zones and Economic Stages," in *Prehistoric Europe: The Economic Basis* (London: Methuen and Co., 1952; Stanford, Calif.: Stanford University Press, 1952), reprinted in *Man in Adaptation*, *I*, Cohen.

62. For some general surveys, see Aloys A. Michel, *The Indus Rivers: A Study of the Effects of Partition* (New Haven: Yale University Press, 1967); A. K. Snelgrove, ed., *Indus River Symposium*, Transactions of the Society of Mining Engineers, vol. 244 (American Institute of Mining Engineers, 1969); C. Hart Schaaf and R. H. Fifield, *The Lower Mekong: Challenge to Cooperation in Southeast Asia* (New York: D. Van Nostrand Co., 1963); Edward H. Spicer, "Developmental Change and Cultural Integration," in *Perpectives in Developmental Change*, ed. Art Gallaher, Jr. (Lexington, Ky.: University of Kentucky Press, 1968); N. Rubin and W. Warren, eds., *Dams in Africa* (London: Frank Cass, 1968); Karuna Moy Mukerji and K. John Mammen, *Economics of River Basin Development in India* (Bombay: Vora and Co., Publishers, Pvt., Ltd., 1959).

63. While this section will emphasize natural and human ecological problems associated with tropical rivers, it should be noted that comparable problems have arisen in other climates. A detailed study of the ecological hazards associated with the attempt to settle the Bedouin of Arabia in irrigated areas is provided by Harold F. Heady, "Ecological Consequences of Bedouin Settlement in Saudi Arabia," in *The Careless Technology: Ecology and International Development*, eds. M. T. Farvar & J. P. Milton (New York: Natural History Press, 1971). The result was overuse of water for irrigation by these untrained people and consequent salinization, siltation, reduction of the water table, and extinction of many wild species.

64. *For the African cases*, see David Brokensha, "Volta Resettlement and Anthropological Research," *Human Organization* 22 (1963): 286-90; David Brokensha and Thayer Scudder, "Resettlement," in *Dams in Africa*, Rubin and Warren; Robert A. Fernea, ed., *Contemporary Egyptian Nubia*, HRAFLEX Book no. MR8-001, vol. 1 (New Haven: Human Relations Area Files, 1966); Thayer Scudder, *The Ecology of the Gwembe Tonga*, Rhodes-Livingstone Institute, Kariba Studies, vol. 2 (Manchester: Manchester University Press, 1962); Thayer Scudder, "Man-made Lakes and Social Change," *Engineering and Science* 24 (1966): 19-22; Thayer Scudder, "Man-made Lakes and Population Resettlement in Africa," in *Man-Made Lakes*, Lowe-McConnell; Thayer Scudder, "Social Anthropology, Man-made Lakes and Population Relocation in Africa," *Anthropological Quarterly* 41 (1968): 168-76; Thayer Scudder, "Relocation, Agricultural Intensification, and Anthropological Research," in *The Anthropology of Development in Sub-Saharan Africa*, ed. D. Brokensha & M.

Pearsall, Society for Applied Anthropology, Monograph no. 10 (1969); Thayer Scudder, "Ecology and Development: The Kariba Lake Basin," in *The Careless Technology*, Farvar and Milton; Thayer Scudder and Elizabeth Colson, "The Kariba Dam Project: Resettlement and Local Initiative," in *Technological Innovation and Culture Change*, Bernard and Pelto. For the Mekong, see John E. Bardach, "Some Ecological Implications of Mekong River Development Plans," in *The Careless Technology*, Farvar and Milton; Jasper Ingersoll, *The Social Feasibility of Pa Mong Irrigation*, A report to the U.S. Bureau of Reclaimation and the U.S. Agency for International Development, duplicated (Washington, D.C., 1969); W. R. Derrick Sewell and Gilbert F. White, "The Lower Mekong: An Experiment in International River Development," *International Conciliation* 558 (May 1966); Wilhelm Solheim and Robert Hackenberg, "The Importance of Anthropological Research to the Mekong Valley Project," *France-Asie*, September-October 1961; Joel Halpern and James Hafner, "Preliminary Bibliography of Miscellaneous Research Materials on Laos, with Special Reference to the Mekong Development Scheme," *Centre d' Etude de Sud-Est Asiatique et de l'Extreme Orient*, Brussels, 1971. For brief summaries of various cases, see Julian McCaull, "Conference of the Ecological Aspects of International Development," (UNESCO) *Nature and Resources* 5 (1969): 5-12. Papers on various phenomena associated with man-made lakes can be found in: McConnell, *Man-Made Lakes;* Rubin and Warren, *Dams in Africa*.

65. Scudder, "Social Anthropology, Man-made Lakes and Population Relocation in Africa," p. 168.

66. For a summary, see McCaull, "Conference on the Ecological Aspects of International Development." For details, see Scudder, "Ecology and Development"; Scudder and Colson, "The Kariba Dam Project."

67. Thayer Scudder, personal correspondence.

68. P. B. N. Jackson, "The Establishment of Fisheries in Man-Made Lakes in the Tropics," in *Man-Made Lakes*, Lowe-McConnell.

69. For a study of trypanosomiasis and its ecological and human-settlement effects, see Frank L. Lambrecht, "Aspects of Evolution and Ecology of Tsetse Flies and Trypanosomiasis in Prehistoric African Environment," *Journal of African History* 5 (1964): 1-24.

70. B. B. Waddy, "Medical Problems Arising from the Making of Lakes in the Tropics," in *Man-Made Lakes*, Lowe-McConnell.

71. Ibid.

72. An informative account of schistosomiasis is found in John M. Weir, "The Unconquered Plague," *Rockefeller Foundation Quarterly* 2 (1969): 4-23. For a study of the effects of onchocerciasis (river blindness) on human settlement and ecology, see John M. Hunter, "River Blindness in Nangodi, Northern Ghana," *Geographical Review* 56 (1966): 391-416.

73. McCaull, "Ecological Aspects of International Development"; Henry Van der Schalie, "WHO Project 10: A Case History of a Schistosomiasis Control Project," in *The Careless Technology*, Farvar and Milton.

74. Brokensha and Scudder, "Resettlement"; Scudder, "Man-made Lakes and population Resettlement in Africa."

75. Fernea, *Contemporary Egyptian Nubia*.

76. Scudder, "Man-made Lakes and Population Resettlement in Africa," p. 102.

77. Ibid.

78. Jackson, "The Establishment of Fisheries in Man-Made Lakes in the Tropics," p. 113.

79. For a classic study of "unanticipated consequences," in the TVA program, see Philip Selznick, *TVA and the Grass Roots: A Study in the Sociology of Formal Organization*, University of California Publications in Culture and Society, vol. 3 (Berkeley: University of California Press, 1949).

80. Scudder, "Social Anthropology, Man-made Lakes and Population Relocation in Africa," p. 172.

81. Jasper Ingersoll, "Mekong River Basin Development: Anthropology in a New Setting," *Anthropological Quarterly* 41 (1968): 147-67.

82. Sewell and White, "The Lower Mekong."

83. Ingersoll, *The Social Feasibility of Pa Mong Irrigation.*

84. Ibid., p. 219.

85. Ingersoll, "Mekong River Basin Development."

86. Ibid., p. 168.

87. Ibid., p. 165.

88. Ibid., p. 164.

89. Solheim and Hackenberg, "The Importance of Anthropological Research to the Mekong Valley Project."

90. For example: Bardach, "Some Ecological Implications of Mekong River Development Plans"; John Milton, "Pollution, Public Health, and Nutritional Effects of Mekong Basin Hydro-Development," mimeographed (Washington, D. C.: Smithsonian Institute, 1969); Joel Halpern, "Mekong River Development Schemes for Laos and Thailand," *Internationales Asien Forum* (Munich), Heft 1, Jahrgang 3, Jan. 1972; also published in "Courrier de l'Extreme Orient," *Centre d'Etude du Sud-Est Asiatique et de l'Extreme Orient,* Brussels, 1971, pp. 139-64; Joel Halpern, "Some Reflections on the War in Laos, Anthropological or Otherwise," *Centre d'Etude du Sud-Est Asiatique et de l'Extreme Orient,* Brussels, Public.mensuelle, 4e année, No. 44, 1972.

91. C. Daryll Forde, *Habitat, Economy and Society* (London: Methuen and Co., Ltd., 1934). For similar typological treatments of tribal societies and their economic adaptations, see Elman R. Service, *A Profile of Primitive Culture* (New York: Harper and Brothers, 1958); Richard A. Watson and Patty Jo Watson, *Man and Nature: An Anthropological Essay in Human Ecology* (New York: Harcourt Brace and World, 1969). Some of the best studies of the emergence of various forms of water resource development in tribal societies are being contributed by archeologists, who can trace the evolution of various uses, and their relationships to settlement pattern and population size and movements, through a series of related groups in a given habitat. For an example, see Thomas C. Patterson, "The Emergence of Food Production in Central Peru," in S. Struever, ed., *Prehistoric Agriculture.* (New York: Natural History Press, 1971). For some typical ethnological monographs with considerable information about water use, see Harold C. Conklin, *Hanunoo Agriculture: A Report on an Integral System of Shifting Cultivation in the Philippines,* FAO Series on Shifting Cultivation, vol. 2, FAO Forestry Development Paper, no. 12 (Rome: Food and Agriculture Organization of the United Nations, 1957); John Fee Embree, *Suye Mura: A Japanese Village* (Chicago: University of Chicago Press, 1939); Raymond William Firth, *Primitive Polynesian Economy* (London: Routledge, 1939); Raymond William Firth, *Malay Fishermen: Their Peasant Economy* (London: Kegal, Paul, Trench, Trubner, 1946); Thomas M. Fraser, Jr., *Fishermen of South Thailand, the Malay Villagers* (New York: Holt, Rinehart and Winston, 1966); J. D. Freeman, *Iban Agriculture: A Report on the Shifting Cultivation of Hill Rice by the Iban of Sariwak,* Great Britain Colonial Office, Colonial Research Studies, no. 18 (London: H. M. Stationary Office, 1955); P. H. Gulliver, *The Family Herds: A Study of Two Pastoral Tribes in East Africa, the Jie and Turkana,* International Library of Sociology and Social Reconstruction (London: Routledge and Kegan Paul, 1955); Bronislaw Malinowski, *Argonauts of the Western Pacific* (London: George Routledge, 1932); Bronislaw Malinowski, *Coral Gardens and their Magic* (London, George Allen and Unwin, 1935); Audrey Isabel Richards, *Land, Labour and Diet in Northern Rhodesia: An Economic Study of the Bemba Tribe,* the International Institute of

African Languages and Cultures (London, New York: Oxford University Press, 1939); Ruth M. Underhill, *Social Organization of the Papago Indians* (New York: Columbia University Press, 1939). It should be noted that that emphasis in this paper has been on direct uses of water as providing energy in some form. We have not been concerned with water uses in the sense of fishing or transportation. However, there is a very large ethnological literature on these uses that would deserve a separate review. A recent study of one of the least known technological adaptations to watery coasts and marshland areas, the "mud sled," is provided in Asahitaro Nishimura, "The Most Primitive Means of Transportation in Southeast and East Asia," *Asian Folklore Studies* 28 (1969): 1-93; also, Nishimura, *A Preliminary Report on Current Trends in Marine Anthropology*, Occasional Papers of the Center of Marine Ethnology No. 1, Tokyo, Waseda University, 1973.

92. Bronislaw Malinowski, "Man's Culture and Man's Behavior," *Sigma Xi Quarterly* 29 (1942): 182-96.

93. A case from India is cited by Thomas M. Fraser, Jr., "Sociocultural Parameters in Directed Change," *Human Organization* 22 (1963): 95-104. Another case from the Papago is cited by Henry F. Dobyns, "Thirsty Indians: Introduction of Wells among People of an Arid Region," *Human Organization* 11 (1952): 33-36.

94. Afif Tannous, "Extension Work among the Arab Fellahin," *Human Organization* 3 (1944): 1-12.

95. Sunil K. Basu, "Water Could not Flow: Case Study into Failure of Technological Aid," Government of West Bengal, *Bulletin of the Cultural Research Institute, Scheduled Castes and Tribes Welfare Department* 6 (1967): 43-48.

96. William Caudill, "Patterns of Emotion in Modern Japan," in *Japanese-Culture: Its Development and Characteristics*, ed. R. J. Smith and R. K. Beardsley (Chicago: Aldine Publishing Co., 1962).

97. For collections of cases of this type, see Charles Erasmus, *Man Takes Control: Cultural Development and American Aid* (Minneapolis: University of Minnesota Press, 1961); Arthur H. Niehoff, *A Casebook of Social Change* (Chicago: Aldine Publishing Co., 1966); Edward H. Spicer, ed., *Human Problems in Technological Change* (New York: Russell Sage Foundation, 1952).

98. Tom T. Sasaki, "Changes in Land Use Among the Navajo Indians in the Many Farms Area of the Navajo Reservation," in *Indian and Spanish American Adjustments to Arid and Semi-arid Environments*, ed. C. S. Knowlton, Committee on Desert and Arid Zone Research, Texas Technological College, Contribution no. 7 (1964).

99. Applied anthropological studies that demonstrate this: (Orissa, India) Fraser, "Sociocultural Parameters in Directed Change"; Nityananda Patnaik, "Digging Wells in Barpali, Orissa: An Experience in Rural Reconstruction," *Man in India* 31 (1961): 83-99; (Papago Indians) Dobyns, "Thirsty Indians"; (Iran) Harold B. Allen, *Rural Reconstruction in Action: Experiences in the Near and Middle East* (Ithaca: Cornell University Press, 1953). For a classic study of rejection of wells due to identification with landlords, see Allan R. Holmberg, "The Wells That Failed: Attempt to Establish a Stable Water Supply in Viru Valley, Peru," in *Human Problems in Technological Change*, Spicer. A useful survey of varying responses to irrigation in different societies is provided by: Millon, "Variations in Social Responses."

100. Allen, *Rural Reconstruction in Action*.

101. Henry F. Dobyns, "Blunders with Bolsas: A Case Study of Diffusion of Closed-Basin Agriculture," *Human Organization* 10 (1951): 25-32; Henry F. Dobyns, "Experiment in Conservation: Erosion Control and Forage Production on the Papago Indian Reservation in Arizona," in *Human Problems in Technological Change*, Spicer; Dobyns, "Thirsty Indians."

102. Holmberg, "The Wells That Failed."

103. Beardsley, "Rice-Growing Communities of Japan and Spain"; Evenari, "Ancient Agriculture in the Negev."

104. See, for example, the rather simplistic formulations in Henry Orenstein, "Notes on the Ecology of Irrigation Agriculture in Contemporary Peasant Societies," *American Anthropologist* 67 (1965): 1531.

105. John W. Bennett, *Northern Plainsmen: Adaptive Strategy and Agrarian Life* (Chicago: Aldine Publishing Co., 1969), chap. 9.

106. That the amount of irrigation practiced by farmers varies with the cost, below a certain level of rainfall, is shown in a paper on well irrigation in Texas by Jack P. Gibbs, "Human Ecology and Rational Economic Behavior: Agricultural Practices as a Case in Point," *Rural Sociology* 29 (1964): 138-51. This example of "economic rationality" suggests the need for consideration of rationalizing models in sociological analysis in other instances where they apply. The study is a good one, but Gibbs does not consider the effects of such rationality on the water supply, which in this part of Texas is diminishing due to reduction of ground water supplies by the wells. "Community economic rationality" must consider the effect of individual maximization on the hydraulic commons.

107. Some anthropologists also tend to generalize about the social effects of technology, in a search for what is called "techno-environmental determinism" by Harris, in *The Rise of Anthropological Theory*. There is nothing wrong with this search, providing one is aware of the level of generality on which he is examining the problem. Where the generalizations are based on microsocial levels, they are subject to continual refutation on the basis of differing constellations of institutional reinforcements and modifiers. An example of misplaced generalization is found in the literature on the relationships of cooperation, competition, and conflict over water in irrigation management. The generalization that canal irrigation leads to conflict between farmers and a diminishing of cooperation is proposed by H. Orenstein "Notes on the Ecology of Irrigation in Contemporary Peasant Societies"; and that conflict over water provided the most important cause of interfamily and intercommunity quarrels in traditional China is concluded by Hsiao Kung-Chan, *Rural China: Imperial Control in the Nineteenth Century* (Seattle: University of Washington Press, 1960). A review of these positions is found in Burton Pasternak, "Social Consequences of Equalizing Irrigation Access," *Human Organization* 27 (1968): 332-43. He properly notes that irrigation will be the source of *both* competition and cooperation, but then presents his own data in order to show that, "equalization of access to irrigation water is associated with a reduction of conflict over water" (p. 342) in a Taiwan village—another broad generalization. He fails to give sufficient attention to the increasing dedication to commercialization in Taiwan agriculture, which might be the key factor in this case.

108. Garrett Hardin, "The Tragedy of the Commons," *Science* 162 (1968): 1243-48.

109. Tom T. Sasaki and J. Adair, "New Land to Farm: Agricultural Practices Among the Navajo Indians of New Mexico," in *Human Problems in Technological Change*, Spicer.

110. Alex Weingrod, *Reluctant Pioneers: Village Development in Israel* (Ithaca: Cornell University Press, 1966).

111. Clarence J. Glacken, "Reflections on the Man-Nature Theme as an Object for Study," in *Future Environments of North America*, ed. F. F. Darling and J. P. Milton (New York: Natural History Press, 1966).

112. For a discussion of the issues, see Kenneth E. Boulding, "Economics and Ecology," in *Future Environments of North America*, Darling and Milton.

113. For information on the increase in the popularity of water-based recreation, see Marion Clawson, "Economics and Environmental Impacts of Increasing

Leisure Activities," in *Future Environments of North America*, Darling and Milton.
114. Raymond F. Dasmann, "Man in North America," in *Future Environments of North America*, Darling and Milton, pp. 330-31.
115. For a study of American water management techniques, see Gilbert F. White, *Strategies of American Water Management* (Ann Arbor, Mich.: University of Michigan Press, 1969).

3 Economics and Economists in Water Resources Development

Stephen C. Smith

PAST CONTRIBUTIONS

What have economists contributed to water resources development? Which water development problems might move toward solution with the assistance of economists? What are the professional incentives and rewards for increased involvement of economists in water-related research?

Important questions have been asked the participants of the symposium. Issues and concepts are exposed which are not frequently probed. At the heart of the questions is the use of the term *water resources development*. This concept has been a frequent frame of reference and it has been in common parlance among "water circles" for over three-quarters of a century.[1] Too often their attitude has been that development means construction or that construction itself is the prime and unqualified means for achieving water-oriented objectives.

The pertinent question is how the contribution of the economists to the water resources field is to be judged. Economists have generally preferred to see their role in terms of establishing criteria for evaluating development, for deciding whether development is appropriate, and if so, which development design is optimum. The criteria they have worked to establish have been only partly successful in distinguishing desirable from undesirable developments. The social context has not always been adequately assessed and many factors have not been observable through the economist's system of perception; economic models have been rudimentary in simulating the economic effects of technical and biological relationships.

The presumption that water development is to be sought as an end in itself is central to many of the water planning controversies of the last two decades. This attitude has split professional interests, often pitting economists against noneconomists in both academic and bureaucratic circles. It has limited the employment of economists in water management agencies. It has led to adulation of development on one hand and charges of boondoggling on the other.

Many professional economists would say that they do not want to be judged by their contributions to water resources development—that this criterion is not appropriate because it miscasts the role of the economist as a professional. His prime concern is not just development in the sense of increasing the supply of water or building structures to reduce flood damage. Thus, he has been reluctant to place himself within an organization in which he felt the goal orientation was fixed on the single concept of development; he limited his role in water development agencies by looking elsewhere for employment. Likewise, water management and water development agencies have been reluctant to employ professionals whose orientation would explicitly raise fundamental questions about basic agency policy. Nevertheless, more economists are working on water resources problems today than there were two decades ago, and a large professional literature has been spawned.

Economic Language and Concepts

The literature and language of economics and the use of economic concepts must be reviewed to assess the contribution of economists. This point will be explored in this paper by developing a management concept which encompasses the common term *development*. An understanding of these resource management issues is crucial, as today's perception of water problems is broadening to include many of the pressing issues of environmental management.

Economics and economic concepts, as well as the concern of some economists, have a long history of involvement with water resources. Ancient history records many instances where investment in water was the major form of capital improvement in arid nations.[2] Even in a humid area, early English economists and governments were concerned with improving harbors and draining swamps and lowlands. Conflicts of interest similar to those of today were also evident during these early times; however, the rationale behind these early projects was basically economic. The economic objectives may have been officially expressed in terms of water supply, a better harbor, or a drained marsh for farm use, or they may have been expressed in the sense of Albert Galletin's evaluation in 1790 of "internal improvements" (largely dealing with inland waterways in the United States), or in the terms of the Flood Control Act of 1936—"the benefits to whomsoever they may accrue should exceed the costs." The translations of the latter legislative directive into administrative application, initiated a stream of theoretical and empirical effort of a formal economic nature.

Some may argue that it is not valid to differentiate between the language of economics and economic concepts. Clearly, concepts are embodied in language. The distinction is made, however, because at certain times the language of economics is used but economic concepts are ignored. It is often in this sense that agencies have used the term *economic justification*. The question of "should I or shouldn't I build" has been answered on some other basis. Agency employees are given to understand that all efforts should be bent toward supporting decisions already made. Since economics has achieved some social status, agency leadership is likely to perceive the role of economists in terms of clinching the argument against those who oppose the project with economic language and, better still, by expressing all values in a numerical form favorable to the project.

As a consequence, economic language has been used extensively in the water resources field to rationalize or provide justification for decisions dictated by other than formal considerations. Such language may be found in project studies and has been brought into river basin studies and high-level policy arguments over project selection. Much of the language give-and-take is concerned with assessing the magnitude of income multipliers or choosing an appropriate balance between the weighting to be given national income criteria and that to be given income distributional effects or regional impact. The pressure in making these assessments has been to emphasize factors favoring projects and to minimize those that do not.

No cynicism is implied. First, persons of good judgment recognize that economics does not incorporate all values. Second, from the fact that language and concepts are intertwined, the weight of logical concepts establishes criteria for judging the language. Thus, deviations between the language and concept become apparent to those knowledgeable about water development. Knowing the existence of such deviations has a heavy impact upon policy, for logical concepts have their own power. Of course, it is knowing this interaction of language and concept which makes the tie with the professional economist necessary. In essence, his role is *to bring the economic criteria to life* in the practice of decision making. However, the economist may become very disheartened if he is a "true believer" in economics and finds out that his usefulness to an agency is only for purposes of enunciating a litany of *justification*—to find benefits in bureaucratic parlance! In this sense, the economist may resent the fact that the major criterion for judging his professional skill is his ability to force a project that really should be rejected into an economic mold that portrays a sound project. His frustration may be heightened because of the nature of his training; his academic background may not have imparted an understanding of the role of economics in the policy process or the economics of policy.

This characterization of economic language, concepts, and economists is all too true. Its truth is substantiated in the employment by water development agencies of too few economists, assignments of economists to the wrong jobs, and improper application of economic concepts to the workaday tasks in water resources. To quote a song of the day, "Is that all there is?" No. If you said, "That is all there is," you would misread the lives of many earnest men dedicated to the application of their talents.

Development Alternatives

For the most part, economists have been asked to contribute to "water development." They generally have not been asked to study the full range of alternatives free of the constraints of agency objectives. Economists have not been asked to address the question of demands for the full range of water services in an unrestricted fashion, and since demand studies raise difficult questions, few have stepped in on their own. Professional pressures from within the discipline, however, would have economists explore a wide variety of alternative solutions to meeting the demands and investigate alternatives inside and outside of the agency's institutional assignment. Consequently, as a group, agency economists and academic— research economists have frequently raised the annoying questions which eventually led to a rethinking of development policy and organizational objectives.

Economists have contributed to water resource development by being internal as well as outside critics and working to expand awareness of policy possibilities. They have developed an economic rationale for comparing development alternatives which, in modern theoretical terms and in practical applications, date back to the late 1930s and the 1940s. An early major contribution in the 1940s appears in both the reports and the dissenting comment of the Committee on The Central Valley Project in California.[3] The economic rationale has continued to evolve and to be reported in government documents and professional journals,[4] and the Water Resources Council has recently developed revisions to the procedures for benefit-cost analysis. The benefit-cost rationale, that benefits when they exceed costs point toward increased national income, is incorporated into the decision process—into the reports designed to provide information for directing government investment—project by project. From the beginning, the benefit-cost system of evaluation has been rooted in the economic theory developed by Hicks, Marshall, Pareto, Carlson, Pigou, DuPuit, and others.

In this contribution, microeconomics played a major role. It provided theoretical constructs whereby biological production or engineering production could be logically tied to a general theory of production, capital growth, and valuation. The contributions to action, to water development, if you will, were of two types: 1) exposing on paper a hypothesized flow of economic activity that provided both a check on project merit and information essential for informed debate as to whether a project should or should not be built, and 2) establishing procedures for project formulation analysis aimed to provide rules for sizing, shaping, and assembling the project itself.[5]

Simply, benefit-cost procedures were to be used to analyze a water management plan to determine whether the economy was better off with it than without it. The literature on the approach is extensive with books of note by Eckstein, McKean, Hirshleifer, and others; and most recently by Arrow and Kurz.[6] Many other books delineate such special problems as river system development and the economics of water quality.[7] As part of the process of analyzing the merit of a plan, it became important that alternative ways to achieve the postulated objective be analyzed, that each component of each alternative be investigated to select the most efficient, and that all benefits and costs be identified and counted. Recently, the article by Kneese defined a "partial-general-model" as an aid to the management of water as a waste receptor.[8]

Economists were not unmindful that merit could not be evaluated for projects in isolation. A theory grounded on system equilibrium or grounded on an interactive system with spiral change over time forced them to take a broader view. Early literature noted that projects might affect the product market (for outputs supplied by projects) and/or the factor market (for inputs required by projects) or merely substitute economic activity in one location or sector for that in another without making any net contribution to national income.

The expansion of the scope of the economist's contribution to water resources planning was taking place when national and regional income accounting and macroeconomics were coming into their own. The formalistic analysis of interaction slowly gave way to meaningful interpretation for policy purposes as "basin analysis" became more acceptable and demanding. For example, the suggestion that the basin be treated as a firm was explored in the early 1950s. Also, it was recognized that watershed boundaries were not acceptable as economic boundaries in defining the relationships between the hydrologic system and the economic system. Added to these economic concepts was the system of social decision making which used economic and hydrologic systems as tools to achieve ends with direct, local payoff to "real" interests and "real" people (construction, farm, transportation, and other groups). More recently the development of simulation techniques has given pragmatic policy assistance.

Economic evaluation has many complexities and subtleties even for goods regularly traded in the market. The economist's problems have been compounded as he has been forced to face the necessity of assigning economic value to the nonmarket products and services derived from water. Concurrently, the need to compare alternative systems of project development led to a continuous discussion about the appropriate way for comparing values occurring at different points in time. Thus, the discount rate and interest rate literature has flourished with major efforts allocated to carefully combing the issues relating to social and private time-preference, alternative ways to assess public investments, and systems for handling uncertainties. Arrow's theoretical work is a recent addition.[9]

The fact that the discount rates used are a matter of practical concern to the public is illustrated by the testimony to the Water Resources Council and by the economic tableau attached to project reports. Argument over the rate of construction activity and over which economic groups will benefit from the investment frequently has hinged around the question of the appropriate discount rate to use in economic evaluation. Advocates seriously differed with stated preferences from a zero rate to a rate as high as ten percent or more.

Financial Analysis

The question of "should it or shouldn't it be constructed" is not the only question economists have been asked. Financial questions loom large and to many a noneconomist, questions related to paying the bills are very important and, at times, more important than the issues of evaluating net returns. Through a system of cost allocation, costs are assigned to project purposes or to users by geographic specification. These, in turn, are reflected in cost sharing agreements among the parties participating in the project and in prices charged for services and in tax rates levied by local government. These operational questions of dealing with joint costs and bargaining among interest groups for service continue to be uncomfortable arenas for many economists and of little or no theoretical interest to most of them.[10] The question of "who should pay and how" has not been as exciting to economists as determining project optimality, formulation, and contribution to the national economy.

The ground of financial analysis is still fertile, however. Its cultivation is becoming interesting again with probing questions exploring issues such as charges on effluent discharge, the effects of alternative financial arrangements upon income distribution, and the feedback of distributional effects to policy. For example, second-round operational design objectives may originate from the cost allocation procedure. Too many professional economists limited their vision with the screen of "evaluation" and "efficiency" theory. They did not look at the whole system as a public-private complex where the market is part, but not the total, decision institution. Too few looked at the total system closely enough to understand the way it functions—namely, that cost allocation, repayment, and pricing analyses have significant feedback roles and effects upon project design, formulation, and evaluation. Agency economists have long struggled with these issues with little power to change the law, congressional committee structure, and other forces.

Economic Institutions and the Law

As a third area of contribution of economists and economics, literature has been developed dealing with the problems of economic organization and the law. This field has been particularly important over the past forty years and remains so today. Its importance stems from the public character of water service; the flow characteristics (time and quality patterns) of the physical resource; the interaction of water with soil, animals, plants, and topography; the geographic patterns of surplus and deficient areas; and the fact that water is a necessity for life and human survival. All of these relationships do not make water resources amenable to fitting neatly into our prime economic institutions of private property and the market, although both private property rights and the market institution play important roles. Public organizations (including public utilities and federal, state, and local agencies) have provided most water services because of the widespread view of water as a public good. Many factors have contributed to water becoming viewed as a public good: the concept of monopoly, the esthetic and nonmarket values relating to water, the downstream externalities of water use, and the value judgment of many that water should be supplied at cost in the sense of a cooperative.

Studies of the organizations and their economic roles have contributed to water management and legislation. For example, analysis of public districts dates back to the early part of the century in California and other western states. More recently economic organizational studies, economics of water law, and the economics of water administration have had important impacts.[11]

Economists have also played significant roles in institution building as analysts, counselors to men of action, and as social scientists in studying human behavior. Also, they have aided in designing and suggesting organizational arrangements which attempt to make water management more responsive to the pattern of demand. For example, in the West economists have been important in developing local, state, and federal water management laws and organizations. In the Midwest economists assisted in developing Iowa's system of water law; in Wisconsin the shoreland zoning laws were developed in consultation with economists. In the East, agency and university economists have worked on the design of basin water management systems. Today they are on the forefront, suggesting and working with policy groups on many problems such as water quality management. The Delaware River and Chesapeake Bay have received particular attention.

Analytical Techniques

Finally, economists and economics have been working for at least a decade and a half to apply the quantitative techniques of operations research, simulation, input-output analysis, and systems analysis to problems of water management. For example, operations research has aided in suggesting operating rules for water resource management systems which would be optimal in an economic sense.[12] Input-output analysis has developed a tableau of economic activity for a geographic area and traced out the impact of water development or quality management on all sectors of the regional or local economy. Insight has been gained into the magnitudes and types of local or regional economic effects. Alternative management systems have been tested for their economic consequences.[13]

The first promise of these analytical techniques was overly bold, for early students in this field, even though they were the master of the method and of the computer, had not yet become familiar with the problems. The gap between theoretical economic models and practical reality still exists (overemphasis on efficiency devoid of human constraints and defined to fit the model formulations rather than prototype characteristics, approximations that divorce models from reality, technical coefficients, lack of dynamic character), but progress has been made through persistent research. Over this fifteen-year period of time, economists have learned more about their data and more about hydrology, engineering, plant science, and most recently, ecology. This familiarity has led to a better interdisciplinary understanding and a closer integration with theory. But the interdisciplinary emphasis is still young, and the development of an integrated water management system which truly begins to satisfy the full range of demands for information at the political and data levels, to say nothing about handling daily operational situations, has only reached a crude approximation of precision. A beginning has been made, but the limitations are still so clear that we often feel progress has been small.

INFLUENCE OF CONTRIBUTIONS

The symposium planners also asked whether or not policy makers are currently aware of the work of economists. The response is yes. A companion question should also be asked—Are economists aware of water resources policy? Again, the response must be yes. But from both vantage points, areas of noncommunication and a lack of understanding exist. Economists have found it hard to realize that their models do not encompass "all that is." The policy process itself is like the market, a system for representing interests in the allocation of resources. The model of the system is not that of the theoretical entrepreneur sitting atop a firm. The analytical models of the firm are helpful in giving insight but, in and of themselves, do not give policy prescriptions.

On the other hand, many of the interests in the policy process use economics mainly as justification for decisions in which formal economics did not play a major part. For example, many a dam has been built to the physical capacity of the site rather than to the economist's "economic" height. The reason for going to the physical capacity may be strong, but its articulation is frequently on grounds which misrepresent the true desire— namely the ethos of construction. In this context, economics may not be permitted to contribute to the decision process in a theoretically appropriate way. In dealing with the issue of how high to build a dam, engineers were early to recognize that sites are scarce resources, while economists gave more attention to the timing of investment. Also, the economist frequently gave a low weight to the entrepreneur's sense of maintaining organizational capacity by having projects "in the construction line."

An important way for economics and economists to have an influence upon the decision process is for the agencies to hire and use economists throughout all echelons of decision making. Two major decision foci should receive special attention as the competence of economists is brought to bear upon policy. One is the Congress and the upper echelon of the executive offices. The other is at the local level where studies are formulated and authorized plans are implemented.

Influence by economists and economics has been felt by the upper executive group in terms of understanding basic concepts, and upon lower echelon groups concerned with applying basic concepts as well as data and microproblems—for example, production economics of irrigation agriculture. Attention at the congressional level will be important in the future with respect to establishing policy and procedures for including national income along with considerations of distributing economic and political benefits and weighting ecological impacts. But even with better economic understanding at the top, agency action still cannot really incorporate the appropriate ideas unless economists are participants at all levels of policy making and execution, from the initial studies through subsequent review and feedback to operations. It is very hard for water resources management to be better than the initial concept and input at the lower organizational levels. This position is stressed with full recognition of the organizational force which may be placed upon professional modes of thinking as well as the professional inflexibility and insensitivity which may inhibit day-to-day operations.

Of course, the effect of professional literature upon policy is significant—most significant. This literature is read by congressmen and agency personnel. In fact, many of the studies reported have been financially supported by operating water agencies. Examples of the latter range from many small studies to such major works as the Harvard water studies described by Arthur Maass and others.[14] These reports are read by agency personnel as buyers of a product they sponsor and for ideas to solve problems.

CHALLENGING PROBLEMS

The second question—What are the major water resources development problems which might move toward solutions with assistance from economists?—can only be fully answered through a complete review of what economists have done thus far. The footnotes in this chapter and those in each work cited expose a vast literature, and most articles suggest more problems worthy of additional research than they resolve by providing final answers. Clearly, there are many technical problems demanding solution.

Production Economic Relationships

Developing the production economic relationships associated with water services, particularly the inclusion of the many aspects of environmental quality, has become increasingly significant. Improving the handling of those nonmarket factors which are deemed critical, making input-output analyses and systems analyses more sensitive to the dynamics of change and to environmental issues, and improving the integration of economic simulation with other simulated or actual systems as they relate to water management are commonly cited areas of increased effort.

Many problems relating to the technical aspects of economic theory demand solution; in the aggregate their resolution is of major import. The understanding gained through such incrementalism has saved us from blunders by improving our foresight. However, today is distinctly different from the past in terms of the considerations shaping the direction of public and private water investment. The publics to be served or injured from water management are forming new interest groups as once predominant externalities are now considered in the light of new ecological insights and new technical capabilities. Thus, major issues are brought into a new focus.

A problem of high national priority may be simply stated. We need to develop a broad national concept of water resources management with an ecological context on the one hand and a socioeconomic frame of reference on the other hand. Because this statement is simple, its meaning may be misunderstood. It does not have the ring of novelty nor of sharp departure from the past; it is both novel and untried.

Today's water problems are still defined in terms of service objectives such as flood control, water supply, water quality control, and recreation; or in terms of socioeconomic organizational objectives such as income distributional effects, repayment, and cost-allocation issues; or in terms of the analysis of economic optimality and external effects through input-output analysis, economic base studies, production functions, and more recently, environmental impacts. It is these subset problems which have received the major attention. Economics has been related to each. The economist initially was asked to deal with establishing priorities in public investment, but effectively he could do little more than set a minimum standard criterion. Subsequently, economists worked on the other issues noted. These issues, singly or in the aggregate, do not constitute water resources management; they are only some of the components.

For the most part, projects have been considered individually and formulated to accomplish a set of water service objectives. Inputs available from upstream and outputs required downstream have largely determined project design. Illustrating early efforts, broader systems analyses encompassing a number of projects have been developed with water accounting studies used to match time patterns of available inflow against requirements for total outflow (for example, the system studies on the Tennessee River, the Missouri River, the Columbia River, and others, starting in the 1920s and 1930s). Basin studies have sought to integrate projects to increase physical output and economic efficiency. However, project selection for regional benefit complicates the struggle for power between the executive and Congress over the items of exchange in the larger game of bargaining for items in the federal budget. Setting priorities with basin or regional criteria changes the federal-local game of political economy. Thus, selecting projects mainly on the basis of system contribution has moved slowly.

The planning of integrated projects is not new, and those who gloss over early efforts, or say nothing has been done, are failing to build intellectually and operationally upon valuable experience. Nevertheless, past experience cannot be the complete model for tomorrow. The required level of integration will increase. More importantly, the pressure to examine a wider variety of operating systems will increase with growing competitive pressure for the use of public dollars and a limited resource and because of the relatively greater significance of externalities which comes with technological growth. In situations where externalities become very pervasive, they are weak in providing the strong cohensive force to establish the new bonds of common interest needed for organizational innovation. To meet these demands, a new—operational—concept of water resources management is needed and is being developed.

The Holistic Approach

Management entails a process of decision making centered on the allocation and use of the resource water. Water management is the process by which the resource is defined and put to use in combination with other resources. It is a process for determining priority services and objectives from the congressional to the local level without taking the services rendered nor the technology of management nor the institutions of management as given. At the national level, water management is concerned with the utilization of the nation's water resource as a whole and its relationship to other management systems. Each subset of issues and problems is approached within the macrocontext of management for all uses. The holistic approach is a frame of reference, an attitude. It is not an administrative proposal for bureaucratic reorganization, but each bureau should assume this point of view as it attacks the problems of its special interest and competence. The overriding concept should be the management of the total resource, using the property categories (private, public, common, fugitive, and so fourth) as instruments of public action.

Nor can water resources be isolated from other resources when the holistic concept prevails. Everything cannot be handled simultaneously, but the holistic concept can give direction to the process of creating national policy as well as to individualized microactivities. When an agency adopts this approach to planning water management, the agency context or constraints should not inflexibly predetermine management analysis. For example, a construction agency may recommend the purchase of floodplain land as a better alternative than building a levee or dam. Using a subsidy to change an industrial process may be better for water quality management than building a municipal waste treatment facility. The distinctiveness of the holistic approach is in more than giving unprejudiced consideration of a wide range of alternatives to accomplish given goals. Rather, the approach of the analyst is to examine a variety of goal-means mixes in a process unrestrained by legislative or bureaucratic rules in goal determinations. These rules cannot be forgotten in comparing management schemes; they are the channels for action and creating policy, but they are not given, or immutable.

The important point, however, is the creation of an attitude that the resource is our responsibility and we manage it as a matter of public policy. We decide to leave it alone or to make it flow uphill. Such an approach opens alternatives to action rather than cutting them off. The concern is with establishing a process for setting goals rather than dealing only with hypothesized "given goals" in analysis and design.

Economists can play a significant role in the development of such an approach. They can work with other disciplines to link an understanding of the economic system with that of the other relevant systems. Notwithstanding all of the attention given to water resources development as a production process, the need for further study remains significant. For example, added attention must be devoted to the concept of demand (what people want by intensity of desire from water resource management) as well as to the supply-cost (what people are willing to sacrifice by degree of willingness). Most attention has been given to production linkages (how to produce what people want), but without doubt many production relationships are far from being clearly understood. In many cases they are unknown in any specific sense. The requirement for greater understanding of macroecological systems creates a demand for new production and cost knowledge which must be conceptualized and specified in quantitative and not just symbolic form. The work requirement for the biological and physical scientist is great. Experience suggests that attention will be given to these supply-cost areas by teams of engineers, economists, computer specialists, and others. Economists must play a full and creative role to make certain that the "hard" data meet the test of usefulness in making decisions.

Three sets of relationships are particularly significant. These deal with 1) integrating large management systems to provide more efficiently for the many uses of water on the supply-cost side; 2) understanding and testing the ecological restraints to the supply-cost relationships, and 3) exploring new production relationships and new technical opportunities and evaluating their potential for overcoming existing problems. Within the present system of water quality management, the economist contributes in making cost studies which have evaluative impact upon the water quality standards which are being adopted and enforced throughout the nation.

Of course, environmental questions are currently receiving much attention. The cost relationships involving alternatives for dealing with environmental issues on large-system bases are just coming to the fore. Cost tradeoff functions for decision evaluation have been and will continue to be practical tools in making day-to-day decisions. The economics of the environment is a new concern only in the sense that its recognition has been made much more pervasive by the increased strength of the social force behind taking such issues into account. Many newly perceived environmental effects have been acknowledged, and research has been directed toward integrating them into operations. Significant antecedents for these studies are found in an economic literature going back for at least two decades. Economists have long contributed to the specification of such policy criteria as the safe minimum standard.[15] Also, the literature on externalities is not new.[16] The applications of the concept of externalities and its limitations should be understood in relationship to production processes which change over time intervals as well as in suggesting channels for institutional or organizational adjustment to handle environmental problems.[17]

The supply-cost side will receive much attention, and the resulting analyses will be integrated into many water decisions. The economist can be productive in this process by providing important analyses of costs of decision alternatives within the larger systems. This should give the economist insight into significant technical feedback systems which have not yet been explicitly defined. The cost allocation process, for example, is such a system which combines both economics and the art of technical design; the real design objective may be an agreed cost allocation and site capacity. The economist should know these systems and how they function in action and should understand the market mechanisms. On the latter point, the economist can do a service by explaining the social context of the market and other allocative institutions to other professions. However, he must be careful that his market orientation in a classical-economic model sense does not blind him to operational realities which may be better understood by other professionals. Here the economist is the learner; but after learning, he can become the better interpreter for policy analysis.

Another major area of assistance by economists is the development of systems of economic incentives to achieve social objectives. To begin with, a great deal of study is required to explore the effects of alternative systems on decisions on social objectives. This is a most interesting and yet frustrating field because of the necessity to understand how demands are integrated into the social fabric. Understanding the forces creating the demands for water management is a major challenge. It is even more challenging when the economist must integrate his understanding into managing specific water management systems, into designing capital investments, or into utilizing nonstructural measures, which are suggested or enforced as rules of behavior; e.g. floodplain zoning, water rights, and so forth. One line of work must link water management into the whole economic system and relate water services to the market-commercial character of the economy. Another avenue of endeavor will link the nonmarket organizational structures (largely governmental action) for reflecting demand and will look toward improving these structures to achieve desired water service.

Frequently, the economist can be of greater assistance in creating an organization to reflect these demands and the competing forces behind them than he can in giving numerical estimates of future demands based on past trends when the forces for shift are strong. Management decisions are based on assessments of possible future consequences, but the record of past success in assessing the future has had its bleak spots. Part of this uncertainty in foreseeing the future can be absorbed through creating an adaptive organization. This type of organizational innovation is urgently needed to bring together common interests in system management. The development of an adaptive organizational system of water management which will respond to the full range of upcoming shifts in water demand is a major task. The organization must define responsibility and establish effective procedures for dealing with the quality, volume, and timing of flow with decision rules to handle effluent discharge. It must find the most efficient index of point quality change, with a system of charges, subsidies, and rules.

PROFESSIONAL INCENTIVES

What are the professional incentives for economists to work on water resources problems? The incentives derive first from a basic concern and interest in people and their economic problems. They are associated with a special interest in resource economics emphasizing water resources issues. The desire to work at the interface between people and their resources is made stronger by a growing recognition of the crucial significance of resource management as a critical issue of maintaining the economy. Admittedly, these problems have not been the concern of most economists, and there is no reason that they should have been central economic issues. On the other hand, there is no reason for the general economist to depreciate the significance of resource problems as unimportant. The number of prominent economists who have devoted time to these issues is significant. In fact, resource management is in center focus on the national scene today. Resource management problems will not be solved unless their economic aspects are resolved in a theoretically and operationally practical manner. Too frequently discussions of resource policy are polarized between economic and noneconomic points of view, with a resulting disservice to those seeking solutions to pressing social problems.

Water is essential, pervasive, and an increasingly limited resource (in an economic sense).[18] A central knot to be cut is economic if true crisis is to be avoided. A successful effort will require technical innovation and major change in current production processes and the economic structure of production and institutions. Both technical innovation and institutional change are directly related to the structure and functioning of our economic system. The challenge has never been greater than it is today for economists to focus upon these critical problems. The opportunity is much broader than estimating benefits and costs for public investment, although this shall continue to be important. The problem is to integrate the many facets of water management into a new economic system of incentive penalties, prohibitions, and opportunities. The use of water as a waste carrier is slowly being integrated with other management functions. Alternative institutions for performing this function are under discussion. New rules and regulations, court action, effluent charges, and the establishment of rights to discharge, as well as to direct citizen action, are all being considered and initiated.

The problems are socially significant, and for this reason alone they will attract the attention of economists who feel a challenge to apply economics to real, increasingly important problems in today's society. The increased social perception of resource-related issues will provide an important incentive. It will attract those economists who enjoy working on the interchange between public and private decision making as well as those with social and technical viewpoints.

Professional Rewards

Job availability, salary, and status in scientific circles are some of the rewards of water resource economists. There are and have been jobs for resource economists in government agencies, consulting firms, and a few industries as well as in the university community. The primary problem economists have had in functioning in government agencies has been noted. Another significant point, however, is the need to have agency economists working on problems at all levels and to have them in groups or teams where they can interact with each other. Locating a single economist where his primary interaction is with other professional groups at times has merit, but for the most part this has not been the most productive arrangement. In the current situation, locating a small group of economists in industry or government to work on problems as an economic task force is an organizational structure to be commended. Such arrangements yield higher incentive for the professional economists.

In the academic communities of the large Land Grant Universities, departments of agricultural economics or planning are frequently the units where resource economists are located. Economics departments have faculty with such interests, but these individuals are fewer in number. With the availability of research money, the water economist can frequently attract research funding and support which in turn gives incentive to his interest. Also, water as the substance for the transport of many elements in nature has received special attention in professional circles.

Academic Incentives

The question of colleague pressure to contribute to theoretical and empirical problems of the discipline rather than to solving resource management problems is real. How this pressure is handled hinges upon the intellectual capability and interest of the individual economist. One good way for an economist to push theoretical work further is to interact with real world problems. Theorizing and testing is a continuous interchange for the productive individual. For example, the June 1970 issue of the American Economic Review carries an article of direct interest by Kenneth J. Arrow and Robert C. Lind, "Uncertainty and the Evaluation of Public Investment Decisions." The recognition achieved by authors of the literature cited in the footnotes to the article illustrates the point and this is just a small sample of professional contributions. The concern with resource issues, including water, has received substantial attention in the professional literature, and one can well anticipate that this interest will rise. Yet, because resource applications are not at the central core of economic theory nor do they represent the only social issue demanding the attention of economists, one would only expect substantial but not central concern from the profession.

Although not asked, but a part of this whole issue, is the education of economists. To generate professional interest, challenging courses in resource economics must continue to be developed within the curricula of the nation's universities. During the last decade and a half, expansion has been evident in departments of economics, agricultural economics, and within programs in engineering economy. These courses of study must continue to be imaginative and relevant to the problems of the future in order to ensure sustained professional interest.

1. For example, reclamation law was predicated on the objective of developing the West in the 1902 Reclamation Act as was such earlier legislation in western states as California's Wright Act in 1887.

2. Many of the details are presented in the anthropology paper in this series.

3. S. V. Ciriacy-Wantrup, *California Central Valley Project Studies*, U. S. Bureau of Reclamation (1947). These reports contain basic concepts for benefit-cost analysis and cost allocation.

4. For reviews of some of this literature and major authors see S. C. Smith and Emory Castle, *Water Resources Development* (Ames, Iowa: Iowa State University Press, 1964), p. 463; Allen V. Kneese and S. C. Smith, *Water Research* (Baltimore: Johns Hopkins Press, 1966), p. 526. Also many economic journals such as *The American Economic Review, The Quarterly Journal of Economics, Land Economics, The Journal of Political Economics, The American Journal of Agricultural Economics* or resource journals such as *Water Resources Research* and *Natural Resources* contain

significant articles. Recent examples include: Robert J. Kalter, et al., *Criteria for Federal Evaluation of Resource Investments* (Ithaca, N. Y.: Cornell University, 1969) Water Resources and Marine Sciences Center; William B. Lord and Stephen C. Smith, "Tools of the Trade in Policy Decision: PPBS, a Case in Point," *American Journal of Agricultural Economics*, pp. 1427-33; Robert J. Kalter and Thomas H. Stevens, "Resource Investments, Impact Distribution, and Evaluation Concepts," *American Journal of Agricultural Economics*, May 1971, pp. 206-15; A. Myrick Freeman and Robert H. Haveman, "Benefit-Cost Analysis and Multiple Objectives: Current Issues in Water Resources Planning," *Water Resources Research*, December 1970, p. 1533; Turvey and Prest, "Cost Benefit Analysis: A Survey," *Economic Journal* 75 (1965): 683-735.

5. Much of the basic literature was developed in the 1930s and 1940s by engineering economists such as Eugene Grant.

6. Otto Eckstein, *Water Resource Development: The Economics of Project Evaluation* (Cambridge, Mass.: Harvard University Press, 1958); Roland N. McKean, *Efficiency in Government Through Systems Analysis with Emphasis on Water Resource Development* (New York: Wiley & Sons, 1958); J. Hirshleifer, J. C. DeHaven, and J. W. Milliman, *Water Supply: Economics, Technology and Policy* (Chicago: University of Chicago Press, 1960); Kenneth J. Arrow and Mordecai Kurz, *Public Investment, The Rate of Return, and Optimal Fiscal Policy* (Baltimore: Johns Hopkins Press, 1970); Joint Economic Committee of Congress, *The Analysis and Evaluation of Public Expenditures: The PPBS System*, Subcommittee on Economy in Government of the Joint Economic Committee, Congress of the United States, 1969.

7. John Krutilla and Otto Eckstein, *Multiple Purpose River Development* (Baltimore: Johns Hopkins Press, 1958); Charles W. Howe, *Interbasin Transfers of Water, Economic Issues and Impacts* (Baltimore: Johns Hopkins Press, 1971), p. 196; Allen V. Kneese and Blair T. Bower, *Managing Water Quality: Economics, Technology, Institutions* (Baltimore: Johns Hopkins Press, 1968).

8. Allen V. Kneese, "Environmental Pollution: Economics and Policy," *American Economic Review*, May 1971, pp. 153-66.

9. Arrow and Kurz, *Public Investment.*

10. S. V. Ciriacy-Wantrup, "Cost Allocation in Relation to Western Water Policies," *Journal of Farm Economics* 36, no. 1 (1954): 108-29.

11. Stephen C. Smith, *The Public District in Integrating Ground and Surface Water Management: A Case Study in Santa Clara County*, Giannini Foundation Report no. 252 (Berkeley: University of California Press, 1963), p. 135; S. V. Ciriacy-Wantrup, "Concepts Used as Economic Criteria for a System of Water Rights," *Land Economics* 32, no. 5 (1956); L. M. Hartman and D. Seastne, *Water Transfers, Economic Efficiency and Alternative Institutions* (Baltimore: Johns Hopkins Press, 1970); J. H. Dales, *Pollution, Property, and Prices* (Toronto: University of Toronto Press, 1968).

12. To illustrate an application to ground water resources: Oscar Burt, "Groundwater Storage Control under Institutional Restrictions," *Water Resources Research*, December 1970, p. 1540.

13. Critiques of these methods are well known in the literature. The discussions between pages 167-77 in the May 1971, *American Economic Review* raise many of the significant points.

14. Arthur Maass, et al., *Design of Water Resource Systems* (Cambridge, Mass.: Harvard University Press, 1962).

15. S. V. Ciriacy-Wantrup, *Resource Conservation, Economics and Policies*, Division of Agricultural Sciences, Agricultural Experiment Station (University of California-Berkeley, 1963), p. 395; S. V. Ciriacy-Wantrup and James J. Parsons, *Natural Resources, Quality and Quantity* (Berkeley: University of California Press, 1967), p. 217.

16. E. J. Mishan, "The Postwar Literature on Externalities: An Interpretative Essay," *The Journal of Economic Literature*, March 1971, pp. 1-28.

17. Kneese, "Environmental Pollution," *American Economic Review*, May 1971, pp. 153-66; S. V. Ciriacy-Wantrup, "The Economics of Environmental Policy," *Land Economics* XLVII, no. 1 (February 1971): 36-45.

18. This is the central issue behind the effort of the United Nations to declare 1975 as an International Water Development year.

4 Role of Geography in Water Resources Management

Gilbert F. White

If, as many of us think likely, the mode of planning water resources use is in a state of major flux, it is important to recognize the directions of those trends before assessing the contributions of academic disciplines to water management. To my mind, at least three main changes are in process in public activities dealing with water resources. First, emphasis upon the canvass of alternative aims and methods of managing water is increasing. Second, the attention given to direct use of scientific and technological research as a tool in water management is growing. Third, basic attitudes of man toward the manipulation of his environment are undergoing such rapid transformation that the whole system of expressing public preferences is being revised.

THREE TRENDS IN WATER MANAGEMENT

As evidence for these fundamental alterations in methods of water planning and management in the United States, I would cite the expanding tendency to deal with multiple *aims* in preparing metropolitan and river basin plans, the new attention to multiple *means* in several sectors of water planning, and the systematic inclusion of research as an element in both planning and operating activities. The profound changes in public valuation of environment hardly require description. So widespread are they that the majestically broad field of environmental quality resembles the

Oklahoma Land Rush as earnest teams of scholars and scientists—disciplinary and interdisciplinary—hurry to stake out their claims.

In the detailed planning of the water resources of the Susquehanna Basin and in the longer-term, cooperative, federal-state studies looking to a Type 1 framework for the North Atlantic drainage basins, the Corps of Engineers has taken the lead in outlining programs which recognize at the outset the possibility of more than one public aim for manipulating water resources. In these instances, explicit analysis is directed toward the effects on the program of seeking to attain regional economic development in contrast to national economic efficiency and of putting first priority on enhancement of the quality of the human environment in contrast to either of these other goals. In doing so, the Corps has made manifest the kinds of suggestions put forward by the Committee on Water of the National Academy of Sciences.[1] The Susquehanna and North Atlantic studies demonstrate both the possibilities and the complications of this more far-reaching type of analysis. It would be a mistake to think that the approach of comparing a wide range of alternatives (as embodied in those studies and as represented in such investigations as that by Davis [1967] on the Potomac[2]) has won full acceptance within the professional groups responsible for water management. The Bureau of Reclamation has stoutly resisted this approach, and within the Corps the acceptance is slow. However, there can be no doubt that the idea has caught hold and that serious experimental efforts are being made to plan from this broader perspective in ways which will meet rigorous analytical criteria and which will be acceptable to those citizen groups and government agencies finally responsible for adopting programs and policies.

The approach of multiple means to achieving one goal is demonstrated in the new national policy for reduction of flood losses.[3] In essence, it seeks to explore and weigh comparatively all the possible measures—structural as well as nonstructural—for achieving a given aim. Where the aim is management of flood losses in the interest of national economic efficiency or regional development, it includes upstream land treatment, levees, channel improvements, and dams, along with flood warnings and emergency evacuation, flood-proofing of buildings, land-use regulation, and public information activities. No strictly comparable policy has been adopted in other sectors of water management, but the Potomac studies exemplify the applicability of multiple means to dealing with water pollution. Agricultural economists have pointed out for a long time the large number of means available for dealing with problems of arid lands and with improvements in the productivity of soils subject to either excess or deficient moisture. There have been a few systematic trials in metropolitan areas, as witness the comprehensive studies of water use and control in northeastern Illinois and the investigations of waste disposal in the New York metropolitan region.[4] With increasing emphasis in water resources planning upon serving metropolitan areas in contrast to drainage basin areas, still greater stress on the comparison of multiple means may be expected. To a greater extent than the variety of citizen and government groups participating in river basin planning, active groups in metropolitan areas are likely to be oriented to seeking explicit human goals instead of the traditional development objectives. People are shifting their attention from engineering design to social outcomes. To be sure, they can become engrossed in simplified and often self-defeating technological solutions (as with public housing), but their concern for the social impacts is more direct and articulate.

For demonstration of the second visible change in public water policy—increasing attention to conscious, systematic use of scientific and technological research as an instrument of water management—one need only point to the federal research programs on weather modification and on the desalting of briny water. These two programs are among the earliest in the history of the United States to devote research to intentional change in the character of water management by developing new techniques. In this regard they are fundamentally different from other research programs of the Bureau of Reclamation and Soil Conservation Service, which seek primarily to improve existing techniques for water storage or for water disposal.

Finally, while strategy has shifted from single-purpose methods to multiple methods of reaching multiple goals and from construction to science and technology, there has been a profound movement in value preferences with respect to quality of environment. This change, known to all of us, has had a sweeping effect upon the character of engineering planning, economic analysis, and the role of citizens' groups in water resources management. No other trend in water planning has had as diffuse an effect, and none has moved so rapidly. It is symptomatic of a much broader change in our society in which prevailing concepts of the relation of man to his environment are being transformed subtly and pervasively. The view of man as the conqueror and the manager has been modified to a call for man to become the harmonizer and reconciler in a complex ecosystem.

The roots for this broad change are not well understood. They may be an expression, in part, of the means to look beyond economic necessity. The increased affluence of our society and increased leisure permits additional time for consideration of differences of quality of living environment. The roots of change also may draw from a deep anxiety about the capacity of man's ponderous bureaucracies to deal with both social and physical aspects of the environment. Repressed concern for his failure to master his enlarged capacities to organize society may be expressed as articulate indignation at degradations of environmental quality which only a few decades ago were tolerated with little complaint. Whatever the causes, and they merit a separate volume, the influence of this trend is great.

SOME CHARACTERISTICS OF RESEARCH ON WATER MANAGEMENT

Along with these observations on the changing modes of water resources planning come a few general and critical comments on the relevance of contemporary research in dealing with water management. Perhaps the most significant comment is that much of the current investigation of water problems is characterized by attention to description, normative appraisals, and technological improvements to the exclusion of searching and thoughtful appraisal of the effects of actions already taken by man. There is no lack of engineering plans for redistributing water and silt by operating on the hydrologic cycle. Most such plans now are accompanied by analyses, varying in degrees of sophistication, which purport to show the economic efficiency of whatever alternatives are proposed. Under the National Environmental Protection Act of 1969, environmental impact statements are also required. However, the level of sophistication found in the early statements has been quite low. In contrast to these studies required for every project, only a handful of studies systematically examined results of such plans once they were approved and executed. The optimum is sought in estimates rather than in performance.

A few studies have been made on the actual distribution of direct and indirect benefits from irrigation projects.[5] There has been a reconnaissance investigation of the effects of activities under the Flood Control Act of 1936.[6] Even where the Economic Research Service attempted evaluations of selected watershed improvement projects, it emphasized the performance of technical works rather than the impacts upon either ecosystems or their human components. More common have been retrospective appraisals of the effectiveness of the administrative organization of river basin investigations of which Hart's study of the Missouri Basin is a good example.[7] The economic impacts have been gauged in a few instances.[8] However, the number of detailed examinations of the full range of consequences of a water project—human and biological and physical—is extraordinarily small. Indeed, no studies so far may be regarded as prototypes for investigations which would probe deeply into the ecological significance of water improvements. They are needed desperately, and their design has only begun. A technologically oriented world has been so intrigued with the pursuit of refined methods for calculating optimal solutions that it has neglected to find out what happened after implementation of the previously planned actions. There is virtually no evidence as to what would have happened without the investment and very little as to the validity of predictions of results. It is extremely difficult to make postaudits, and the methodology is far less advanced than for normative appraisal. Thus, preoccupation with means of computing flood-control benefits has obscured the question about the degree to which, and under what circumstances, the benefits as hypothesized by econometricians ever were realized.

How much social science research on water resources development has had any substantial effect upon either public policy or methods of preparing programs for public action? This inquiry should be carried even unto the gates of the economic fortress. For while there has been widespread acceptance among government agencies of the desirability of carrying out refined economic analysis of benefits and costs, and a new framework of evaluation is being developed for application by the federal agencies, there are reasons for sober doubt as to the actual effects of economic analysis upon types of solutions proposed and finally adopted by the Congress or by state legislative agencies. It is sometimes argued that, by and large, the advanced economic appraisal has served chiefly to buttress conclusions arrived at by other paths, and that only rarely has it modified radically the investment patterns or design procedures of government agencies. I am prepared to change my mind on this when presented with adequate evidence. It now seems likely that changes in public preference with respect to water quality or recreation or dependence on large dams has had far greater effect than has the refinement of economic analysis.

There has been a good deal of talk about the desirability of interdisciplinary collaboration in research on natural resources. That hope has been intertwined with much of the planning for water resources institutes, as they have been established in all of our states. So far, there is scant evidence that interdisciplinary or multidisciplinary collaboration has been notably fruitful. Interdisciplinary research has not been prominent, and a goodly proportion of its results seem interdisciplinary or collaborative only in the sense that authors speaking from different standpoints and using different styles of analysis publish materials appearing within the covers of the same book or journal. Seminal exchange of ideas or methods among the disciplines as they affect water management has been lacking. The exceptions are few in number. As one who believes strongly in the need for interdisciplinary approaches and who has joined in experiments with them, I feel it is important to work more intently and sensitively to enhance these interdisciplinary goals.

To sum up these observations, much of the current social science research on water resources is distinguished by emphasis on normative analysis to the exclusion of critical examination of results. There is doubt as to the influence of this research upon public action. Its ventures in interdisciplinary collaboration have been interesting more for their aspiration than for achievement.

REVIEWS OF GEOGRAPHICAL CONTRIBUTIONS

Against this background, what contributions have geographers made to water resources management? The quick answer is that their help has been modest. What contributions might be expected in the future? Here the response is more encouraging. However, the incentives for increased involvement by geographers are relatively weak at this stage, and it seems likely that how the needed interdisciplinary research takes shape will help determine whether incentives become stronger.

It is tempting to report a wide spectrum of geographic investigations which touch in some way on the use and control of water. Most regional geographical studies make reference to water, and a large number of research papers describe systems of water use, as with irrigation or municipal water supplies, or discuss the size and implications of new water projects such as canals and dams. Reference to them can be found in the standard bibliographies. The larger list may be narrowed to a smaller number of studies on the basis of their actual or likely utility in contributing to better water management. Noting those that clearly have affected public action is easy because the number is small; tracing the indirect influence of ideas and findings is more difficult; and estimating the possible effects of a yet unused piece of work is plain speculation. Here I confess to a personal bias in favor of research which yields results clearly capable of shaping the direction or quality of public action.[9]

For those who would like a detailed description of geographic thinking about water resources and of contributions which geographers have made or might make to water development, I suggest four works. The first is a volume of essays in the fields of hydrology, geomorphology, and socio-economic geography, edited by Richard J. Chorley, under the title of

Water, Earth and Man.[10] This book brings together papers by a number of geographers and associated hydrologists, engineers, and economists, chiefly British. Together, they provide the viewpoint of geographers on the interrelation of hydrologic, geomorphic, and human systems and note some contributions geographers can make to actual water management. Much material from other disciplines is organized in a geographic framework. The reader must extract from the descriptive papers the specific points at which geographers have been active and productive.

A second review is that completed by W. R. Derrick Sewell as part of an investigation for the Policy and Planning Branch of the Canadian Department of Energy, Mines and Resources on *Social Science Priorities in Water Management Research.*[11] In that study, Sewell appraises possible contributions of geographers to water resources activities. He notes the record of activity to date in the Canadian sphere and refers to work elsewhere which has possible application in Canada. His description of specific methods and problem solving is concrete, and his references to illustrative work are extensive. Canadian geographers have been active in applying geographic learning to water problems, on a per capita basis probably more so than their colleagues in any other large nation. They have not made major advances in method, but their university departments have been vigorous in developing centers of specialization on water problems.

A third analysis is that prepared by a committee of the National Academy of Sciences and the Social Science Research Council on *The Behavioral and Social Sciences: Outlook and Needs.*[12] The general volume is accompanied by separate reports, including one on the state of geographical research.[13] In these reports, there is selective reference to contributions of geography to water resources management, and those are more detailed than in the preceding two reviews. While fewer in number, the reports on water resources management have the merit of describing significant research that affects other aspects of society and the environment. Therefore, they give a kind of perspective not found in the studies of water resources activities alone.

The fourth survey is one which I made in 1962, basing it on an analysis of world geographical literature and illustrating the conclusions by applying them to the international experiment in river development in the Lower Mekong.[14] In that appraisal, I tried to examine geographic studies in terms of six major elements in individual and public decision making. The model was based on the assumption that every decision with respect to resource management involves 1) some perception by the manager of the range of choice open to him, 2) an estimate of available resources, 3) an estimate of available technology, 4) an appraisal of economic efficiency, and 5) an assessment of spatial linkages with other resource uses. Each of these five elements is regarded as related to the others and as being affected by a sixth, social guides, which restricts or encourages them. If water decisions can be described in such a framework, then the significance of a discipline can be judged in terms of its role in changing each of the six elements in the decision. Obviously, there are other frameworks in which research might be appraised. This one is convenient, and it focuses attention on the decision-making process. The conclusion then was as follows:

I am not interested in staking out professional claims in this domain of science. What does seem important is to recognize intellectual problems which call for solution, and which because of their relation to spatial distributions and human adjustment to differences in physical environment are of interest to geographers.

What are the types of geographical analysis which seem especially pertinent to river development and currently promising for advancement? Beyond atlas compilation of background data, the range of choice for methods of river management can be defined more accurately by studies of homologues and by regional and historical studies of water management. Resource estimates can be improved by refining the mapping of water balance, hydrological characteristics of terrain and land use, and by examining the nature and distribution of human perception of resources. The application of new technology can be strengthened by discovery and partial explanation of variations in patterns of water use and disposal. Benefit-cost analysis can be sharpened by finding normalities in the spatial variations of water use, control, and demand. The effects of water management upon the stream system and upon movements of human activities within and outside the basin can be identified more clearly. Possible responses of land and water management practice to changes in social guides in different environments can be estimated from critical regional studies. In these and other ways geographical analysis can aid in so deepening our understanding of the flows of water, silt, people and goods and of their setting, that as each is altered by human initiative we may recognize a bit more precisely the likely consequences to the interconnected systems.

Every change in landscape or resource use on a large scale disturbs a complex set of relationships. To do so is not necessarily to do wrong by upsetting a "natural equilibrium." The existing situation may in effect be out of equilibrium as in the case of shifting cultivation in the Lower Mekong plateaus, or a new, more productive relationship may be established, as where permanent irrigation rice culture replaces hazardous wet-season cropping. The decision to change may, however, go far wide of the intended goal of lasting human betterment if the strategy of development is built upon narrow and distorted models of these relationships. Nothing less than a system analysis of the whole complex of natural and social processes at work will yield in the long run a sound basis for decision, and it is toward this that we should move.

At this time those conclusions should be modified by referring to new work accomplished or unfolding, and by suggesting several directions seem particularly promising in the light of recent research or its applications.

THE RANGE OF CHOICE

To earlier studies of homologues of conditions encountered in developing basin plans should be added the work of geographers and others in systematically expanding the range of choice explored in river basin planning. This view is exemplified in the approach to the public choice in planning the Colorado Basin as reported by the Committee on Water.[15]

The committee called for a procedure by which the theoretical array of actions that could be taken to meet specified social aims would be compared according to their consequences. These major Colorado Basin alternatives are illustrated in the figure on page 111. When, for example, questions are raised as to why additional quantities of Colorado River water should be delivered to the Phoenix area rather than to Yuma, or why the water should be used for agriculture in a region where urbanization is the dominant force, all other aspects of planning for the basin are affected. From his habit of systematically examining the whole range of possible human adjustments to similar sets of conditions, the geographer poses such inquiry.

Thoughtful regional and historical studies may indicate in more detail the experience in exploring different choices in river basin planning; Michel's study of the Indus basin is the outstanding example.[16] It reviews the international and national efforts to divide Indus waters and points out underlying causes of conflict.

An example of research assisting in public decision is the work by geographers on the range of adjustments in floodplain use.[17] Comparative analysis showed that adjustments could include bearing the loss; modifying the flood flow by upstream land treatment; controlling the flows by engineering works; modifying the loss by emergency evacuation, flood warnings, altering building design, and land-use changes; and distributing the losses over time or among more people by insurance and public relief. The geographic studies supported the formulation and acceptance of new federal policy for dealing with management of flood losses as embodied in the report of the Task Force on Federal Flood Control Policy.[18] The same approach found international discussion and partial acceptance in the work of the United Nations Seminar in Tbilisi in September and October of 1969.[19] Geographic studies of adjustments to floods first identified the range of choice, asked what had been the effect of public policies upon actual floodplain use, noted that the results in terms of national flood losses had been the opposite of those intended, and then set out to learn why the results were as they were.[20] Alternative choices open to the public in dealing with floods were explored, and the studies led into other

Colorado Basin Alternatives

GOALS	ALTERNATIVE SOLUTIONS*							
	Do Nothing	Store and Pump Water	Increase Water Supply†	Change Present Water Use	Manage Pop. & Land Use	Save Water	Pricing of Water	Redistributed Funds & Taxes
National Economic Efficiency	□	□	□	□	□	□	□	□
Income Redistribution								
Encourage Regional Growth	□	□	□	□	□	□	□	□
Help Local Communities	□	□	□	□	□	□	□	□
Rescue Areas of Decline	□	□	□	□	□	□	□	□
Promote Family-Sized Farms	□	□	□	□	□	□	□	□
Preservation Esthetics								
Preserve Landscape	□	□	□	□	□	□	□	□
Political Equity								
Commitment to Mexico	□	□	□	□	□	□	□	□
Allocations to Basin States	□	□	□	□	□	□	□	□
Rights of Indians	□	□	□	□	□	□	□	□
Maintain Regional Political Arrangements	□	□	□	□	□	□	□	□
Control of the River	□	□	□	□	□	□	□	□

*Not necessarily mutually exclusive.
†Includes: importation, desalting, weather modification.
Source: *Water and Choice in the Colorado Basin*, p. 56.

aspects of the problem of environmental perception. The work was inter-disciplinary in the sense that the collaboration of lawyers, engineers, psychologists, and sociologists was enlisted. The incentives were simple geographical questions as to why the use of floodplains varied as it did in the face of the known flood hazard and why public policy concentrated upon two choices to the virtual exclusion of other alternatives. Out of it came a better understanding of the effects of different public policies on flood losses.

RESOURCE ESTIMATES

With respect to resource estimates, geographers have helped in improvements in the mapping of water balance, particularly in the Soviet Union.[21] The first comprehensive analysis of water balance in relation to river regimen has been drawn together by a group cooperating in the International Hydrological Decade.[22] Notwithstanding increased interest in the application of remote sensing devices to the improvement of estimates of resources over very large areas, the results have not yet been applied in any significant way. Much research and discriminating experiment lies ahead.

The compilation of atlases and related materials about river basins continues to provide basic data for both physical and social planning. The products are most visible in reports assembled by the area redevelopment group in the Department of Commerce, the Upper Great Lakes Commission, the Appalachian Commission, and in the preparation of such volumes as the *Atlas of the Physical, Economic and Social Resources of the Lower Mekong* by the Resource Appraisal Unit of the Corps of Engineers.[23] These not only assemble much information useful in other steps of the planning process but also organize it according to criteria judged by the geographer to be significant to later analysis. Of a different style are the collection of papers describing aspects of a basin, such as that for the Wabash Basin.[24] Compilations can be no better than the conceptual framework within which the data is assembled, and their rigorous use, in contrast to their browsing value, deserves more careful examination.

Perhaps the most interesting aspect of work on resource estimates has been the analysis of human perception of natural resources. As exemplified by Kates's work on perception of flood hazard and Saarinen's work on perception of drought, this analysis seeks to understand how the same dimension of environment appears to various people and what accounts for the differences.[25] In elucidating how resource managers perceive the physical events associated with excessess or shortages of water (for example, a rare flood or a severe drought), there has been a deepening of knowledge of how managers—both individual and public—make their decisions.[26] There also has been a change in the view of what sorts of data are significant to managers and what forms of presentation are important to them.[27] Thus, in the study of floods attention is given to what kinds of maps and supplemental information on flood hazard are most meaningful to those people called upon to use information about flood hazard in arriving at decisions about locations of new buildings and industrial activity.

Mapping of flood hazard has resulted in part from stimulus by geographers. In collaboration with the U.S. Geological Survey, Sheaffer planned the first comprehensive mapping of flood hazard in an entire metropolitan area, in this case northeastern Illinois.[28] Ohya has extended his classification of floodplains based on geomorphological data to many parts of Japan and to sectors of the Lower Mekong, South Korea, and the delta of the Ganges-Brahmaputra.[29] The geographical skill has been to combine a knowledge of physical parameters of the water resource with insight into ways in which the data, if properly presented, can promote wiser choice among possible adjustments to possible time patterns in resource availability or excess.

TECHNOLOGY

In studying the variations in patterns of technology of water use and disposal, geographers have added to our knowledge about the location and spread of different management techniques. The classic work of Ackerman and Löf[30] first outlined the major techniques of water management and indicated ways in which they vary among different environments. More detailed studies have had direct application to the planning of water improvements, although by and large, they have been more descriptive than analytic. Confronted with spatial variation in water technology, a geographer may look for patterns of diffusion or for differences in the conditions affecting adoption of an innovation. So far as the explanation is valid, it serves as a basis for public policy in managing the technology.

Thus, there have been a few investigations of the conditions that account for differential application of technology in water use in industry, in households, and in irrigation. Wong's study of the factors affecting application of water-saving techniques by industrial water users threw light on the likely effects of different types of public action designed to reduce withdrawals.[31] Bowden's examination of diffusion of pump and sprinkler irrigation innovations in the High Plains showed how individuals may

respond to commercial advances.[32] Sheaffer's appraisal of possible techniques for reduction of flood losses by flood-proofing, supported by the
Tennessee Valley Authority, later led to a change in the Corps of
Engineers' policy in providing technical assistance for such techniques,
including the issuance of a handbook.[33]

ECONOMIC EFFICIENCY

Economic analysis of water resources investment has been enhanced by
several studies which recognize the significance of externalities resulting
from the investment. Going beyond ordinary market calculations, geographers have developed methods to estimate the effects of dams upon
wildlife and upon recreational use. The studies of social impacts of fish
preservation expenditures in the Pacific Northwest, and of the relation of
travel time to reservoir use illustrate the insights to be gained from
examination of spatial factors in flows of costs and gains.[34] In this way
geographers have aided in predictions as to certain consequences of new
construction. The efficiency of various water supply networks in the New
York metropolitan area also has been appraised.[35]

Since economic theory commonly assumes rational man seeking to
optimize his net returns, studies of the conditions in which other types of
decisions are made may illuminate the process of choices. Geographers
have done some work along these lines in helping to explain how resource
users cope with hazard and uncertainty. The promising investigation conducted by Russell, Arey, and Kates in the Northeast revealed the way in
which communities responded to the drought conditions of 1967.[36] While
this study was primarily an analysis of economic effects, it went much
further to review the political implications and forms of adjustment to
water shortage. Burton's and Theiler's studies of what happened in farming
areas protected from floods direct attention to the unanticipated consequences of construction.[37] Construction had been justified by a benefit-
cost analysis, assuming changes in land use that later proved inadequate as
a measure of consequences.

SPATIAL LINKAGES

Ideally, every public agency charged with implementing water management measures would like to be able to predict the effects of each
contemplated action upon the interlocking systems of land and water in
the entire river basin or other affected area before choosing from among
the alternatives and undertaking one of them. The requisite knowledge

never is fully in hand, and to acquire it would call for study by experts from many disciplines. Yet, this type of broadly based interdisciplinary approach is what we must seek. Along with ecologists, geographers look for the full range of linkages, and like the ecologists, lack the skill to measure many of them satisfactorily. Notwithstanding those limitations, they have added to our appreciation of the number and types of relevant linkages among environmental factors.

Wolman has continued his studies of effects of water regulation upon sediment movement and accumulation downstream from dams.[38] The long-term alterations of streams through storage and channelization are difficult to discern and often are either neglected or handled by rough rule-of-thumb estimates. In a few areas, notably the Meramac Basin of Missouri, a more systematic canvass has been made of social effects of reservoirs in a larger area.[39] This is one of the few basin studies to be directed primarily by geographers.

Geographers have had a hand in the organization of comprehensive studies of the effect of man-made lakes on the African continent, notably in the reservoirs created by the High Aswan, Kainji, and Volta dams. In the field of weather modification, geographers took the lead in initiating interdisciplinary examinations of possible consequences of modifying parameters of weather or climate when social aspects of weather modification first were subject to National Science Foundation review.[40] They also are active in identifying aspects of those atmospheric systems which would be most susceptible to or most significantly affected by human modification.

SOCIAL GUIDES

Any finding which throws light on the results of a public policy of education or regulation offers grist for the mill of public decision, and in this sense any study that traces the consequences of a water management project helps shape the social guide for future management. Geographers have influenced policy by that means in the instances noted above. In addition, they had a hand in the drafting of the new National Water Act in the United Kingdom. Several participated in the basic staff studies for the Senate Select Committee on National Water Resources which led to the framing of the Water Resources Planning Act of 1965.[41] They have helped organize water districts in Ontario.[42] The appraisals by Farmer of irrigation project results has changed public policy in Ceylon where heavy investment in new settlements in the arid zone had failed to yield the anticipated benefits.[43]

The record of accomplishment as reported here is not highly impressive, but it indicates several lines of investigation which have borne fruit in the operating procedures and policies of government agencies. Geographic work during the last decade has contributed significantly to the whole shift in strategies of water management toward exploring alternatives in means as well as in aims. It has helped examine the spatial implications of diffusing technology and of social linkages. And it has had a small part in assessing the significance for water resources planning of changes in attitudes towards the environment.

FUTURE CONTRIBUTIONS

In looking to the future, it may be asked what conjunction of events accounts for geographic research with respect to water problems having taken the turns that it has so far. Some aspects of water management, such as pollution, have been largely neglected, while others, such as floods, have received extensive attention. The explanation seems to lie partly in the serendipity of individual professional careers, and partly in the fact that certain problems lend themselves to geographical analysis more than others.

Perhaps the distinguishing feature of geographic contributions has been a holistic view. In preparing and compiling estimates of resources for river basins, in examining the whole range of choice available in water management, in developing schemes for canvassing all alternative adjustments in a metropolitan area, and in the planning of investigations of impacts of African reservoirs, the geographer has tended to stress the intermeshed systems of land, water, and human life. When one part of the system is manipulated by a water project or policy, sensitive readjustments occur throughout other parts of the system. This was the essential contribution of Barrows in the late 1930s in planning the historic Columbia Basin joint investigation which was the first integrated attempt by federal and state agencies to examine all the impacts of a major storage project then under construction.[44] It was a principal task of those who took part in the studies of the President's Water Resources Policy Commission and organized the cooperative review by government officers of ten large river basins.[45] The same view shows in discussions of policies for integrated river development as they first took shape in the activities of the National Resources Planning Board and as they later were reflected in the United Nations' part in river development.[46] It probably continues to be a salient but not unique value of the geographers' participation. Obviously, workers in other disciplines have emphasized the same view. In practical terms, to bring a geographer into an interdisciplinary investigation often increases the likelihood that the investigation will take a comprehensive view of human and natural phenomena in their interlocking relationships.

The geographer also has been in a distinctive way a major exponent of the need for assessing the full range of alternatives in water management. This might be expected from his habit of comparative examination of types of adjustments to similar environments or similar adjustments to different environments from one part of the world to another. This attitude happens to have found a concrete expression in geographic studies in the water field.

In the years immediately ahead geographers promise to make contributions to understanding differential perception of environment and differential evaluation of environmental features. The accomplishments and problems of studying environmental perception are well summarized by Craik in the latest volume of *New Directions in Psychology*.[47] These reviews show that no one disipline has claim to a unique corner of the field of environmental perception. It is an area in which geographers, psychologists, sociologists, architects, and others mix with impunity and with general cordiality.

SKILLS AND INCENTIVES

Insofar as a regional study lays bare the processes by which men shape the spatial patterns of land use and landscape appearance, it provides a basis for predicting the consequences of altering one portion of the landscape on the other portions. Actual application of the study requires searching analysis as well as careful description, and the job should be done from a perspective that ensures a breadth of view. Among the skills which figure in geographic research on water management are comparative analysis of human adjustments and resource decisions, spatial analysis of networks, methods of measuring environmental perception, modeling of cultural diffusion, and cartographic synthesis of large amounts of data.

In some respects, the drift of contemporary inquiry toward comprehensive study of the impacts of human intervention on the environment brings traditional geographic study into new prominence. More workers in other disciplines are cultivating a similar view, and there is greater interest in use of geographic skills.

In these circumstances, it is possible that the response to wider adoption of geographic methods in water management might come through their application by people trained in other disciplines. The incentives for strenuous expansion of these methods by geoographers themselves are mixed. While the sense of urgency about environmental problems gives the methods heightened importance, there is a strong inclination for geographers to pursue lines that enhance the image of their discipline as being rigorous or quantitative. Many of the questions studied in water management are viewed by geographers as offering fewer rewards from that standpoint. There is more emphasis on theory building and on the refinement of quantitative measures. However, to the extent that effective interdisciplinary ventures can be organized, the demand for geographic thinking is likely to increase.

Support for geographic research on water has been relatively minor compared to support for other lines of geographic study. Typically, if the work is to be pertinent, it requires collaboration with investigators in other disciplines, and thus does not lend itself to the devotion of a single investigator. When geographers have sought funding for cooperative studies they generally have been successful, but they have had to take the initiative. In the long run, the demands made upon researchers from all the social sciences will be linked with the kinds of questions asked by water planning agencies, and these, in turn, will be influenced by interest groups involved in making the final decision. If these groups are satisfied to regard water management as a discreet, conventional field serving ambiguous ends, there will be little need for research on alternatives and their consequences and little disposition to strive for holistic assessments of them. To the extent that alternative aims and means are studied with conviction and without preconceived selection, the appetite for guidance from the findings of social research will enlarge.

The promise far exceeds the record. Yet, the record is substantial enough to warrant arguing that a program of investigation of water resources management altervatives which does not take into account the analytical techniques that geographers have developed is bound to be inadequate. To put the conclusion succinctly, any group establishing a research program in water management or carrying out a comprehensive river basin planning investigation is likely to gain from the viewpoints and skills of geographers. Geographers may keep the group from overlooking major aspects of relationship among natural and social systems in the area to be manipulated by water management. They can aid in conscientiously examining the full range of choice open to society in dealing with water, including engineering works as well as readjustments in patterns of land use, water use, or in social constraints affecting such use. They may bring new understandings of the ways in which managers of resources perceive the resource and therefore respond to new information or social incentives and constraints in use of the resource. Geographers will not assure cool and comprehensive consideration of all these points. However, they have demonstrated that they have a significant and unique contribution to make. They also have shown a capacity to work with other disciplines in probing for new answers to the puzzle of man's interrelationship with water and land.

The author is grateful to W. R. Derrick Sewell for comments on an early draft of this article.

1. National Academy of Sciences, Committee on Water, *Alternatives in Water Management* (Washington, D.C.: National Academy of Sciences, 1966).

2. Robert K. Davis, *The Range of Choice in Water Management* (Baltimore: Johns Hopkins Press, 1968).

3. President's Task Force on Federal Flood Control Policy, *A Unified National Program for Managing Flood Losses* (Washington, D.C.: Government Printing Office, 1966).

4. John R. Sheaffer and Arthur J. Zeizel, *The Water Resource in Northeastern Illinois: Planning its Use* (Chicago: The Northeastern Illinois Planning Commission, 1966); Report of the Second Regional Plan, *Waste Management: Generation and Disposal of Solid, Liquid and Gaseous Wastes in the New York Region* (New York: Regional Plan Association, 1968).

5. Marion E. Marts, "Use of Indirect Benefit Analysis in Establishing Repayment Responsibility for Irrigation Projects," *Economic Geography* 32 (1956): 95-114.

6. Gilbert F. White et al., *Changes in Urban Occupance of Flood Plains in the United States* (Chicago: University of Chicago Department of Geography, 1958).

7. Henry C. Hart, *The Dark Missouri* (Madison: University of Wisconsin, 1957).

8. Robert H. Haveman and John V. Krutilla, *Unemployment, Idle Capacity, and the Evaluation of Public Expenditures* (Baltimore: Johns Hopkins Press, 1968).

9. Gilbert F. White, *Strategies of American Water Management* (Ann Arbor, Mich.: University of Michigan Press, 1969).

10. Richard J. Chorley, *Water, Earth and Man* (London: Methuen, 1969).

11. W. R. Derrick Sewell, Richard W. Judy, and Lionel Quellet, *Water Management Research: Social Science Priorities* (Ottawa: Department of Energy, Mines and Resources, 1969).

12. Behavioral and Social Sciences Survey Committee, *The Behavioral and Social Sciences: Outlook and Needs* (Englewood Cliffs, N.J.: Prentice-Hall, 1969).

13. Edward J. Taaffe, *Geography: The Behavioral and Social Sciences Survey* (Englewood Cliffs, N.J.: Prentice-Hall, 1970).

14. Gilbert F. White, "Geographical Contributions to River Basin Development," *Geographical Journal* 129(1963): 412-36.

15. National Academy of Sciences, Committee on Water, *Water and Choice in the Colorado Basin* (Washington, D.C.: National Academy of Sciences, 1968).

16. Aloys Michel, *The Indus Rivers: A Study of the Effects of Partition* (New Haven: Yale University Press, 1967).

17. David H. Miller, "Cultural Hydrology: A Review," *Economic Geography* 42 (1966): 85-88.

18. U.S. President's Task Force on Flood Control Policy, *Managing Flood Losses*, 89th Congress, 2nd Session, House Document no. 465.

19. Gilbert F. White, "Recent Developments in Flood Plain Research," *Geographical Review* 60 (1970): 440-43.

20. Gilbert F. White, "Formation and Role of Public Attitudes," in *Environmental Quality in a Growing Economy*, ed. Henry Jarrett (Baltimore: Johns Hopkins Press, 1966), pp. 105-27.

21. J. I. Lvovich, "The Water Balance of the Land," *Materialiek IIIs' 'zdu Geogr. Obsch.* (U.S.S.R., 1959).

22. Reiner Keller, *Report on World Water Balance* (Freiburg: International Geographical Union, Commission on International Hydrological Decade, 1969).

23. United Nations, *Atlas of the Physical, Economic and Social Resources Aspects of the Lower Mekong Basin* (Bangkok and Washington, D.C.: United Nations, 1968).

24. Ronald R. Boyce, ed., *Regional Development and the Wabash Basin* (Urbana: University of Illinois Press, 1964).

25. Robert W. Kates, *Hazard and Choice Perception in Flood Plain Management* (Chicago: University of Chicago Department of Geography, 1962); Robert W. Kates, "Variation in Flood Hazard Perception: Implications for Rational Flood-plain Use," *Special Organization of Land Uses: The Willamette Valley* (Corvallis: The University of Oregon, 1964); Thomas F. Saarinen, *Perception of the Drought Hazard on the Great Plains* (Chicago: University of Chicago Department of Geography, 1966).

26. Ian Burton and Robert W. Kates, "Perception of Natural Hazards in Resource Management," *Natural Resources Journal* (1964): 412-41.

27. Duane Baumann, *The Recreational Use of Domestic Water Supply Reservoirs: Perception and Choice* (Chicago: University of Chicago Department of Geography, 1969); Robert C. Lucas, "Wilderness Perception and Use: The Example of the Boundary Water Canoe Area," *Natural Resources Journal* (1964): 394-411.

28. John R. Sheaffer, "Economic Feasibility and Use of Flood Maps," *Highway Research Record*, no. 58 (1964): 44-46.

29. Masahiko Ohya, *Report on the Geomorphological Flood Analysis of the Nakton River Basin* (Southern Korea, n.p.: Food and Agricultural Organization, 1970).

30. Edward A. Ackerman and George Löf, *Technology in American Water Development* (Baltimore: Johns Hopkins Press, 1959).

31. Shue Tuck Wong, *Perception of Choice and Factors Affecting Industrial Water Supply Decisions in Northeastern Illinois* (Chicago: University of Chicago Department of Geography, 1969).

32. Leonard W. Bowden, *Diffusion of the Decision to Irrigate: Simulation of the Spread of a New Resource Management Practice in the Colorado Northern High Plains* (Chicago: University of Chicago Department of Geography, 1965).

33. John R. Sheaffer, *Introduction to Flood Proofing: An Outline of Principles and Methods* (Chicago: University of Chicago Center for Urban Studies, 1967).

34. Marion E. Marts and W. R. Derrick Sewell, "The Application of Benefit-Cost Analysis to Fish Preservation Expenditures: A Neglected Aspect of River Basin Investment Decision," *Land Economics* 35, no. 1 (February 1959): 48-55; Edward L. Ullman, "Geographical Prediction and Theory: The Measure of Recreational Benefits in the Meramac Basin," *Problems and Trends in American Geography*, ed. Saul Cohen (New York: Basic Books, 1967), pp. 146-73.

35. Leonard Zobler et al., *Benefits from Integrated Water Management in Urban Areas* (New York: Barnard College, 1969).

36. Clifford Russell, David Arey, and Robert W. Kates, *Drought and Water Supply* (Baltimore: Johns Hopkins Press, 1970).

37. Ian Burton, *Types of Agricultural Occupance of Flood Plains in the United States* (Chicago: University of Chicago Department of Geography, 1962); Donald Theiler, "Effects of Flood Protection on the Land Use in the Coon Creek Wisconsin Watershed," *Water Resources Research* 5(1969): 1216-22.

38. M. Gordon Wolman, "Two Problems Involving River Channel Changes and Background Observations," *Quantitative Geography: Part II*, ed. W. L. Garrison and D. F. Marble (Evanston: Northwestern University, 1967).

39. Donald J. Volk, *The Meramac Basin: Water and Economic Development* (St. Louis: Meramac Basin Research Project, 1962).

40. W. R. Derrick Sewell, ed., *Human Dimensions of Weather Modification* (Chicago: University of Chicago Department of Geography, 1966).

41. U.S. Senate, Select Committee on National Water Resources, *Report, 87th Congress, 1st Session, Report No. 29* (Washington, D.C.: Government Printing Office, 1961).

42. E. G. Pleva, "Multiple Purpose Land and Water Districts in Ontario," *Comparisons in Resource Management*, ed. Henry Jarrett (Baltimore: Johns Hopkins Press, 1961), pp. 189-207.

43. B. H. Farmer, *Pioneer Colonization in Ceylon, a Study in Asian Agrarian Problems* (London: Oxford University Press, 1957).

44. U.S. Bureau of Reclamation, *Columbia Basin Joint Investigations: Character and Scope* (Washington, D.C.: Bureau of Reclamation, 1941).

45. U.S. President's Water Resources Policy Commission, *Ten Rivers in America's Future* (Washington, D.C.: Government Printing Office, 1950).

46. United Nations, *Integrated River Basin Development: Report by a Panel of Experts* (New York: United Nations Department of Economic and Social Affairs, 1958)

47. Kenneth H. Craik, "Environmental Psychology," in *New Directions in Psychology*, ed. S. M. Newcomb (New York: Holt, Rinehart and Winston, 1970).

5 Toward a Political Science of Water Resources Decisions

Henry C. Hart

What is the current state of the political analysis of American dealings with water? The quantity of work is mounting rapidly after a slump in the 1960s. The influence of political analysis upon decisions is still weak, notably weaker than in the 1950s. Its influence upon political science, too, is weaker than it was in the 1950s. Is the currently renewed activity of political scientists likely to attain both kinds of influence, or either? Assuming that the answer depends at least partly upon whether the new modes of analysis are converging toward some ordering (or perhaps rival orderings) of knowledge in this policy field, it is necessary to defer answering these questions until an attempt is made to discover such orderings.

The task is to plot the interface of an academic discipline and a public policy and management problem area. The search for orderings will not review all current scholarship regarding governmental solutions to water problems, as that would call for examination of much work by economists, agency personnel, professionals in the law, and city planners. It is only necessary to draw on these sources here and there on issues neglected by political scientists. For reasons of convenience, the review will only include work done with regard to the United States and will concentrate upon recent years in the hope of detecting directions of likely advance or frustration.

Meanwhile, a glance back twenty years will give a rough standard by which to judge the current interest in water among political scientists. It will also pose the question of whether water resources research produced in the 1970s can be organized under the old political science concepts.

Water policy questions certainly captured a larger share of the attention of political scientists twenty years ago than they do now. In 1950 the *American Political Science Review* published a symposium on the subject. One of the three authors, Charles McKinley, who devoted his research career to the field, was shortly thereafter elected president of the American Political Science Association.[1] Both intensive book-length studies of particular river basins and evaluations of particular agencies provided raw material for political generalization.[2] The political scientists who did these studies agreed to a remarkable extent on the questions to be asked and even on the answers. Executive organization was studied with a view to hierarchical consolidation, legislative processes with a view to general public attention and accountability, and intergovernmental relations with a view to demarcation of clear fields of responsibility for each level of government and comity between them. Admittedly, these last were somewhat conflicting.

The work of the 1950s was oriented toward reform in government structures. Political scientists influenced authoritative recommendations: the two Hoover Commissions (1949 and 1955) and the President's Water Resources Policy Commission (1950). Reforms were not enacted. At the end of the decade, some of these political scientists began to put their talents to other uses. As one of the most active of them explained: "Until further political analyses disclose a way in which Congress might accommodate the patent need for more reasonable arrangements for consideration of water resources programs, we can revert to relatively apolitical modes of analysis."[3]

Political scientists dealing with the politics and government of water were less prominent in the profession during the decade of the 1960s, but not altogether inactive. Case studies written during this period described and evaluated by the accepted criteria the performance of federal and state water resource development efforts.[4] The resulting monographs are now a valuable resource for the political scientist who wishes to test generalizations against a body of diverse American experiences. Looking back, however, a political scientist has to report that his discipline was not much affected by these studies. Furthermore, the mark on national government decisions governing water was made increasingly, during the 1960s, by economists. At a time when organizational reforms had been frustrated, economists were improving basin-wide planning and investment decisions by benefit-cost analysis, one of those "relatively apolitical modes of analysis."

A POLITICAL CALCULUS FOR ECONOMIC MAN

One political scientist who worked vigorously on water problems during the 1960s was Vincent Ostrom. For that reason, but even more for the theoretical issues it raises, his work is a good entry point for reviewing that decade. He studied a new body of legal, governmental, political and economic experience—the remarkably creative achievements of the urban and rural water supply institutions of California. The ideas of economists had stimulated the use of benefit-cost analysis as a tool in political decision making. Ostrom departed radically from conventional political science in that he made a largely economic analysis of political decisions.

The actors in his system accept government constraints when it becomes clear that individualistic exploitation of a common-pool resource threatens all. Otherwise they resemble the "economic man" of classical economics. Participants in water decisions, as Ostrom conceives them, are rational and self-interested. To be sure, they may be uncertain as to the consequences of some of the alternatives before them. They know their value preferences, however, and insofar as they have information, seek steadfastly to maximize them.[5] This is not the view of the American voter that has gradually emerged from the survey literature. It quite directly challenges Arthur Maass's assumption that the preferences of participants are not given, "but that institutions themselves influence the preferences."[6] On the other hand, Ostrom's view is shared by a group of political economists now writing in the journal *Public Choice*. More important, Ostrom offers convincing evidence that the actors he observed in California behaved this way.

He focuses upon the public entrepreneurs who distribute water rather than upon individual water consumers. In California these entrepreneurs number in the thousands: mutual irrigation companies, cooperatives, municipal water utilities, and public districts. They overlap one another, larger units wholesaling or furnishing supplementary supplies to local ones. Retail distributors vary from dwarf to giant. Ostrom calls the whole complex the "California water industry." It is not managed by hierarchical authority. On the contrary, it is a "community" of political as well as economic entrepreneurs, whose member firms litigate, negotiate legislative constraints, and get new enterprises chartered when individualistic activities seriously threaten common supplies. Such behavior "requires a highly knowledgeable understanding of the strategic opportunities that can be realized through each of the decision-making structures that are available in a political system."[7] It is the public enterprise units, not individual consumers and voters, that are making the decisions. Ostrom's assumptions of rationality, knowledge, and self-aware maximizing fit fairly well.

Even though some water distribution enterprises serve irrigators and some serve urban consumers, all supply paying customers. The diversions hurt such other users as fishermen, but these other sectors are not in the industry. If their injuries are significant and they know it, they will demand redress of the legislature or of the state agencies.

What kind of redress? Again, in a very useful 1967 paper contributed to a Social Science Research Council conference on the role of political scientists in analyzing policies, Ostrom proposed an economic calculus. All political action carries some cost. Following Buchanan and Tullock, he distinguished costs to those constrained by the action (which decline as more of them participate in the decision) from costs of making the decision (which rise as more participate). This is a rationale by which one can conceive of the expensiveness of an all-encompassing hierarchy at one extreme and of unanimity at the opposite extreme. There is no clear discrimination, however, among a wide range of intermediate solutions: majority rule, negotiation among political leaders or leaders of other groups or agencies, or litigation. These more realistic alternatives require other criteria for comparing their differential capabilities. Ostrom himself is not confident that the least-cost political solution can be calculated once the game is widened. "If the terms and conditions inherent in political action create an incentive to raid the public treasury in order to avoid the economic costs inherent in allocating common-pool water supplies to their respective uses, the political process does not provide an appropriate calculus in the short run to bring individual incentives into harmony with the aggregate social welfare, but may instead serve to magnify or distort the allocational problem."[8]

In his 1967 paper, as well as in a later work with Elinor Ostrom,[9] Vincent Ostrom provided a conceptualization of water management decisions which could be useful for the more general analytical tasks of political science. The generality of the conceptualization depends on the location of the concerns of the California water industry in the array of possible water decisions, not only because of the distinctive characteristics of water supply in California, but also because Ostrom's own generalizations are dualistic; decisions have one set of constraints within the industry but approach incalculability when other water uses enter the arena.

CATEGORIZING POLICIES

Fortunately, the political science literature offers a rough map of this policy terrain. Theodore Lowi made the initial, and seminal, contribution in 1964 in reviewing a book on tariff policy making.[10] The policies he called *distributive*, (a later author suggested the name *subsidy policies*,[11]) confer highly divisible public benefits upon particular groups, localities, or individuals without any concern in the minds of decision makers that others are being injured or burdened, or that limited resources are being spent. "The indulged and the deprived ... need never come into direct confrontation." Lowi used "rivers and harbors" legislation as an example. Ostrom's phrase *raid the treasury* leaves little doubt he was warning against this kind of decision.

A second category of policies confers benefits on specified parties in the knowledge that other parties are, in the process, being deprived. Lowi called these policies *regulatory*. The decision is made by application of a general rule that threatens or protects all of a certain set of firms or groups—for example, interstate shippers, importers of watches—and they bargain and form shifting coalitions within and among interests to participate in the decision. "Since the most stable lines of perceived common impact are the basic sectors of the economy, regulatory decisions are cumulative largely along sectoral lines."[12] In most cases, a sector would be an industry.

California legislation facilitating the growth of the water industry seems in one way to be such sectoral policy. But it is not enacted with awareness of the counter-interest being foreclosed. Robert Salisbury, refining Lowi's theory, provides for just such decisions in a subcategory *self-regulatory*. "Self-regulatory policies also impose constraints upon a group, but are perceived only to increase, not decrease, the beneficial options to the group. ... In the self-regulatory policy situation, only a small group, such as lawyers or oil companies, makes demands, and typically there is no opposition."[13] The language could scarcely better fit a case noted by Ostrom and Ostrom. Faced with entry of salt water into a depleted underground basin, water supply utilities in Los Angeles County gradually, after litigation and negotiation, agreed upon a new overlying governmental district for water replenishment. It would recharge the basin by injecting purified waste water, monitor withdrawals by all local utilities, and recoup the cost by a combination of pumpage charges and a property tax increment in the benefited zone. The legislature merely ratified the intricately negotiated agreement.

Lowi's final category is *redistributive* policies. Decisions of this kind deliberately burden and benefit still broader social formations, approaching society-wide classes. The income tax and the social security system are examples. Whereas the textile industry or the American Bar Association might be mobilized to fight a regulatory battle, contestants in the making of redistributive policy would be as inclusive as the National Association of Manufacturers or the AFL-CIO.

Lowi shows that the America of the open frontier was characterized by distributive policies. For a single, durable policy issue, the tariff, he is able to point to a shift, dating from the 1930s, toward a sectoral, regulatory context. Are all decisions gravitating toward redistributive significance? Lowi can see societal reasons why they are; Salisbury can show that the distribution of power in our constitutional order, plus the open-ended characteristics of our economy, keep injecting elements of distribution, regulation, and self-regulation.

Has water policy shifted from one category to another? An initial use of the Lowi-Salisbury schema is to suggest that the dominant critiques of the 1950s were challenging traditional distributive policies of the rivers and harbors type in the name of a regulatory approach to electricity, regional development, soil erosion, transportation, and flood prevention. Ostrom put forward self-regulation as an alternative. But in what combination of circumstances is the alternative operative?

CATEGORIZING DECISION METHODS

Vincent Ostrom offers a characterization of the whole decision process for water. We have asked whether it was not derived from observations of policies of a particular type. The case studies of other political scientists cover alternative policy types, to be sure, but they also tend to focus on legislative decisions, or executive organization, or interest groups, or public opinion. They do so because most of the regularities or political behavior are recorded in terms of decision processes. In order to see independent studies as apposite, we need, therefore, a second categorizing theory that sorts out collective processes of policy decision. Fortunately, the literature contains a systematic classification of these processes, prepared fifteen years ago by an economist, Charles E. Lindblom, and a political scientist, Robert A. Dahl. Their work not only relates to water resources decisions but combines economic and political thinking to characterize the alternative methods for understanding and controlling the whole of the public economy. Their concepts have achieved durability in the professional repertoire of policy analysis.[14] They provide a convenient outline for the next section of this chapter. The four major methods of decision in their scheme are: 1) market allocation of priced goods; 2) bargaining or negotiation among leaders; 3) control of nonleaders by leaders, or hierarchy; and 4) control of leaders by nonleaders through elective representation, which Dahl and Lindblom call *polyarchy*.[15]

MARKET PROCESSES

Understanding the political implications of deciding water questions through market processes requires a review of the American experience with the surrogate market technique, benefit-cost analysis. We can learn something from the fact that, as Arthur Maass reminds us, the technique was developed first to deal with water decisions. "Thus when in 1963 Robert Dorfman organized the Brookings Institution's first conference on measuring benefits of government investment, he excluded papers on water resources, because the great need was to bring analysis in other areas of public investment up to the level already achieved in the design of water resource systems."[16]

Aaron Wildavsky carries the point further. He credits benefit-cost analysis of water projects with sparking the drive toward programming-planning-budgeting in the Kennedy and Johnson administrations. He also suggests why the technique was first applied to water projects. Water projects were not aimed at a substantive purpose (as were education, defense, even certain kinds of recreation) so evident and so desirable to policy makers as to provide a dimension along which projects could be arranged in priority order.[17] Only in a situation in which project goals did not posses this intrinsic merit could a putative dollar balance guide decision. Wildavsky's point has meaning in our conceptual scheme. Water projects were distributive policies. No general rules guided decisions; no general sectoral interests cumulated demands or resistance. Decision processes had fragmented long before. Projects were selected not by the budget (controlled hierarcy), not by Congress as a body, but by committees and subcommittees.[18] The interesting political question in this light is whether such a policy does not imply a decision process so fragmented as to abort the process it was designed for: measurement of all projects by a single, purpose-neutral yardstick.

In the 1960s a number of economists and political scientists shifted attention from the estimation of benefits and costs to the greater reliance upon actual prices set in functioning water markets. This was a principal thrust of Ostrom's work. At Resources for the Future, Irving Fox as early as 1962 proposed the redesign of institutions for water resource development in which a central role would be played by the release of "market-like" forces.[19] He meant that public investment should respond to demonstrated willingness of beneficiaries to pay for project benefits. He saw the market as weighing certain values more validly and more certainly than could planners' calculations of benefits.[20]

This was also a principal thrust of Ostrom's work. "In many cases we need to add to the voting strength of the ballot box by an opportunity to bid with our dollars for the services which we value."[21] In Ostrom's view, water uses range from the directly marketable to the inherently unmarketable (such as flood control) with most occupying a middle ground where pricing can function to allocate uses, but only through a set of politically arranged constraints.[22] He envisioned a "community of users," drawn into a common decision process by their realization that they were tapping a common property, negotiating the terms of such constraints, then getting legislative sanction. In our language, and based on the actual behavior of California water supply utilities, a market for water was a means of self-regulation by an industrial sector.

A slightly (but significantly) different view of the political processes by which a needed market can be brought into operation has been taken by an influential group of economists following the initiative of Allen V. Kneese. They advocate effluent charges. According to Kneese, "we must devise ways of reflecting the costs of using resources that are the common property of everyone, like our watercourses, directly in the decision-making of industries, local governments, and consumers.[23] The group argues that there is an even stronger case for "internalizing the externalities" of discharging liquid wastes than of depleting a common water supply. The municipal sewage disposal system or the industrial polluter inevitably make delicate and constantly changing *qualitative* impacts upon the common body of water into which they discharge. The cost of the quality of the river, lake, or estuary can only be balanced against an in-plant cost of cleaning an effluent by those with intimate knowledge of both sets of costs. Kneese and other economists who have thought most systematically about pricing the use of water to dispose of wastes do not envision a community of polluters hammering out a proposal and bringing it to a legislature. Kneese thinks a federal law setting minimum effluent charges would be a likely first step, followed by regional agencies set up by states under federal stimulus. The agencies would actually manage the body of water as well as administer effluent price schedules.

Kneese and the economists are thinking of a market brought into operation as regulatory policy; Ostrom conceives a self-regulatory objective. Why the difference? One reason has to do with differing types of competition for Ostrom's "common-pool flow-resource." A simplification will highlight the difference: As water supply utility A finds the ground water level in its well falling, A sees the external costs visited upon it by utility B, a firm in the same industry. B also sees A's external costs to

B. Not so with firms or cities C and D discharging effluents to the same stream or lake. C's effluent creates no direct costs to D. Eventually E, F and G—water supply utilities, downstream riparian property owners and unorganized but voting boaters and swimmers—feel the external impacts. Those who complain are not in the set of users (industry or sector) creating the impact. The distinction is actually one of the most venerable in American political theory, so old it has now been forgotten. John Dewey based his explanation of the rise of communities of concern making demands for government action upon the collective perception of just such serious and lasting, indirect (third party) consequences of social and economic transactions. He called these communities of concern "publics."[24] Translated into these terms, Ostrom is saying that when externalities run to those putting a common body of water to the same (or the same class of) use, the industry will seek to regulate itself. Kneese is saying that when the externalities run to third parties a public arises to exert government controls. The technique is the same in both cases: publicly administered prices. The difference in the diagnosis of the necessary political condition for the use of that technique has to do with the social meaning of *common-pool*.

The easy conclusion that problems of water supply spawn an industry, while problems of water quality give rise to a public, short-circuits the argument. Detroit, for example, has a metropolitian utility that wholesales water to its suburbs. No market has emerged significantly affecting retail pricing. Some suburbs mark up water seventy percent while others, without economic reason, mark up water from the same source 280 percent.[25] It is perceptions that determine whether an industry or a public is evoked. Ostrom points out that users in the West regard water as a scarce commodity. The Detroit study suggests that in the Great Lakes area water supply is perceived to be readily available in almost unlimited quantities. There may be crucial differences in perceived water availability not only from region to region but from time to time. Kneese points to a trend he calls "congestion" with reference to our environment. If he is correct, everyone will eventually come to see all resources as exhaustable.

To the extent that groups outside an industry regard each use of water as a deprivation to them, one important precondition is satisfied for making regulatory rather than distributive or self-regulatory policies. Regulation could create a market apart from the initiative of the public or private entrepreneurs of a water industry, and not necessarily on their terms.

THE BARGAINING PROCESS

If the concept of "a government of laws and not of men" once kept American political scientists from looking for processes of negotiation in decisions regarding water, that barrier exists no longer. Stimulated by the interest shown in this approach at Resources for the Future, Matthew Holden in 1966 published his *Pollution Control as a Bargaining Process*. Social scientists had long been explaining some environmental resource decisions as bargaining, but Holden found *regulatory* powers being wielded in ways that could best be understood as bargaining. State and perhaps national agencies regulating water pollution "tend to engage in some loose interchange (bargaining) with regulated parties until they find a settlement which is tolerable to them all."[26] He found some bargains to be tacit and some explicit, but he found that they all "limit, if they do not explicity repeal, the larger decision (e.g., a legislative act)."[27]

Within four years economists Robert Dorfman and Henry Jacoby had furnished a rather full and precise model of the processes by which a water pollution control agency (hypothetical, but not atypical) might bargain with polluters for a particular allocation of effluent discharges to attain a particular stream quality classification. They maintain that the bargaining might lead to a "feasible alternative that is preferred by some interested parties and that is regarded as equally beneficial by all." Because the decision process gets down to "pulling, hauling, and compromising to ascertain the decision that best reconciles the interests of all concerned,"[28] predicting the likely outcome from among the limited number of alternatives involves assigning to each bargaining agency a weight in the decision process. By this assumption and by benefit-cost analysis, one decision is found to be more likely than others.

Dorfman and Jacoby do not consider their model to represent a different decision process than Holden's. How is it that they conceive their actors as optimizing policy, whereas Holden sees his as limiting or repealing it? Dorfman and Jacoby conceive policy as general, subject to interpretation in the specific case. Second, they assume representative functions for the pollution control agency while Holden views the agency as a hierarchical representative of the state. Both studies specify perfectly plausible contexts in which a particular decision might be made. Neither takes its conceptualization far enough to put the decision into a larger context of public institutional growth or changes. That kind of conceptualization requires information on whether the bargain can be made the subject of an issue-appeal by representatives to voters (polyarchy), and if so, in what decision arena: city, state, or federal. One also needs to know whether the bargain thwarts the coordinative or technical interpretation of water quality being hammered out in the administrative staff of the state or federal departments concerned or whether (as is equally likely) bargaining complements polyarchy and hierarchy.

It becomes all the more important to see each decision method in the context of policy content and other decision methods when one turns from the interpretation to the making of legislative policy—to the input side of the political system. Ostrom's picture of the California water industry provides one point of comparison in that the industry meets its occasional needs for social control of water enterprises primarily by bargaining through to agreed forms of legal constraint which the state legislature then ratifies. "Governmental authorities are relied on primarily to establish veto points, to determine bargaining positions, and to validate negotiated settlements."[29]

Bargaining is also at the heart of a superficially different kind of water decision, authorization of the Central Arizona Project, as Helen Ingram records and interprets it. "Commitment and unity within the locality is practically a prerequisite for broadening support," she tells us.[30] Compare Ostrom's: "In the absence of a consensus among a community of water users the judgment is frequently expressed that 'We are not ready to go to Sacramento yet.' "[31] But closer attention reveals a significant difference. The California water industry confronted its members' conflicts of interest and finally negotiated a distribution of burdens and benefits among them. Not so those directly affected by the Central Arizona Project. Even when it emerged that California might be deprived of water in dry years, the initial solution of project proponents was to import water from outside— from the Columbia.[32] (Of course, Senator Jackson stopped that.) The distinction is clearly between a self-regulatory policy in Ostrom's case, and the distributive one Ingram explicitly presents. She writes that combinations to achieve consent for water development are built upon mutual non-interference. "This is pork barrel in the purest sense, for a pork barrel is a container of unrelated items."[33]

The distributive bargain was ultimately disrupted by another set of participants, the preservers of the natural environment. They fought a major battle against the Grand Canyon dams and won, against a small dam on the Gila River and lost. They did not bargain very much, for bargaining requires trading among leaders. Conservationist leaders had neither latitude nor desire to negotiate over what seemed to them irreplaceable. As Ingram expresses their view: "A compromise of wilderness was an irretrievable loss."[34] They had a leader, Congressman Saylor of Pennsylvania, free to cultivate a conservationist following since he had few potential water projects in his district. The conservationists, however, had no government agency staff working to identify alternatives to the Central Arizona Project and prepare defenses of those alternatives. They had a national constituency, but it was thin in particular states. It held together to fight the Grand Canyon dams, which stirred national opinion. It split—New Mexico preservationists versus Congressman Saylor—upon a compromise of the non-national issue of the Gila River dam.[35]

Political scientists recording water decisions have described bargains of limitless variety: agency with agency alloting jurisdictions;[36] local water officals in a water users' association;[37] chairman with chairman allotting congressional committee jurisdiction;[38] city water utility with suburb over extension of service;[39] chairman with other members of federal-state river basin commission over commission powers;[40] and among advocates of various bills in a state legislature.[41] Such accounts, however, add to a general knowledge of politics only as they specify in general terms the resources at the command of the bargainers, the content of the bargain, and the relation of the bargain to other methods of political decision.

HIERARCHY

Most of the water resources work of political scientists in the 1950s studied or advocated hierarchical unification. Executive control was the means, and unification of the river basin, or the full range of water (sometimes water and land) programs of the state or nation, was the goal. Few political scientists today study the executive unification of water programs. Irving Howards and Edward Kaynor, comparing four regional water supply systems with five conflicted situations come to the forthright conclusion that unification does not matter: "Give the researcher a thorough briefing on physical setting, historical sequences, socio-economic background, and values and skills of decision makers, and he will be able to predict within reasonable limits what will be decided with no knowledge whatever of the institutional framework within which the decisions are to be made."[42]

Interest did not fall off because hiearchical unification had already been attained, as that had not happened. In the most obvious subject for executive integration, control of the water stored behind the several dams on a river, an inventory of the reservoirs on sixteen major rivers in the United States published by the U.S. Geological Survey and analyzed by Frank Munger and Ann Houghton found that only five river reservoir systems were under unified control: Colorado of Texas (Lower Colorado River Authority), Cumberland and Missouri (Corps of Engineers),

Tennessee (Tennessee Valley Authority), and Wisconsin (state-chartered private authority). The criterion was modest, that seventy-five percent or more of the reservoir storage be under single control.[43]

One gets the contrary impression that political scientists are no longer studying integrated hierarchical control of water resources because the subject is losing the intrinsic unity it once seemed to possess. The two reasons are alternative technologies and ecological continuities. As technology added alternative means for the accomplishment of any development objective, water became less viable as a focus of political organization. For example, thermal plants so overshadowed hydroelectric energy as to supplant the idea of the river basin as an electrification unit. Only domestic water supply remains as a technologically unpre-empted basis of departmentalization, and even that may be administered as an instrument to achieve goals that are not water-oriented. More recently human pressure upon and awareness of ecological cycles have involved water programs as links in larger environmental chains. The thermal pollution of lake, stream, or estuary by the condenser water of a fuel-fired generating station can be reduced by building a cooling tower, but that will pollute the air. Hierarchical control in water resources units cannot encompass these broader issues; some other approach thus has to be used in the end.

Elizabeth Haskell and her associates in their fascinating *Managing the Environment: Nine States Look for New Answers* discuss how states have dealt with this situation.[44] Comparative analysis is possible at the state level because enough change has occured for the changed present to be compared with the past. Among states, change of one kind can be compared with a change of another and with no change.

The dominant change has been administrative consolidation. Five of Haskell's nine states moved in that direction around 1970, but it was consolidation of environmental quality programs, not of water programs. Environmental programs may include—it varies from state to state— pollution control (water, air, and solid waste), land use, and the conservation and management of fish, wildlife, forests, and natural areas. A major thrust and a powerful justification for all these administrative consolidations was to avoid fragmented activities and to make program administration match "the integrative way problems occur in the environment."[45] Those with long memories will recall the "seamless web" of resource relations in the river basin widely discussed at the time of passage of the TVA Act. The jurisdiction, forty years later, is altered.

Furthermore, the comparative study uncovers overt arguments against hierarchical unification even of programs deemed to be closely interrelated. Illinois has a standard-setting Pollution Control Board, an Environmental Protection Agency to prosecute violators and give assistance to those trying to clean up their wastes, plus the Illinois Institute for Environmental Quality to do supportive research. "Illinois' system is designed to create a competitive system of government. Functions overlap intentionally to increase state officials' motivation. The public spotlight and state funds are the rewards for which officials compete."[46] Wisconsin in 1970 organized pollution control, including water pollution, with the old fish, game, forest, and park programs, and the control of extraction of water from wells and streams into a single superdepartment. Minnesota, with a similar tradition of semi-independent boards and weak governor, deliberately organized pollution control in a single-purpose Pollution Control Agency. Two reasons were advanced in Minnesota: 1) Its purpose clear, each agency will function as an advocate of whatever state action is necessary to that end. 2) Single purpose agencies will attract, hear, and define each major public interest. Other agencies, the governor, the legislature and the public can then take sides.[47] The case which carried the day for departmental integration in New York and Wisconsin ran in the direction of building a support base. "If sportsmen, wilderness buffs, and bird fanciers can be united with 'new environmentalists' who are concerned about pollution, urban areas and legal action, then a strong political coalition can be welded within the state."[48]

Even among nine state there is experience enough for proposing a few relationships but scientists have not done it yet. For a sample set of experience data, note the following. The governor was a prime mover in New York, as was the governor's task force in Wisconsin. A legislative committee had the greatest share of initiative in Minnesota. A law professor sparked change in Michigan. The first two states enlarged hierarchies, Minnesota preserved interagency competition, and the Michigan law put decisions in the hands of the state courts. Immediate, no doubt contingent, explanations are thus suggested for a comparative study that selects the nature of the administrative reform as the dependent variables.

Elizabeth Haskell's data also suggests the varying conditions under which a single consequence, more vigorous enforcement of pollution control law, may proceed from quite different, even opposite, directions of organization change. At the extremes, competition among single-purpose agencies does not invigorate enforcement if part of the anti-pollution authority is left in the hands of a promotional agency responsive to a politically powerful and organized interest: oil pollution control in the Illinois Department of Mines and Minerals and pesticide regulation in an interagency board controlled by the Illinois Department of Agriculture, for example.[49] Hierarchical integration of control activities here would strengthen enforcement.

Short of such an extreme condition, explanations for vigorous anti-pollution enforcement are not direct or simple. Even the nine cases, however, suggest propositions worth studying further. One set of explanations, for example, might be derived from public attitudes of concern over pollution: the salience, specificity, wide or narrow distribution of such attitudes, and the state of organization of antipollution interests. If public concern is high, shared among almost all politically active groups, and brought to bear at many points in the political process, one suspects that departmentalization makes little difference. Both Wisconsin and Minnesota seem to approach this extreme.[50] If public support is new, not shared by some powerful groups, and much more widespread among individual voters than among lobbyists and political insiders, then strong executive leadership through department head and governor may be the only way to crystallize such sentiments into persistent legislative and administrative effectiveness even though they might have been strongly expressed at the polls.

Other explanations for clear policy and vigorous enforcement may be found in the differing capabilities of various political institutions to reconcile value-loaded conflicts among interests, organized and latent. If such capability is concentrated in the governorship (as seems true in New York) executive consolidation may be indicated. If the legislature is organized to do much of this job through its leadership, its committee organization, and the expertise acquired by some of its members, then several advocate departments bringing their disputes before it may be favorable for program development. Minnesota approaches this situation.[51]

One rationale for a superdepartment "is that such a structure is more efficient because it allows tradeoffs on natural resource issues to be made on a rational, nonpolitical basis within the context of one department."[52] For example, if enforcement of effluent discharge standards is departmentalized with water withdrawal permits, the permits can be used as a lever for enforcement. This view sees bargaining as a means of gaining compliance with policy, not as an erosion of policy. At the other extreme from the superdepartment (equipped with a wide array of tradeoffs) one might conceive of the state courts (having plenty of room to negotiate on judgments but no side payments).[53] It is, however, premature to call for research of this complexity until we know whether side payments are in fact put to the use specified above.

We have been thinking of unifying administrative activities under single direction as though it were a simple variable. Interstate comparisons make clear, however, that consolidation is not unidimensional. The consolidations of 1970 were not of water programs, but of environmental-quality programs, including air and solid waste. They were often achieved by dividing water *quantity* programs (permits to withdraw, assistance for water supply) from the water *quality* mission of an enviromental protection agency. Furthermore, hierarchical integration at any level of government may be had at the cost of reducing hierarchical control by another level. "Many of the new powers that states are beginning to assume have been shifted entirely or in part from local governments, the usual strategy being first to set up a state-local partnership."[54] The horizontal integration of programs within state administration may then require transferring some program responsibilities out of single-purpose bureaus.[55] Disintegration in the administrative hierarchy, furthermore, may succeed in bringing under administrative control authority formerly designated entirely to the courts. Illinois's Pollution Control Board is split organizationally from the Environmental Protection Agency. Only thus could it achieve a quasi-judicial, quasi-legislative character allowing it to substitute "for the lower court in Illinois, for findings of fact and issuing fines with appeals to appellate courts."[56]

Finally, the *scope* of hierarchical control is by no means the only variable affected by organizational change or choice. To be sure, most political scientists, working on reorganization studies initiated by, or serving, chief executives have concerned themselves with consolidating executive control. But the design of administrative organization is also the design of 1) roles, including agency roles as well as jobs; 2) careers; and 3) interpersonal relationships. The study of all three has been neglected in examining institutional change affecting water programs.

The power of an official's role, developed by his life career, to cancel organization structure ordered by the President and Congress was demonstrated neatly by Robert H. Pealy some years ago. Two federal-state basin planning commissions were chartered on the some day and given the same mandate in law and presidential directive. They had analogous memberships: federal officials of existing construction agencies, state representatives, and an outside chairman appointed by the President. The Texas Commission, however, succeeded merely in collating the plans of the federal agencies. The Southeast River Basins Commission accomplished its own planning. Why the difference? One reason was contextual. The Southeast Commission had more physical options, less organized interest-commitment to any of them, and more public apathy. To planners the context was more open. A second reason was a difference in the roles federal members brought with them to the commissions. Texas Commission members were advocates of plans long decided and promoted by their agencies. The one Southeast Commission member (Soil Conservation Service) whose role had already been so rigidly defined soon made himself appear a maverick. He did not set the tone of the commission. Pealy's account offers evidence that temporary organization is vulnerable to pre-existing role sets.[57]

What of relatively permanent hierarchies? Elizabeth Haskell's study gives us one relevant experience common to several states. A principal reason to reorganize water pollution control was to displace the role endemic to control officers working in departments of health, that of "consulting sanitary engineer."[58] The role was reinforced by career expectations (the top opportunity in government was health department head). The role included some enforcement techniques (reviewing plant designs) but rejected others (prosecution in the courts, publicity of violations). The interesting point is that "consulting sanitary engineers" were to be transformed into "water quality enforcers" not by replacing them, but by putting them in a different hierarchy. With hierarchy, leadership changed, but so did promotion criteria, the occupational mix of colleagues, patterns of interest group access, and style of communicating with the public. A study of the role changes that resulted would be interesting in the light of the doubt some have expressed of the value of federal redepartmentalization on the ground that it could only unite some water programs by separating others. Quite apart from that issue, its effects *might* be of critical importance to official roles. We need to find out.

Hierarchy is the one of the four Dahl and Lindblom decision methods now being re-examined by some political scientists. There is a movement among younger students of public administration to stress associational criteria rather than hierarchical criteria for organization. They would shift attention from authority to the stimulus provided by colleagues, from policy direction to the creativity of the individual, from control to the security to innovate. Whatever may be the ultimate fate of these propositions in our understanding of public administration, they are now stimulating critiques of administrative consolidation, partly coinciding with the critiques made from the perspective of maximizing public access and controversy. David C. Ranney has addressed a recent criticism to Wisconsin's superdepartment of natural resources from this perspective.[59]

This fact may be loosely connected to a rather surprising blank in present political science research. Six years ago Irving Fox very clearly specified the kind of administrative agency he thought would be needed to perform the tasks of water quality management. He felt that the agency must be "capable of administering a highly integrated set of policies and measures" which he listed.[60] Since then much work has been done on this question, including useful international comparative studies of just such integrated managerial agencies in the Ruhr[61] and in England.[62] Except for the consideration of Maryland's very interesting Environmental Service (a sort of statewide sanitary district) in Elizabeth Haskell's review of the experience of nine states, the research and the advocacy has come from economists and ecologists.

POLYARCHY, OR ELECTIVE REPRESENTATION

Many well-informed observers of the politics of water decisions in Washington began to detect a new political climate in about 1969. In that year Congress multiplied almost by four the appropriation requests of Presidents Johnson and Nixon for grants to build sewage treatment plants, $214 million to $800 million. The unusual action had the earmarks of response to the grassroots; "it was accomplished through none of the established power centers in Washington," said the New York Times.[63] The increase was petitioned for by 222 members of the House of Representatives, pressed hard by an ad hoc group called the Citizens Crusade for Clean Water.[64] Simultaneously, evidence was mounting that the stanchest supporters of the traditional engineering developments, the rivers and harbors interests, were politically frustrated. The ranking Democrat on the House Public Works Committee told the Ohio Valley Improvement Association, a gathering of 250 river-oriented businessmen and government officials, that it was time for most of the civil works projects to be taken from the hands of the Corps of Engineers and turned over to local governments using federal funds. The Congressman, Kenneth Grey of Illinois, declared that "the Corps has not been able to push projects through Congress for funding."[65]

These two signals of change in political power in 1969 cannot be unrelated. Funding of Corps's flood-control reservoirs, local flood protection works and navigation channels (for example, the Cross-Florida Barge Canal), funding of the Bureau's storage and diversion projects, and funding of the small watershed projects of the Soil Conservation Service are being blocked by objections from conservationists. Conservationists are multifariously organized. They have spokesmen in Congress and in various of its committees. They have exerted power, though in somewhat different directions, in the reorganization of state governments. The venerable constituencies, groups, access points, agencies, and political spokesmen of the water project construction programs seem at last to have met countervailing powers. If so, it is a turning point in American political history, probably more consequential than the transformation of tariff politics Lowi perceived.

Distributive policies are giving way to regulatory. Lowi has shown that American political scientists constructed a model of decision making which precisely fits the regulatory policy situation: the pluralist model. "The regulatory arena appears to be composed of a multiplicity of groups organized around . . . 'shared attitudes.' Within this narrower context of regulatory decisions, one can even go so far as to accept the most extreme pluralist statement that policy tends to be a residue of the interplay of group conflict.[66] Several implications arise from pluralist theory. Since many groups challenge many groups, wide participation is assured. But since the challenges tend to be tangential, not head-on as in redistributive policies, they can be resolved in a fragmented decision arena. The epitome of such an arena is Congress, Congress acting as a whole. A committee might be able to decide a distributive policy. A redistributive policy would likely be too divisive for the fragmented Congress; only an executive-led coalition could resolve its extensive confrontation.

Are not our fragmented policy institutions, then, ideally suited for the kind of decisions water questions have newly come to pose? It might be prudent exercise, before we jump to that conclusion, to consider an alternative possibility. Perhaps the emerging policy issues, those now producing deadlock, are not regulatory but redistributive. Is America dividing into two schools of thought whose conflict is not tangential but head-on, into a group structure not plural but polarizing? Lynton Caldwell, the political scientist who has given this matter the most thought, believes that "as the United States moved into the decade of the 1970s it became increasingly clear that an indefinite period of tension and conflict could be expected between the nation's historical commitment to unfettered economic growth and the new and growing concern for the quality for life."[67] This would seem to be a sufficient sign to warrant our casting about in studies of water decisions for a model not of pluralism but of conflict, not of regulatory but of redistributive policy.

There is in the contemporary research literature at least one such model.[68] It is the product of political scientists working with sociologists to explain as much as possible of a large body of actual polyarchical decision making. The evidence gradually turned them away from their initial social-psychological explanations (alienated voters) to political explanations (community decision structures). The issue upon which the research compares 515 cities' decision processes is the fluoridation of the municipal water supply.[69] It is an issue that provides a very large number of comparable observations of the processes of election and representation at work in a context of conflicting popular values and perceptions.

Authors Crain, Katz, and Rosenthal frankly consider fluoridation to be good. "[A] majority of the American public approves of it; the medical profession is nearly unanimous in its support; and local government officials rarely oppose it."[70] But once a controversy started, fluoridation has usually lost. What causes success (a profluoridation decision)?

Advocacy by the mayor is the best single predictor of success.[71] Strong executive leadership is a matter of institutional structure: a longer term for mayor, absence of other elected officials, partisan election. All these conditions favor fluoridation. The last is particularly interesting, for Crain, Katz, and Rosenthal find that partisan elections centralize power in the hands of the mayor and also reduce direct citizen participation.[72]

The second explanation for success goes deeper into the social structure and general political traditions of the city. It contradicts much conventional wisdom. It is not uneducated "blue-collar" cities that have the most controversy and defeat the most referenda. On the contrary, "the most educated communities have the most trouble with fluoridation"[73] Further, what is most unorthodox in the American tradition, popular participation as such, is counterproductive. In the 600 cases in which fluoridation was put on the ballot since 1960, it was defeated sixty percent of the time. The authors conclude that "broad popular participation, particularly in the absence of strong executive leadership and an institutionalized channel for the expression of opposition, spells defeat to fluoridation. It does so because fluoridation is a technical issue, the advantages of which are rather small from the citizen's point of view (and even less than that as far as political capital is concerned), and because the opposition can easily implant doubt. Doubt takes root and blossoms the more the issue is discussed."[74]

This brings us to the third area of findings: the nature of the issue as people perceive it. Fluoridation is not salient to most citizens. "Fluoridation is perceived as treatment for a minor disease. It is not enacted, as smallpox legislation often was, after a particularly severe epidemic. The issue itself contains little to frighten the public into support and little incentive for the public official to support it at a personal risk. . . . Finally, of course, we are dealing with . . . the fear of illness and death [adding "rat poison" to the water] . . . about as basic and important as any emotion ever tapped by a political campaign."[75]

The tinder is ignited by nationally organized groups whose local members tend to be at the fringe of the community establishment: the chiropractors, food faddists, Christian Scientists, and to a lesser extent, the radical right. Interestingly, because opponents are so totally and emotionally committed, while proponents are detached, many organizations sit out the unexpectedly bitter fight because they are not prepared for a sharp internal quarrel. Thus, the third finding is that the issue is too technical and peripheral for most institutional leaders to become involved until the few who feel passionately about it take command of the popularization process.[76]

A few proponents of dams, diversions, or generating plants who have been through a battle with the Sierra Club may need no further argument to identify their own cause with fluoridation. But we must test the validity of the analogy.

There is no obvious category for fluoridation among Lowi's policy types. The broad polarization of the whole community that characterizes redistribution is fleeting; it cuts across the durable ties of peak associations, parties, and classes. On the other hand, fluoridation is no distributive decision as it imposes good or ill upon all who use water, without individual escape. This last characteristic fits many conservationists' perceptions of federal water projects, which they see as foreclosing such other options as wild rivers, fisheries, or simply enjoyment of natural beauty by generations to come. There is an ecological perspective which sees inescapable general goods or ills in every water modification. The following points of comparison with fluoridation will provide instructive tests of the relevance to water quality decisions of the pluralist versus the conflict model.

1) Both decisions are seen by many as closing individual options. (In welfare economics terms the effects are indivisible). Fluoridation imposes itself on all water users, without individual escape. Conservationists see many dam, thermal-electric, and channel rectification projects in a similar light. An oversimple ecological framework puts every water modification in terms of far-reaching goods or ills, perhaps irreversible.

2) The seriousness of ecological damages, beyond the question of indivisibility, is an extraordinarily technical matter. For many effects, science simply cannot answer. The effects of fluoridation are comparatively well established. Yet even here there is a shadow of disagreement among "experts"—for instance, an article by a dentist published by *Harpers*. Once the question enters public controversy, it is no longer divided into technical consequences to be determined by the experts and preferences among those predicted consequences to be selected by voters.

On the contrary, the very fact that the issue is put to public vote suggests *prima facie* that there must be a doubt. If there is a doubt, it is safer for the layman to say no.[77] This is true even though, in one community surveyed, more than half the *opponents* said they would prefer that the decision be made by experts. It is difficult to believe that the subtler, more debatable issues of ecological damage can escape this public reaction.

3) Water quality is definitely more salient to most voters than fluoridation. A 1965 Harris poll covering eleven different issues found that forty-three percent of the national sample *often* or *sometimes* felt concern for the issue *pollution of rivers and streams*. In 1970 a slightly differently worded question drew responses of concern about water pollution from ninety percent of the sample. The 1970 survey showed that fifty-three percent of the sample regarded air and water pollution as among issues of the highest priority.[78] This should help link constituent interests to the positions formulated by group leaders and decision makers outside the heat of bitter controversy. A related distinction from fluoridation attitude structures is that water quality concerns are more salient to high-status people than to low. The same is true of economic development attitudes toward water. This finding, too, fits the pluralist better than the conflict model.

4) As to the key questions of depth and extent of attitude conflicts, available information is very limited. In contrast with Lynton Caldwell's view that America is in for a sustained and pervasive clash of basic values (growth versus environmental quality) is the belief of J. Clarence Davies. Many people, he thinks, unite against pollution because "it is a way of avoiding thinking about more divisive matters."[79] There is certainly, here, a vital area capable of being explored by attitude surveys, both cross-sectional and in terms of patterns of influence. One hint as to the meaning of these divergent interpretations is provided by the low degree of opinion crystallization toward specific demands upon the government. It may be that people agree *something* should be done about pollution, but that they will not really perceive a conflict until they experience brownouts.

5) Is the pattern of interest-group membership, leadership, and activity pluralist or conflicted? Again, we do not have the knowledge needed to answer. Lynton Caldwell lists the National Reclamation Association (founded 1932) with the Sierra Club (founded 1892) in a long roster of conservation organizations. Obviously, something has changed. The case studies available show both old and new conservationist groups in the 1960s militantly confronting the pressures for projects. This activity may be pluralist, or it may suit the conflict model. We need to learn the extent

of overlapping memberships; the strength in linking constituencies to decision makers of militant, single-issue groups as compared to broad-spectrum broker groups; the proportion of combative versus majority-building techniques used; and exclusive versus shared access-points to governments.

6) The functioning of congressional committees dealing with water policies has yielded two institutional studies, neither yet published. James T. Murphy is examining the significance of political party in the work of the House Public Works Committee.[80] Richard F. Fenno, Jr. has included the House Interior Committee in a comparative study of several quite different committees.[81] Both studies provide evidence that these two committees still play a part characteristic of distributive policy making. Members of the committee are all trying, Fenno reports, not to make policy but to get bills onto the House floor and passed. The second committee strategy is "to provide, in the context of conservation legislation, reasonable protection for the private users of land and water resources." "The easterners want to turn the West into a vast playground where they can come to play. . . . You're talking about our livelihood." The committee, heavy with westerners, is not a body in which water quality issues will be raised or solved. But Fenno can see a possible change not far away. "A burgeoning conservation movement may change the Committee's second strategic premise. More Easterners may be attracted to the Committee, or Westerners may come to define their constituency interests as basically preservationist."

Davies makes it evident that such a change has already taken place in the Senate Committee on Public Works, largely through the work of Senator Muskie's subcommittee. Senator Jackson's Interior Committee has also proved itself capable of facing and resolving regulatory policy issues.[82]

7) Congressional committees are known to be fragmented but judgments differ on the consequences of that fragmentation. A 1970 symposium at the University of Washington produced the opinion that "the congressional committee system hinders rather than assists the careful evaluation of environmental legislation."[83] Political scientist J. Clarence Davies makes the same description of fragmented jurisdiction, but finds differing outcomes. In air and water pollution control (unlike anti-poverty legislation, for example) "it was Congress that led and the administration that followed."[84]

8) Consideration of presidential intervention in the representative decision process leads to a tentative conclusion quite different from that of the fluoridation study. During the Eisenhower years, as two accounts

agree, Congress's initiatives for water quality legislation met not presidential indifference but active presidential opposition. President Eisenhower made a national issue of his opposition to grants to the states for sewer and sewage treatment plant construction. He drew the state department heads into the controversy, even the governors. "The turning point appeared to come when a significant element of conservative opinion yielded to the compulsion of the facts that pointed to national action. . . . In water pollution control, it was the state administrative agencies and the governors."[85] Eisenhower's veto of Congressman Blatnik's water pollution control bill (authorizing grants totaling $90 million per year for sewage treatment plant construction) in 1960 thrust the issue into the presidential election. Kennedy campaigned on it. Party lines thus drawn enabled Blatnik to win in the face of normally fractured congressional leadership.[86] Presidential intervention was strong, though negative. State executive intervention was strong and positive, and parties articulated interests in Congress and the campaign. Such broad-purpose interest groups as the National League of Municipalities and the AFL-CIO became very active. After 1960, Kennedy and Johnson made extraordinary use of presidential task forces to work out legislative positions across the divided purposes of the executive agencies.[87]

While this description of recent legislative history is too short to draw conclusions, it suggests the early stages of the great national division, if there is to be one. It does prove that the positive leadership of the elected executive is not a sine qua non for water quality legislation as it proved to be for pro-fluoridation outcomes. Nevertheless, a solution reconciling these environmental concerns with an energy plan for the next decade or two might be quite impossible without presidential leadership.

While present knowledge is insufficient to exclude either the pluralist or the conflict model, it suggests a profile of relevance for each. In new water quality issues the trend to bring out conflicts in basic values holds more potential for conflict than did the fluoridation issue. People are more concerned about water quality, and more durably concerned. Plural groups and plural committees of Congress are seized perennially with the issue of water quality, and this makes representation a much more powerful element in the processes of polyarchy than it has been for fluoridation. The knowledge is not so polarized into blacks and whites as it tended to be for fluoridation, but it still falls pitifully short of permitting policy to be set in the light of known consequences. James Sundquist concluded that "the basic problem is knowing what to do."[88]

There is another respect, too, in which neither pluralism nor conflict seems to possess an answer. However volatile the controversy over fluoridation, one ground rule was fixed. The arena of policy combat was the city. Defining the arena in which contemporary water controversies will be fought out, however, is at least half the battle.

DECISION ARENAS

Polyarchy, as is clear from Dahl's original definition, "control of leaders by nonleaders," is linkage politics. Those with power to act, the representatives, must be made responsible to a large number of voters who may be powerless on the specific issue up for decision. Formally specified constituencies are essential to a representative system, and in our tradition these are territorial. The conflict model suggests the further requirement that linkages not only be formally delimited, but be stable over considerable periods. Only thus could representative policy makers be judged on many issues, multi-interest groups come to carry a significant share of the linkage, and parties hold representatives to account or mobilize support for them. To whatever degree one accepts the conflict model, it adds to the need for institutionalizing polyarchical arenas.

It is worth noting that the market, bargaining, and hierarchical processes can function perfectly well without formally contituted arenas. The point is clearly illustrated in a case study, *Urban Water Policies and Decision-Making in the Detroit Metropolitan Region*,[89] written from a quite different perspective. In 1959 the Detroit Water Board decided to supply the entire metropolitan area. This was an administrative decision, quite clearly marked by a change in general manager. By 1968 roughly half the agency's business was in the suburbs. The service area is fixed partly by market processes (Will it be cheaper for Ypsilanti to purchase water from Detroit?), partly by negotiation (Flint was able to extract the concession that it be the sole distributor of Detroit water in its county because Detroit needed to justify a large supply main in Flint's direction), as well as by administrative policy.

The legislature has not been called upon to delimit the area. But without a legally constituted metropolitan constituency the Water Board cannot formally represent any voters save Detroit's. Of its seven members, three are suburban residents, but they are appointed by Detroit's mayor. Flint leaders resisted joining the larger system partly because of "a fear that, without representation on the Detroit Water Board, Flint would have no control or influence over rates,"[90] and one may speculate that Detroit had to delegate a substantial administrative, marketing, and negotiating authority to Flint (wholesaling Detroit water in Flint's county) in lieu of representation. The reason was that representation would require a more fundamental constitutional change, modifying the system's accountability to the Detroit voters.

When the constitutional fences separating the jurisdictions of the national, state, and local governments were lowered during the New Deal, political scientists began considering whether there are other criteria by which to assess the effects of alternative federal allocations. One criterion—Through what representatives can voters maintain control?—was addressed by this author fifteen years ago.[91] The three principal determinants were intensity of public interest, commonness of public interest, and potential engagement of established political units in decisions. Intensity of interest varied with physical and economic capacity of the available technology to use water to benefit the population, with the disaster-producing capabilities of water, and with the conscious participation of people in putting water to use. Intense interests might, however, conflict. Commonness of interest varied generally with the social cohesion of the basin populace, directly with the social cohesion of those benefited to those displaced or burdened, and inversely with the approximation of water uses to a zero-sum game. Intensity of interest could be conceived as a multiplier of these factors. The degree to which existing political systems could be expected to engage in water decisions varied with the conformity of the basin to their boundaries and with the relative importance of water uses (in terms of their perceived purposes) to other programs on their agendas.

The Basin as a Decision Arena

All the controversy over the Tennessee Valley Authority never made clear the elected representatives through which the decentralized federal administrative hierarchy can be held responsible to voters in the affected area. The most likely answer is the congressional delegation from the Tennessee River basin districts and states. No comprehensive study shows whether they have functioned in this role or upon what questions voters have expected them to function.

We do have some relevant studies of river basin commissions which, because they were to be set up through interstate compacts, could theoretically represent voters via participating state governments. A systematic study of the potential of the Delaware River basin to function as a representative decision arena preceded and guided the design of the interstate-federal institution.[92] That study raised with some precision the question of the intensity of public concerns with water programs. "How many Delaware area Congressmen would be willing to trade a vote on civil rights, or on labor-management relations, or an aid to distressed areas for a vote on Delaware water?"[93] The study team of political scientists led by Roscoe Martin did not find the answer, but they did demonstrate a means of observing the emergent polyarchical capabilities of a decision arena: the concerns and interrelations of its relevant interest groups. From 156 of these groups, they ascertained the scope of their water interests; from a smaller group of seventy-two, the intensity (in terms of willingness to act) of their interest; and from eighty-five, their tendencies to cooperate with other such groups.[94] One may further speculate (this point was not directly researched) that the activeness and reciprocal influence of interest groups with regard to the Delaware were facilitated by the centrality of the great city of Philadelphia to the basin and to water interests in it.

In an innovative article on the Wabash basin, Daniel Elazar related to the basin's capabilities as a decision arena certain indicators of political culture which he defined in terms of measurable expectations relevant to public participation in resource development—localism in government, assumption that a region must grow or decay, for example. The Indiana-Illinois compact, creating an interstate commission for the Wabash, took effect in 1959. Demographically, the Wabash basin centering in Indianapolis, might seem a potentially cohesive region, but Elazar's indicators suggested it had little unity. The degrees to which this lack of cohesiveness can be attributed to intrabasin disjunctions in political culture or to the weakness of the potential contribution of the proposed river development to economic growth could only be learned from a more inclusive investigation. Elazar, however, has shown that analyses of relevant aspects of political culture belong in research upon the political capabilities of basin decision arenas.[95]

Recent experiences have begun to confirm the positive contribution of commonness of interest to the viability of special basin units of representation. Both the Ruhr river associations and the English River Authorities represent municipalities (the Ruhr associations, also industries) in the management of water quality for basin units. These overseas cases, and the strong recommendations they have prompted for American states and regions, apply to highly urbanized watersheds, whose people are overwhelmingly on the same side in the deep division between growth and quality of the environment.[96] It is conceivable that the Delaware River Basin Commission may, with its announced plans to clean up the river, evoke this kind of constituency.[97]

Metropolitan Water as a Decision Arena

For decades political scientists have studied the various forms of metropolitan government and their consequences, who supports them, who opposes them, and why. Perhaps because the most acute and realistic analyses have so often been ignored, political scientists have had to be recalled to the subject in the water context by members of other disciplines. In 1968, for instance, the Engineering Foundation and the Urban Hydrology Research Council of the American Society of Civil Engineers conducted a research conference on Water and Metropolitan Man. William Whipple, Jr., a former Corps of Engineers officer now heading the Rutgers Water Resources Research Institute concluded in his summary of the conference: "An engineering forum is certainly not the best place to recommend the fundamental reorganization of our system of government. But it seems entirely suitable to recommend research into the present institutional handicaps to proper water and waste disposal in metropolitan areas."[98]

The rise of this interest in metropolitan institutions for water is understandable. New demands call for new technologies for diversion, storage, purification, waste collection and treatment. Water taken from the river, lake, or estuary for urban use becomes a subsystem overshadowing the economic and ecological significance of the natural flows.[99] These costly processes are characterized by great economies of scale. A water treatment plant for a town of 60,000 to 100,000 people costs two-and-a-half times as much per capita as one designed to serve 600,000 to one million people.[100] Economies of scale apply also to waste disposal, and may be available as a practical alternative since waste treatment plants now must often be built de novo. Among highly industrial states, only New York and Texas do not already have the majority of their sewered populations served by some form of cooperative waste-handling arrangements.[101]

Arrangements across local government lines have mainly taken the form of special, single-purpose districts. The 1967 Census of Governments counted 1,220 sewage districts and 2,112 water supply districts, plus 292 combining sewage and water supply functions.[102] The need for multipurpose management of urban water is as evident now as the value of multipurpose river basin planning was three decades ago. Urban water management involves programs for recycling water, ground water recharge, recreational use of storage reservoirs (which may be the only way to gain local acceptance for their siting), and enhancing recreational values through effluent treatment. It also involves the whole gamut of interdependencies among street layout, land-use controls, common and storm sewer design and the safe disposal of flood flows. Speakers in the Engineering Foundation's 1970 conference on Urban Water Resources Management took multiple water purposes to be the planning unit.[103]

Two considerations carry the definition of *multipurpose* farther than the design of urban water subsystems. Ecological considerations bring some urban planners to consider the entire urban environment as a system for management. Harvey Perloff points to these interrelations within such a system:

> One resource may be substituted for another (air-cooling for water-cooling);
>
> A resource decision by or for one set of users affects the users of other resources in the urbanized area ("One firm's or one suburb's welfare is another's illfare");
>
> A residual may be transformed or moved, it cannot be eliminated (washing smokestack discharges creates water-borne wastes);
>
> Conserving any environmental value may be done in a variety of ways, among which there are trade-offs.[104]

The case for metropolitan planning is persuasive. It is a case, however, not merely for water but for environmental planning. The administrative implications are clear: "Finally, it might be necessary to design an institution or institutions to perform management functions and to supply it with appropriate policy instruments. The latter would include authority to regulate emissions, levy charges or taxes on them, and implement (or encourage other agencies to implement) large-scale regional measures."[105]

We have been considering the management of metropolitan water (or the metropolitan environment) as an end. Those who wrestle with the intransigent problem of intergovernment relations would like to use it as an instrument to induce desired patterns both of urban growth and of metropolitan political organization. This perspective was proposed ten years ago by the U.S. Advisory Commission on Intergovernmental Relations, though it has never been more than a recommendation. "The potential of water and waste disposal facilities as a tool for shaping communities has been ignored in most urban communities."[106] How great is this potential? Walker and Wengert make, for the Detroit metropolitan area, an assessment contrasting with the Advisory Commission's. "It must be recognized that for institutional and many other reasons, water supply policy is a very weak weapon in the struggle for more rational land use. Those making water supply decisions are usually ill-equipped . . . and the public is just not ready in most situations to accept dynamic, forward-looking land-use planning and control, and would not sanction attempts to use water supply as a positive force in this connection."[107] It is possible in the Detroit case, as it is always possible in the account of a single experience, to find distinctive historical circumstances to explain why metropolitan water supply cannot provide inducement to metropolitan community formation. The Detroit Water Board decided to become metropolitan upon its own initiative after Wayne County had entered the business, and it had to make concessions to win acceptance as a metropolitan service agency. The more important conclusion is that we have no comparative, and hence discriminating, appraisals of the power of water management services to induce community formation. The political scientist is unable to meet the demand already voiced by the public water supply planning engineer. "The urban water manager needs help to assess the role of water in the solution of the other urban problems of housing, welfare, race, and economic motivation. Maybe urban water, as a strength, should assist the other elements to create a better total environment."[108]

Ecologists, urban planners, and forward-looking urban water managers perceive a general direction of movement toward metropolitan water management. It is not management of water supply and quality in the natural flowage of appropriate streams, lakes, or estuaries. It is not the management of water in the metropolitan region. It is rather, as Lyle Craine finds it in an older urbanized nation, England, two new arenas of decision, basin and metropolitan, interlocked.[109] It remains for political science to suggest a possible path from single-purpose metropolitan management, or multipurpose metropolitan planning, to multipurpose metropolitan decision arenas.

General Government Arenas in Interrelation

One strategy for moving toward metropolitan government would have the federal government, and under its stimulus the state governments, define the direction of movement, offer incentives, and end present disincentives. A political scientist in the White House, Daniel Patrick Moynihan, stated such a policy in this way: "A national urban policy must look first to the vitality of the elected governments of the urban areas, and must seek to increase their capacity for independent, effective, and creative action. This suggests an effort to find some way out of the present fragmentation, and a certain restraint on the creation of federally-financed 'competitive governments.' "[110] A political scientist making policy in the Department of Housing and Urban Development, Robert Wood, made clear that such a new strategy for "the development of new communities" would deploy water supply and sewage service as instruments.[111]

At the state level there have been, meanwhile, organizational changes to make such a program feasible. In 1972, twenty-five states created departments of local government or community affairs; there were four in 1965.

Such a policy of "community-defining federalism"[112] would produce the positive goal toward which forward-looking water managers seek to direct their physical plans. There still remain, however, within the field of water resources and water management, the federal disincentives to decision in general political arenas. One illustration is at the metropolitan level and involves rivers and harbors policy. The other has its impact upon a state polyarchy and involves reclamation policy.

Guy J. Kelnhofer, a regional planner, studied the various meanings of the Chattahoochee River to the Atlanta metropolis in the 1960s. He assessed the public and governmental capabilities to act in knowledge of those meanings.[113] His conclusions were blunt. The Chattahoochee was merely a public utility, supplying water and carrying off sewage. There was no public concern and no arena in which narrow interests were brought to encounter each other. Water management, too, was fragmented. Altanta's environment and economy were likely to be altered by a navigation dam which would put the lower part of the metropolis at the head of a still-water pool. The local agency responsible for sewage disposal opposed the dam vigorously. The Atlanta Water Department favored it. There was no city policy, let alone a metropolitan one. "With the backing of the Atlanta Freight Bureau, a private organization has been formed to promote . . . the extension of navigation to Atlanta, a development that would permanently foreclose a variety of alternative metropolitan uses of the River. Whether this particular type of development . . . would serve the best interests of the Atlanta Area is a question that is unlikely to receive serious and objective debate in the Atlanta Metropolitan Area."[114] Why unlikely? Atlanta is not, among large American cities, either leaderless or indifferent to its environs. Kelnhofer tells us, "Because Federal rather than local funds will be used to finance most of the work under present policies, there is little incentive for the metropolitan public to subject these projects to the same searching scrutiny that attend investment proposals for local public works."[115] It is indicative of the sterility of the method by which the national decision is *supposed* to balance local impacts, that the benefit-cost ratio for the Chattahoochee navigation project was negative. But the District Engineer of the Corps of Engineers continued to advocate the project, asserting, "there is not the slightest doubt in my mind that the economic benefits will more than justify the construction costs."[116]

Kelnhofer is concerned with a general problem of intergovernmental relations, not with a single case or a single federal program in its local impact. In 1967 he found that where, as in Denver after the South Platte flood of 1965, a common disaster suddenly created an intermunicipal public will to control a common threat, there was no organization of state government comprehensive of the interdependent needs of water supply, flood damage prevention, and water-quality control. "Were [the metro-politan area] able to define and represent its area-wide interests, it would find . . . that there is no organization designed to manage regional water resources with which it could negotiate for its water requirements. . . . No one pretends that the [Colorado State Water Conservation] Board is likely to be directly concerned with urban water issues."[117]

The impact of the federal reclamation program on intergovernmental relations, examined by political scientist Robert D. Thomas, is analogous.[118] Reclamation is a rural program (though its greatest beneficiaries may be towns in the areas of intensive cultivation). State government is the general government in a position to 1) balance irrigation values against alternative values from other uses of water; 2) apply the methods of general planning to the whole array of physical changes irrigation brings (from road networks and the location of new schools to land-use planning in the mushrooming towns); 3) shift the pattern of agricultural research, extension, and education; and 4) control the power-ful new impact of irrigation upon water quality and water supply in the surface and underground basins. Thomas shows, however, that the state is bypassed. "Water policies in Arizona are established and carried out by a cooperative arrangement between the Bureau of Reclamation and local water-users' associations. The consequences for state officials is exclusion in policy-making at the vital points of problem identification and account-ability."[119]

The Arizona legislators, most of whom Thomas interviewed, are not dissatisfied to be bypassed. On the contrary, reclamation means peopling the desert; it means growth. It is a classic manifestation of one of the two sets of values already mentioned. The reclamation constituency, thanks to the water-users' associations fostered by the United States Bureau of Reclamation, is powerfully organized. Again, the distinctive financing provisions of this program relieve the state of a sense of choice in the use of public funds. The water users are thought of as repaying the cost to the treasury, though in fact they pay a small fraction of the outlay. As more than half the state legislators expect the United States Government to finance water development in Arizona, there is no issue left to engage polyarchy.[120]

These two examples demonstrate the stultifying effect upon local and state polyarchical decision making of distributive policies extended from Washington. Policies which originate in agreements on the mutual nonin-terference of congressmen do not provide further occasion for metro-politan or state governments to evoke, bring into encounter, and resolve competing water interests. In the Atlanta case, local constituencies of federal agencies drew apart from that process. The Arizona outcome was just what Moynihan sought to restrain: "the creation of federally-financed 'competitive governments.' " Community-defining federalism can be thwarted as well as served by water programs.

EVALUATION

This paper began with the goal of discovering the state of political science work on water decision making, focusing on the past ten years. The search was to determine whether any patterns were developing and how patterns might be further developed. Though our organizing concepts were drawn from the general political science literature, some of the work most germane to these concepts turned out to be done by economists, urban and regional planners, and ecologists. Is there any need for a *political science* of water decisions or is it just as adequate to say that the political aspects of water decisions should be studied?

Political science is not essential because of any distinctive methodology. The best work on political aspects has used hypothesis-testing methods common to the social sciences as a whole. Certainly the current fad for interdisciplinary study is more trouble than it is worth unless the addition of another discipline contributes something unavailable from the disciplines which have greater working familiarity with the practical aspects of the problem. Political science can be counted on to contribute a set of concepts oriented toward legitimate power, cleavage and consensus, and ways of seeking collective goals. It will bring to water problems a whole series of partly tested propositions radiating out from these central questions. Will these make a difference?

That question can take two forms. Will it make a difference to water decisions? Second, will it make a difference to political science? By taking these questions one at a time and using illustrative propositions (not the only possible set, but not implausible ones, either), one can more carefully examine what the two kinds of differences might be.

Effects of Political Science upon the Study of Water Decisions

How can knowledge of political science improve water decisions? Well-worn political science concepts provide order to quite a bit of research knowledge concerning water decisions, but the resulting patterns are not necessarily of high priority to the improvement of water decision institutions and processes. It might be fair to begin with an authoritative formulation of the kind of questions most pressing in water resources management and then determine whether the conceptualizations originating from political science contribute answers to these questions. Fortunately, just such a set of questions was carefully developed by a task force of the Universities Council on Water Resources. The chairman of the task force was a political scientist, Ernest A. Englebert, but it was an interdisciplinary team that devoted enough time and discussion to agree upon a perspective. The questions are guided by assumptions of a new concept of ecological interrelatedness, new competition among water demands advanced most powerfully by urbanites, and neglect of the potentialities of water to facilitate planned growth. With regard to the capacity of institutions to make decisions, the task force called for an examination of conflicts of values and how these may be settled. They offered three clear-cut and significant propositions: "1) The decision-making system has a low capacity to handle overt conflict; 2) Goals will not be debated and articulated for institutionalized use except when conflict is unavoidable and is joined; and 3) Conflicting goals usually will be accommodated side-by-side in a pluralistic society."[121] The task force carried this line of analysis no farther, although they must have been aware that the first and third of these propositions (as presently stated) negate or countervail the second.

The concepts provided by political science are useful mainly in suggesting how to disaggregate the three propositions into a consistent system of relationships. The possibility can be illustrated in this manner:

1) Polyarchy may comprise significant variations in conflict-settlement capacities because representatives (for example, chief executives, legislative leaders, or party leaders) may decide questions of potential conflict that if raised for direct voter action would overtax the system. This proposition is at variance with the task force's endorsement of "greater public participation in all phases of decision-making," but it is warranted by experience with fluoridation.

2) Several quite different decision arenas are characteristically available for a particular water decision: national, state, city or (potentially) metropolitan region. Conflict may be unavoidable and may be joined in one of these but not in others. That one seems to be characterized by salience of the issue to representative-voter links, and the issue posed in that arena might be solved even though it raised a conflict.

3) Accommodating conflicting goals side-by-side (and unconfronted) is what Lowi called distributive policy. Conditions under which distributive policy has in fact become regulative or redistributive policy can, hopefully, be learned from comparative policy analysis.

Whether or not political science can answer the political questions enunciated by the task force can only be learned by trying. All that can be claimed for sure is that when confronted with significant political questions which have been given priority by a group of scholars closely in touch with the needs of policy makers in this field, political science can propose ways of searching for answers. That is, nevertheless, a considerable contribution.

Effects of the Study of Water Decisions upon Political Science

The ordering concepts from political science used in this paper went little beyond typologies. Can one expect further work to interrelate these categories so as to contribute to the theory of whole political systems? Are there suggestions of such interrelations in the studies on water? Does this line of research, in other words, promise to move from typologies toward models?

Certainly, research on the politics of water decisions touches theoretical issues close to the heart of political science as a discipline. Some which can be recognized from the work cited above are:

1) Has a cleavage opened across American society (and across other industrialized societies) between those who value growth and those who value the quality of the environment? If so, it would surely shift water-policy questions from the distributive to the regulatory category. Would it shift them further to the redistributive category? Here is the criterion offered by Lowi: "Issues that involve redistribution cut closer than any others along class lines and activate interests in what are roughly class terms. If there is ever any cohesion within the peak associations, it occurs on redistributive issues."[122] We urgently need to find out whether the growth-versus-environmental-quality cleavage coincides with class cleavage or cuts across it. If, as our few case studies suggest, it is the latter, is Lowi's criterion for redistributive policy obsolete? Are the forms of redistributive decisions different if interests are fragmented, not polarized?

In this light, one could, through the study of water management decisions, contribute to the theoretical argument which Seymour Martin Lipset shared with James Madison but not with Karl Marx. It is the argument that cleavages may unite, not split, a society, provided each cleavage divides the parties to other cleavages.

2) One of the liveliest current battles in political science is the challenge from those who believe noncommunist industrial nations are ruled by an elite to the older school who believe politics in the United States is a constrained struggle among overlapping interests. The study of water decisions throws a tangential light on this issue. It suggests circumstances in which interests can become too plural and participation too extensive for decision.

3) Barry Commoner's first Law of Ecology, "Everything is connected to everything else," has, insofar as people act upon it, an important implication for government decisions.[1][2][3] When elected representatives choose one use of water over others, they require information of considerable variety and subtlety, so marshalled as to reveal the consequences of each use. This argues not only for research as such, but also for the hierarchies required to collect data over long periods, to fund research, and to integrate research findings into policy alternatives. Nor can polyarchy function without the market and much negotiation. Dependencies among decision processes also run in other directions. The needed markets can only be brought into operation, and be sustained, by law and much negotiation in establishing a government policy. The desire to minimize duplication of effort in performing this task is beginning to conflict with separation of powers as an American constitutional principle. Are institutions of government in this situation losing their autonomy from one another?

4) The policy of "community-defining federalism" requires each government to foster, within its jurisdiction, decision arenas capable of polyarchy. Water could be used to foster such arenas, but this partly reverses the initiative of American federalism, which was built from local units upward. What difference does such a partial reversal make in the long-term distribution of power? A related issue is the extent to which a unit of political authority evokes or reflects social interdependence and cultural identity, a basic question in the literature on nation building and national integration.

Complementarity of Effects

Clearly the study, through the concepts of political science, of the field of water resource development and management can contribute both to that field and to the discipline. Some work exists but the potential is still unrealized. Fifteen years ago it was possible to explain the neglect of this field by political scientists; the lack of change frustrated them. That explanation no longer holds. Change has taken place in the states. Committees, commissions, even executive agencies are vigorously canvassing possibilities for change in national institutions, but they get few answers as to the consequences of various alternatives in political terms. Why are political scientists not fully engaged on these research problems?

One reason, perhaps, is that contributions to practical decisions and contributions to tested theories of politics have become separated at a stage when each must depend heavily upon the other. One illustration will show that dependence. Three or four decades ago, when water development created relatively significant economic opportunities in a river basin, it was possible to use knowledge of the river basin to infer the appropriate decision arena. Now decision arenas for water questions must more often be considered in terms of the overall capabilities of cities or states, even in terms of the elusive metropolitan governments. It is evident that for some situations, certainly for metropolitan water, two-cycle models will be required. The first cycle will clarify choices as to kinds of metropolitan government institutions needed to manage water; the second cycle will show how water may be used to guide development of such metropolitan institutions. It should be evident, too, that thorough involvement in the resolution of actual problems of water management can highlight otherwise neglected theoretical issues.

Perhaps some political scientists, called on suddenly to answer immediate questions of decision makers, have not had time yet to shape the questions in terms more central to their discipline. As they undertake to do so now, they find a rapidly growing and influential subfield of political science ready to interlink applied with theoretical work. That subfield is the study of public policy. The time has recurred, after more than a decade, when political scientists are in demand to study the heart of the water decision process. The time has arrived when such study can illumine man's political behavior.

1. Arthur Maass, "Congress and Water Resources"; Charles McKinley, "The Valley Authority and Its Alternatives"; and Albert Lepawsky, "Water Resources and American Federalism," vol. 44, (1950), pp. 576-649.

2. Case studies are: C. Herman Pritchett, *Tennessee Valley Authority: A Study in Public Administration* (Chapel Hill: University of North Carolina Press, 1943); Charles McKinley, *Uncle Sam in the Pacific Northwest* (Berkeley: University of California Press, 1952); Vincent Ostrom, *Water and Politics: A Study of Water Policies and Administration in the Development of Los Angeles* (Los Angeles: Haynes Foundation, 1953); Henry C. Hart, *The Dark Missouri* (Madison: University of Wisconsin Press, 1957). Evaluation of an agency (Army Corps of Engineers): Arthur Maass, *Muddy Waters* (Cambridge, Mass.: Harvard University Press, 1952). Generalizations: Arthur Maass, ed., *Area and Power* (Glencoe, Ill.: The Free Press, 1959); and the special issue of *Law and Contemporary Problems* 22 (Summer 1957).

3. James W. Fesler, "National Water Resources Administration," *Law and Contemporary Problems* 22 (1957): 468.

4. An incomplete list, chronologically arranged, will suggest the diversity: Roscoe C. Martin, *Water for New York, A Study in State Administration of Water Resources* (Syracuse: Syracuse University Press, 1960); John I. Thompson, *Public Administration of Water Resources in Texas* (Austin: University of Texas Institute of Public Affairs, 1960); Public Administration Service, *Governmental Administration of Water Resources in the Chicago Metropolitan Area* (Chicago: Public Administration Service, 1963); Dean E. Mann, *The Politics of Water in Arizona* (Tucson: University of Arizona Press, 1963); Robert H. Pealy, *Organization for Comprehensive River Basin Planning: The Texas and Southeast Experiences* (Ann Arbor: University of Michigan

Governmental Studies, 1964); Ernest A. Englebert, *Policy Issues of the Pacific Southwest Water Plan* (Boulder: University of Colorado Press, 1965); Charles McKinley, *The Management of Land and Related Water Resources in Oregon* (Published by the author, 1965); Louis F. Wechsler, *Water Resource Management: The Orange County Experience* (Davis: University of California, Institute of Governmental Affairs, 1968); Helen M. Ingram, *Patterns of Politics in Water Resources Development: A Case Study of New Mexico's Role in the Colorado River Basin Bill* (Alburquerque: University of New Mexico Division of Government Research, 1969).

5. Vincent and Elinor Ostrom, "Public Choice: A Different Approach to the study of Public Administration," *Public Administration Review* 31 (March-April 1971): 205.

6. Arthur Maass, "Public Investment Planning in the United States: Analysis and Critique," *Public Policy* 18 (Winter 1970): 237.

7. Vincent and Elinor Ostrom, "Conditions of Legal and Political Feasibility," multilithed (Bloomington: Indiana University, Department of Political Science, 1969), p. 19.

8. Vincent Ostrom, "Water Resource Development: Some Problems in Economic and Political Analysis of Public Policy," in *Political Science and Public Policy*, ed. Austin Ranney (Chicago: Markham Publishing Co., 1968), pp. 137-41, 148.

9. Ostrom and Ostrom, "Public Choice." The practical thrust of their ideas is attractive: "Should we not begin to look at the police industry, the education industry, the water industry, and other public service industries on the assumption that these industries have a structure that allows for coordination without primary reliance upon hierarchical structures?"

10. Theodore J. Lowi, "American Business, Public Policy, Case-Studies and Political Theory," *World Politics* 16 (1964): 677-715. (Reprinted by Ripley; see note 11.)

11. Randall B. Ripley, ed., *Public Policies and Their Politics* (New York: W. W. Norton & Co., 1966), p. viii.

12. Lowi, reprinted in Ripley, *Public Policies*, pp. 31-32.

13. Robert Salisbury, "The Analysis of Public Policy: A Search for Theories and Roles," in *Political Science and Public Policy*, ed. Austin Ranney (Chicago: Markham Publishing Co., 1968), p. 167.

14. "Four decision-making systems" corresponding to the Dahl-Lindblom categories were used as an analytical framework by the Task Force on Water Resources Evaluation, chaired by the political scientist Ernest A. Englebert of the Universities Council on Water Resources in their report *Evaluation Processes in Water Resources Management and Development* in 1971. See their report, sponsored by the Office of Water Resources Research, U.S. Department of the Interior.

15. Robert A. Dahl and Charles E. Lindblom, *Politics, Economics and Welfare* (New York: Harper and Brothers, 1953).

16. Arthur Maass, "Public Investment Planning in the United States: Analysis and Critique," in *Public Policy* 18 (Winter 1970): 211.

17. Aaron Wildavsky, "Rescuing Policy Analysis from PPBS," *Public Administration Review* 29 (March-April 1969): 189-202.

18. Lowi, reprinted in Ripley, *Public Policies*, p. 30.

19. Irving K. Fox and Lyle E. Craine, "Organizational Arrangements for Water Development," *Natural Resources Journal* 2 (1962): 1-44.

20. Irving K. Fox and O. C. Herfindahl, "Attainment of Efficiency in Satisfying Demands for Water Resources," *American Economic Review* 54 (1964): 198-206; and "New Horizons in Water Resources Administration," *Public Administration Review* 25 (1965): 61-69.

21. Vincent Ostrom, "1964: Western Water Institutions in a Contemporary Perspective," *Proceedings: Western Interstate Water Conference, September, 1964*

(Berkeley: University of California Water Resources Center, 1965), p. 27. Reprinted by Resources for the Future.

22. Ostrom, "Water Resource Development," p. 127.

23. Allen V. Kneese, "Strategies for Environmental Management," *Public Policy* 19 (Winter 1971): 47. His initial proposal was in *The Economics of Regional Water Quality Management* (Baltimore: Johns Hopkins Press, 1964).

24. John Dewey, *The Public and Its Problems* (New York: Henry Holt & Co., 1927).

25. George M. Walker, Jr. and Norman Wengert, *Urban Water Policies and Decision-Making in the Detroit Metropolitan Region* (Ann Arbor: University of Michigan, Office of Research Administration, 1970), pp. 121-33.

26. Matthew Holden, *Pollution Control as a Bargaining Process: An Essay in Regulatory Decision-Making* (Ithaca: Cornell University Water Resources Center, 1966), p. 11.

27. Ibid., p. 43.

28. Robert Dorfman and Henry Jacoby, "A Model of Public Decisions Illustrated by a Water Pollution Policy Problem," in *The Politics of Ecosuicide*, ed. Leslie L. Roos, Jr. (New York: Holt, Rinehart & Winston, Inc., 1971), p. 180.

29. Vincent Ostrom, "Water and Politics—California Style," mimeographed draft of article for *Arts and Architecture* (n.d.), p. 14.

30. Ingram, *Patterns of Politics in Water Resources Development*, p. 14.

31. Ostrom, "Water and Politics," p. 10A.

32. Ingram, Op. cit. pp. 33-36.

33. Ibid., p. 14.

34. Ibid., p. 30.

35. Ibid., chap. 6 and p. 93.

36. Henry C. Hart, *The Dark Missouri* (Madison: University of Wisconsin Press, 1957), chap. 7.

37. Duane Hill, P. O. Foss, and R. L. Meek, *Organizational Adaptation to Change in Public Objectives* (Fort Collins: Colorado Natural Resources Center, 1969).

38. J. Clarence Davies III, *The Politics of Pollution* (New York: Pegasus, 1970), pp. 66-70.

39. Walker and Wengert, *Urban Water Policies*, pp. 170-74.

40. Helen Ingram, *The New England River Basin Commission, A Case Study Looking into the Possibilities and Disabilities* (Springfield, Va.: National Technical Information Service, 1971).

41. Joseph Anthony Miri, *The Politics of Water Supply in Northern New Jersey* (Rutgers: New Jersey Water Resources Research Institute, 1971).

42. Irving Howards and Edward Kaynor, *Institutional Patterns in Evolving Regional Programs for Water Resource Management* (Amherst: University of Massachusetts Water Resources Research Center, 1971), p. 4.

43. Frank Munger and Anne Houghton, "Politics and Organization in Water Resources Administration: A Comparative Study of Decisions," *Water Resources Research* 1 (1965): 337-47.

44. Elizabeth Haskell et al., "Managing the Environment: Nine States Look for New Answers," Multigraphed form published by the author who was then at Woodrow Wilson International Center for Scholars, Washington, D.C., 1971.

45. Ibid., pp. iii, 11.

46. Ibid., pp. 23-24.

47. Ibid., p. 142.

48. Ibid., p. 19.

49. Ibid., p. 28.

50. These states were already controlling the growth of pollution before recent administrative reorganization.

51. Ibid., p. 134.

52. Ibid., pp. 42, 223.

53. Ibid., pp. 2-3.

54. Ibid., p. 4.

55. Ibid., pp. 2-3.

56. Ibid., p. 23

57. Robert H. Pealy, *Organization for Comprehensive River Basin Planning: The Texas and Southeast Experiences* (Ann Arbor: University of Michigan Institute of Public Administration, 1964) Michigan Governmental Studies no. 46.

58. Well brought out in the Illinois case. Haskell, *Managing the Environment*, p. 79. For a contrast between irrigation association officers and urban water supply staff as to definitions of the water agency planning role see Duane W. Hill and R. L. Meek, *Local Water Agencies, Communications Patterns, and the Planning Process* (Fort Collins, Colo.: Environmental Resources Center, 1971), p. 113.

59. David C. Ranney, *An Analysis of Alternative Institutional Patterns for Managing Water Quality on a Regional Systems Basis* (Madison: University of Wisconsin Water Resources Center, 1970).

60. Irving Fox, "We Can Solve Our Water Problems," *Water Resources Research* 2 (1966): 621.

61. Allen V. Kneese and Blair T. Bower, *Managing Water Quality: Economics, Technology, Institutions* (Baltimore: Johns Hopkins Press, 1968).

62. Lyle Craine, *Water Management Innovations in England* (Baltimore: Johns Hopkins Press, 1969).

63. *New York Times*, 29 September 1969.

64. Davies, *The Politics of Pollution*, p. 75. Davies' book is the soundest and most insightful account of air and water pollution control politics in the national arena.

65. Louisville *Courier-Journal*, 24 October 1969.

66. Lowi in Ripley, *Public Policies*, p. 31.

67. Lynton K. Caldwell, *Environment, A Challenge to Modern Society* (Garden City, N.Y.: Doubleday & Co., 1971), p. 225.

68. Robert L. Crain, Elihu Katz, and Donald B. Rosenthal, *The Politics of Community Conflict: The Fluoridation Decision* (New York: The Bobbs-Merrill Co., 1969).

69. This was the number of usable responses from city health officers in the 1,181 cities to which questionnaires were sent. Replies were received from at least one other informant in 200 of the cities.

70. Ibid., pp. 206, 4.

71. Ibid., p. 212.

72. Ibid., p. 203 and chap. 10.

73. Ibid., p. 215.

74. Ibid., p. 228.

75. Ibid., p. 142.

76. Ibid.

77. Ibid., pp. 58, 65.

78. Cecile Trop and Leslie Roos, Jr., "Public Opinion and the Environment," in *The Politics of Ecosuicide*, ed. Leslie Roos, Jr. (New York: Holt, Rinehart & Winston, Inc., 1971), pp. 55, 58, and 60. A slight discrepancy in the references to the 1965 poll is here resolved in a conservative direction.

79. Davies, *The Politics of Pollution*, p. 82.

80. James T. Murphy, "Partisanship and the House Public Works Committee," a paper at the 1968 meeting of the American Political Science Association.

81. Richard F. Fenno, Jr., "Congressmen in Committees," unpublished. Shown to me in manuscript form thanks to the author and Barbara Hinckley.

82. Ingram, *Patterns of Politics in Water Resource Development*, p. 27.

83. Richard A. Cooley and Geoffrey Wandesforde-Smith, eds., *Congress and the Environment* (Seattle: University of Washington Press, 1970), pp. 230-32. Committee consideration is dispersed, but less so than appears at first glance. The 1,289 bills dealing with water introduced in the 89th Congress (1965-66) were referred to thirteen standing committees of the House, to eleven of the Senate. But three-fourths of the bills were assigned to four committees: to Public Works and Interior and Insular Affairs in the two houses, respectively. Data from Theodore Schad and Elizabeth Boswell.

84. Davies, *The Politics of Pollution*, pp. 69-70.

85. James L. Sundquist, *Politics and Policy: The Eisenhower, Kennedy and Johnson Years* (Washington, D.C.: Brookings Institution, 1968), p. 509.

86. M. Kent Jennings, "Legislative Politics and Water Pollution Control," in Frederick N. Cleaveland et al., *Congress and Urban Problems* (Washington, D.C.: Brookings Institution, 1969), pp. 89-93, 101.

87. Davies, *The Politics of Pollution*, pp. 63-64.

88. Sundquist, *Politics and Policy*, p. 536.

89. Walker and Wengert, *Urban Water Policies.*

90. Ibid., p. 171.

91. Henry C. Hart, "Crisis, Community and Consent in Water Politics," *Law and Contemporary Problems* 22: 510-37.

92. Roscoe C. Martin et al., *River Basin Administration and the Delaware* (Syracuse: Syracuse University Press, 1960).

93. Ibid., pp. 375-76.

94. Ibid., pp. 31-36, 55-60.

95. Daniel Elazar, "Influences on Political Values and the Wabash Basin," in *Regional Development and the Wabash Basin*, ed. Ronald R. Boyce (Urbana: University of Illinois Press, 1964), chap. 8.

96. Cf. three articles in *Public Policy* 19 (Winter 1971). Blair T. Bower, *Waste Management* (New York: Regional Plan Association, 1968) recommends a regional authority managing disposal of *all* wastes.

97. This is the view of a skeptical Nader task force: David Zwick and Nancy Benstock, *Water Wasteland* (New York: Grossman Publishers, 1971), p. 130.

98. William Whipple Jr., *Water and Metropolitan Man* (New York: American Society of Civil Engineers, 1969), p. 14.

99. Craine, *Water Management Innovations in England*, p. 17.

100. J. K. Sherwani, "Urban and Industrial Water Supply: Prospects and Possibilities," in *Man's Environment in the Twenty-First Century*, ed. Charles M. Weiss (Chapel Hill: University of North Carolina School of Public Health, 1965), p. 125.

101. U.S. Department of the Interior, Federal Water Pollution Control Administration, *The Cost of Clean Water and its Economic Impact* (Washington, D.C.: Government Printing Office, 1969), pp. 55, 59.

102. U.S. Water Resources Council, *The Nation's Water Resources* (Washington, D.C.: Government Printing Office, 1971), pp. 5, 9, 3.

103. Engineering Foundation, *Urban Water Resources Management, Report on the Third Conference on Urban Water Resources Research* (New York: American Society of Civil Engineers, 1971).

104. Harvey Perloff, "A Framework for Dealing with the Urban Environment: Introductory Statement," in *The Quality of the Urban Environment: Essays on 'New Resources in an Urban Age,'* ed. Harvey Perloff (Baltimore: Johns Hopkins Press, 1969), pp. 5-25.

105. Robert U. Ayres and Allen V. Kneese, "Pollution and Environmental Quality," in Perloff, *Quality of the Urban Environment*, p. 69.

106. U.S. Advisory Commission on Intergovernmental Relations, *Intergovernmental Responsibilities for Water Supply and Sewage Disposal in Metropolitan Areas* (Washington, D.C.: Government Printing Office, 1962), p. 109.

107. Walker, *Urban Water Policies*, p. 111.

108. Robert C. McWhinnie, "Basic Needs of Urban Water Management on the Firing Line," *Water and Metropolitan Man* (New York: American Society of Civil Engineers, 1969), p. 11.

109. Craine, *Water Management Innovations in England*, pp. 10-11.

110. Daniel Patrick Moynihan, "Toward a National Urban Policy," *The Public Interest*, no. 17 (Fall 1969), p. 12.

111. Robert Wood, "Federal Role in the Urban Environment," *Public Administration Review* 18 (1968): 345-46.

112. The phrase was used by Henry Hart, "The Dawn of a Community-Defining Federalism," *The Annals of the American Academy of Political Social Science* 359 (1965): 147-56.

113. Guy J. Kelnhofer, *Metropolitan Planning and River Basin Planning: Some Interrelationships* (Atlanta: Georgia Institute of Technology, 1967).

114. Ibid., pp. 66-71, 101, 103.

115. Ibid., p. 100.

116. Ibid., p. 99.

117. Ibid., pp. 111, 114, 117.

118. Robert D. Thomas, "Federal-Local Cooperation and Its Consequences for State Level Policy Participation: Water Resources in Arizona," *Publius, the Journal of Federalism* 1 (Winter 1972): 77-94.

119. Ibid., pp. 93-94.

120. Ibid., p. 86.

121. Task Force on Water Resources Evaluation of the Universities Council on Water Resources, *Evaluation Processes in Water Resources Management and Development* (Berkeley: The Council, 1971), pp. 20, 22.

122. Ibid., p. 36.

123. Barry Commoner, *The Closing Circle: Nature, Man, and Technology* (New York: Alfred A. Knopf, 1971), p. 33.

6 Recent Sociological Contributions to Water Resources Management and Development

Sue Johnson

The focus of what people want from resources management has in recent years shifted away from the physical performance that engineers have been trained to provide. A new emphasis on social and environmental values has introduced an interdisciplinary flavor into the water planning efforts in the federal agencies. Water resources research is beginning to respond in the types of studies underway, if not in their total number.

Economists, once specializing in better techniques for benefit-cost analysis, are now seeking more complete statements regarding the contributions of water resource development to social welfare. Sociologists and economists have studied institutional aspects of water resource development and management. Political scientists and sociologists have studied effects of projects on the community as well as the community decision-making processes that determine water management policy. Anthropologists and geographers have studied the effects of water resources development through changes to the physical environment; economists and engineers have examined the costs and benefits of water-oriented recreation; and sociologists, the effect of reservoirs on leisure behavior. Ecologists and sociologists have explored the social causes and effects of water pollution. Psychologists have joined the research effort by applying attitude scales and dissonance theory to explain the behavior of water managers.[1]

Sociologists are mentioned more frequently in the above paragraph than any other professional group. This is not wholly arbitrary as sociology is the topic of this paper. Water-resource-oriented research areas of interest to sociologists are wide-ranging in scope, if not in the number of projects. For example, sociological research encompasses studies of tiny communities subjected to weather-modification projects, studies of vast regional water systems like the Tennessee Valley Authority, and theoretical discussions of the political and value bases leading to water pollution, among many others.[2]

Any research directed toward sociological interests—largely the behavior of people in groups—and that applies scientific methods of observation and analysis, or that uses principles generally asserted by sociologists, is of interest. This paper does not purport to be a complete review of the literature; its purpose is to indicate the major concerns of sociologically based, water-oriented research.[3] Attention is concentrated on the more recent contributions and on empirical findings about the relation of society to water resources, although there is also some exploration of sociologically slanted theoretical contributions. A further purpose is to suggest current research needs and to describe areas of potentially fruitful research by sociologists.

From a sociological point of view, the importance of an environmental element lies in the "relationships established among men as they deal with it."[4] "Thus, the meaning of water, the way it is used and enjoyed, rests on the way its attributes intersect with social, political and economic action."[5] At certain points, the sociologist may appear to be encroaching upon the precincts of the economist, the anthropologist, or the political scientist, but such is the contemporary, unavoidable, and not entirely disorderly interface among the social sciences.

Water resource decisions are social in nature and result from the complex interaction of 1) water resource needs, 2) the kinds of development proposed, 3) the kinds and organizational qualities of institutions present or needed to implement the development, 4) the types of communities affected, and 5) the matrices of values, attitudes, and goals of all those involved—including planners, construction workers, administrators, decision makers, and community residents. The characteristics of these five variables affect the viability of any water management system and are the major focus of this paper.

The United States Water Resources Council recently recommended a new approach to the evaluation of alternative proposals to develop or manage water resources.[6] They recommend the replacement of benefit-cost analyses with four objectives, the aims of which are to enhance 1) national economic development, 2) the quality of the environment, 3) social well-being, and 4) regional development. For the water resources planner, these goals are criteria with which to evaluate existing water project performance as well as guidelines for planning future development. For the sociologist, the new criteria provide a framework for evaluating the applicability of sociological findings to water resource development and point to fruitful lines of future inquiry.

REGIONAL SYSTEMS AND THEIR IMPACT

The Tennessee Valley Authority (TVA) is the best known *regional* water resource development system, and social science research on it is quite extensive.[7] Studies focus on linkages to the federal government and other agencies, organizational structure, administrative qualities, fiscal responsibility, and relationships with the communities and institutions in the Tennessee Valley area. The studies have produced a voluminous literature, but this paper will only review selected generalizations that provide yardsticks for possible reference in the development of water management systems elsewhere.[8]

The TVA is a multiproject system designed to achieve a comprehensive regional development goal. Project purposes range from power supply, navigation, flood control, and irrigation to regional economic development, distribution of industry, recreational development, and rural community development.[9]

Part of the TVA's success is attributed to a decentralized relationship to the federal government, giving it an autonomous character as a regional bureaucratic system.[10] This relationship has provided considerable freedom of operation, business efficiency, flexibility, and opportunity for experimentation. All these are in contrast to the usual departmental bureaucracy with inherited policies and routines. The TVA was able from this position to centralize and regionalize, through a common cause, what were previously just adjoining states. It struck a balance between the decentralization that guaranteed its autonomy, and the administrative coordination of a massive intra-regional system, both of which contributed to its success.

A retrospective study twenty-five years after the TVA's inception pointed out that the system of dams had in large part paid for itself by prevention of floods; that ninety-five percent of the valley's farmers used TVA's low-cost electricity; that shipping and industrialization, recreational use, and regional income levels had all increased dramatically; and that the TVA had succeeded well in cooperating with state and local governments.[11]

Perhaps the best-known sociological contribution to water resource development is Phillip Selznick's *TVA and the Grass Roots*, a work which gives considerable insight into how a complicated technical system was organized for and accepted by a region.[12] Selznick explored both formal and informal workings of the organization that contributed to its viability and independence.[13] The TVA, through informal co-optation, brought the county agricultural extension service support base and its constituency into the decision making areas that affected agriculture and surrounding communities, thus enlisting their support and cooperation. Moreover, TVA co-opted city governments and cooperatives, and these became the public links in the distribution of its electricity. The task was accomplished by what appeared publicly as the formal sharing of power while in fact local entities were used instrumentally. However, the TVA was co-opted in return in that TVA values and practices began to reflect those of its constituency. Actually, Selznick's contribution was more to sociology through developing the concept *co-optation*, than to water resources planning, though the insights into the importance of using local leaders to ensure cooperation and participation have served resource development well over time.

Folz has noted that economic growth is more likely to be associated with those large-scale regional development systems having a wide variety of resources available to private exploitation and having proximity to highly industrialized areas and mass markets. Because the development of any one resource cannot guarantee economic growth, coordination of water resources development with other governmental programs is very important if resource development is to achieve its potential.[14]

The fact that many water systems are poorly coordinated and subject to fragmented control has been traditionally lamented by planners.[15] Their complaints suggest that 1) organizations to develop and manage water resources ought to have, for coordination purposes, jurisdiction throughout the entire river basin, urban-defined region, or district; 2) well-planned management requires an interdisciplinary staff working through the auspices of an official public agency; 3) existing agencies and institutions are ill-equipped to manage the large-scale systems required by good water management programs, and thus need the help of outside technical expertise; and 4) despite the known virtues (as demonstrated by the TVA) of comprehensive regional planning, most planning efforts in the United States are too narrow in scope. Kraenzel suggests that even overcoming these obstacles to regional development will be inadequate unless accompanied or even preceded by "true regionalism," a sense of social, political, and economic homogeneity and identity that transcends state lines.[16] In the case of the TVA, the development created the regionalism.[17] Kraenzel also points out that where river basins lack metropolitan centers, improved social policies and increased social justice are not a guaranteed result unless development is accompanied by a true regionalism allocating benefits equitably throughout the area.[18] The major reason that the TVA and systems like it are comparative yardsticks for resource development is undoubtedly because of their success in distributing the benefits so widely.

Water resources planning could certainly profit by the extension of sociological inquiry to answer a number of important questions. If overall regional and national economic development is to be enhanced by large-scale water management systems, what are the effects on the quality of the environment? How can the economic benefits be distributed so that the disadvantaged can profit, too? A larger and very important question is whether new institutional forms are needed to make water management more responsible to the changing needs of society, and if so, what forms should be introduced. Specifically, with regard to water resource management, the question might be whether an autonomous, centralized agency with broad powers superceding all other agency powers is the best unit to plan and manage water resources or whether planning can be handled more efficiently in smaller decentralized segments working through local authority.

RURAL-URBAN ATTITUDES TOWARD
LARGE-SCALE WATER RESOURCE DEVELOPMENT

A study of the Bear River Basin in Utah by Andrews and Geersten helps point to the attitudes people have when affected by large-scale water resource development and gives some idea of the hierarchy of the values people attach to various water uses.[19] The project studied involved the transfer of water from one river basin to another, partly to help supply a large urban center. Interviews of a random sample of householders showed that a majority did not feel it wrong to transfer water from its natural basin to another, but more respondents in the urban area than in the rural area were in favor of the project. The first priority given to water use was for irrigation. A majority thought it wrong to take water away from agriculture for industrial use, though the urban group was more likely to disagree. Mining was given higher priority than was recreation by the rural respondents, though the metropolitan group favored recreation. An earlier study by Burdge, Sitterly, and So found similar rural-urban differences.[20] Urban Ohioans were strongly in favor of constructing reservoirs *if* some provision for recreational use was made, but the farm population had a negative reaction toward converting farmland to other uses.

Andrews and Geersten also studied awareness of the project and its probable consequences. They found greater awareness among the urban members of their sample, the group who favored industrial expansion. The open-country, nonfarm residents least favored such expansion. More older, less-educated people than younger, better-educated respondents were skeptical of the project, although socioeconomic status was not significantly associated with awareness of the project.

The Andrews-Geersten study of the diffusion of ideas about water resource use found the major sources of information were farm journals and the Agricultural Extension Service. The farmer's understanding of water rights was informal and incomplete, but Andrews and Geersten say this lack of knowledge may relate to fear of change in the water-rights system. More generally, Andrews and Gillings found in an earlier study that a farmer's conservatism was due to lack of knowledge about his own relationship to the project.[21] The authors conclude that the general public is not very well informed either about resources or about the relationship of resources to government, and that this lack of knowledge inhibits the effectiveness of public social systems such as those for water resource development.

PUBLIC PARTICIPATION
AND COMMUNITY DECISION MAKING

Several writers stress greater citizen awareness and participation as critical to efficient water resource use. A study of the Delaware Basin listed the four keys to maintaining effective public participation in the development of water resources as 1) real problems, 2) concerned citizenry, 3) dynamic leadership, and 4) cooperative agencies.[22] The second of these is particularly important and the key to a concerned citizenry seems to be twofold. One requirement is that the public have reliable information on the problem lest it fail to act, or act in ways that intensify the difficulty.[23] An effective supplement to the mass media as a means of diffusing information, as illustrated in a Susquehanna basin project, is the holding of workshops where planners can interact with local opinion leaders.[24] The most complete means of diffusion is to identify all those who will be directly affected by plans and proposals, and inform them by mail, direct contact, or some similar approach.[25] The second requirement for concerned citizenry is that the information reveal something that will make people want to participate in decision making.[26]

Conner and Bradley define public participation in planning as "a systematic process which provides an opportunity for citizens, planners, and politicians to share their experience, knowledge, goals, and energy to create a plan for the future which reflects their best judgment at this time and is understood and actively supported by most of the people affected by it."[27] The virtue of this approach is that the public is more likely to accept a plan if it has been active in shaping alternatives. Rejection is more likely if the public has been ignored or has had no voice.[28] With regard to managing our water resources, Hart says that we have been looking erroneously at the details of national departmentalization and executive organization; the key, he says, lies in public interest and attention.[29]

An article by Smith and another by Rogers and Burdge outline ways of influencing opinion and explain the crucial importance of the community decision making process in the acceptance of a water project.[30] Both aspects, diffusion and decision, are necessary to the efficient implementation of needed water resource development, regardless of whether the projects are basin-wide or affect only a single community.

Even if one takes basic public goals as determined through democratic processes, public opinion on the alternative means for achieving those goals has an important bearing on whether the goals can be achieved. Smith says any changes in public opinion come about through the diffusion and acceptance of new ideas, proposals, and practices which are deliberately disseminated among the members of a population. Mass media campaigns are important for would-be change agents, but they must be supplemented by grass-roots organizations where those with the information meet face-to-face with those who will be affected. Starting early to inform, using differing media, and constructing messages that are compatible with existing opinions are effective practices.

A six-stage model is presented by Rogers and Burdge in describing community decision making processes.[31] Their first stage is awareness on the part of a small group that something is needed. The second step is spreading awareness to civic groups and the local political structure. This starts the process in which an idea is shared with more groups, and concrete plans are developed to solve the problem. In the third and more crucial stage, the problem is acknowledged and plans are legitimated by key power holders, the financial and political leaders of the community. The main object at this stage is to minimize opposition from power groups when the project is announced to the public.

Diffusion occurs in the fourth stage during which the general public is informed of the project, through a variety of media and meetings. All arguments and counterarguments need to be covered in this stage because if the public is not fully informed, it may withhold approval, and the project may fail to reach fruition. The fifth stage is one of securing official political approval to proceed. If a referendum or bond election on the community level is required, action is directed toward getting a favorable vote. Even if an election is not required, elected officals must normally sense a consensus for a project before proceeding. The sixth stage is that of evaluation. When projects fail, the reasons are sought, and attempts are made to correct mistakes. More generally, postproject evaluation would be helpful in assessing the "goodness of fit" of benefit-cost analyses and in seeing what factors have been overlooked.

RESERVOIR CONSTRUCTION AND FORCED MIGRATION

The implementation of the TVA projects spurred interest in what happens to people whose homes are threatened by reservoir construction. Satterfield's 1937 article on the relocation of families to provide right-of-way for TVA reservoir construction found that the heads of families to be moved had no industrial experience and were limited to agricultural vocations.[32] Desiring to continue their previous way of living, most of the families resettled near their old homes and this occasioned some subdivision of farms. Some problems of overcrowding occurred in the rural communities to which the families moved. Only about one-third needed financial assistance, though close to half of the migrants needed some kind of help in relocation. Part of the success of TVA no doubt lies in the fact that these human considerations were taken into account, and the agency rendered assistance to persons affected.

This early research as well as several recent studies urge that the effects of water resource development on people's lives be taken into account along with other, more technical, aspects of project performance. As is the case with any innovation being presented to a culture, the success of a project lies, in part, in its acceptance by the community. Smith suggests that data on social variables be used by planners to focus attention on human problems where innovation is occurring and to minimize the conflict between the innovation and other features of the culture involved.[33]

Smith suggested how to do this in a Kentucky county where a reservoir project was soon to be implemented.[34] He studied the community and found that perceptions of costs and benefits differed considerably along predictable lines. Businessmen, downriver farmers who had been flooded, young people, and pleasureseekers from nearby cities were in favor of construction. In other words, those who would benefit looked favorably on the project. The perceptions of costs came mainly from rural residents. A large part of their negativity was based on fear that the community would be changed—outsiders ("undesirables") would come in, and that new shopping centers they would build would get more business than the town. They feared that the natural beauty of the area would be destroyed by the reservoir, that fertile bottom land would be inundated, and that the price of land would rise because outsiders would be buying it. Cemeteries would have to be moved, and a church would be lost.

Those being relocated were subject to considerable stress. Not only were they going to lose their farms, their homes, and possibly their vocations, but they were also suffering during five years of governmental indecision. Homes the government would eventually buy deteriorated because of ignorance about the government's timetable. The fear of having to move increased stress. Smith cites examples of postlocation stress occurring in the prelocation period when people were feeling themselves to be at the mercy of outsiders and were mourning in advance the loss of their homes.

A similar and related study by Burdge and Ludtke about people in the way of reservoir construction in Ohio and Kentucky found that persons with the greatest apprehension over moving were those who identified most strongly with their present homes.[35] Furthermore, the more solicitous people were about moving, the less separation from their community they were willing to accept. It was not so much abstract loyalty to their communities that aroused apprehension as the fact that moving threatened the interactive web of their lives with neighbors, with its predictability, comfort, and known status configurations. Moreover, the authors found that knowledge of the impending project had no effect on misgivings among those who would be required to move. (This contrasts with the other findings that show knowledge of a water resource project engender favorable attitudes within the community.)

Those who looked forward to transferring their status to their next community were those moving to similar places. Residents whose vested interests were being enhanced by the reservoir project anticipated greater social separation upon moving and were more willing to sever previous social bonds. Those with a recent history of mobility and those who were younger were also more willing to move.

Becker and Burdge found, in studying a Kentucky reservoir construction project, that both high socioeconomic status and experience of previous flood damage accompanied favorable attitudes toward the reservoir.[36] Several factors, including familism and traditionalism, associated in that community with rural residence, older age, and lower socioeconomic status, made no difference; they were *not* directly related to attitudes toward reservoir construction.

Webb and Bultena in their study of 146 cases found that farmers facing resettlement as a result of reservoir construction were opposed to the project.[37] However, those who expected increased general life-satisfaction upon moving later developed positive attitudes, as did those who would migrate to places outside the area directly affected by the reservoir.

These studies point out unanticipated consequences of reservoir construction on populations who are forced to move. These psychological, personal, and community costs elude inclusion in benefit-cost reckonings. They represent effects on people for which financial payment alone can never fully compensate. Consideration needs to be given to those who must move into new communities, and better ways are needed to help people suffering from pre- and postmigration stress.

THE IMPACT OF RESERVOIR CONSTRUCTION ON THE COMMUNITY AS A WHOLE

Thomas Hogg reports that a large-scale water project has "surprisingly major" effects on the political systems and social structure in nearby communities, and on the economic balance of the whole surrounding area.[38] Through a set of comprehensive but general statements concerning the social costs and benefits of such undertakings, he describes the process that a community experiences while a nearby major water project is planned, constructed, and set into operation. His sources of data are from studies of two river basins together with related information on water systems in the western United States. The benefits during the construction period accrue to river-basin workers who get the construction jobs, to persons who own retail stores, and to those who provide housing for construction personnel. Later, others may benefit from increases in power output, in industrial product use, and in recreational opportunity. Real estate speculators often benefit as land values rise. However, among persons being relocated, the poor and the aged are usually disadvantaged in that they, more than others, are likely to migrate from the site of possible benefits. The immigration of workers when construction begins causes rents to rise for limited housing, and this affects adversely the poorer people who are not homeowners.

During the planning stage, communities were found making changes in their local governments to reap the benefits from new construction. The typical city increases measures of social control (including zoning), enacts more ordinances, and tries to increase the roles of local government. It asks for more state services and becomes more involved with state regulatory bodies. The recreational, economic, and political offices of state and county government strive to put their inputs into project planning, and there is generally an increased bureaucratization of the community.

In the preconstruction phase, those elements of the society that receive or assume new prerogatives are "modernist-oriented, and market skilled, middle-class." During this period, conflicts of community image and direction, of activity, and social conscience may occur. "Traditional cultures . . . feel severely threatened and justifiably so."[39] The decline of traditional values is hastened by the arrival of new and more mobile people and of new businesses. The newcomers introduce, among other things, alternative role models for youth and disruptions to conventional patterns of socialization. Hogg concludes that social, political, and economic systems tend to become more open and willing to take risks when there is impending development. Many persons, individually, take increased hope from the promise of betterment. Some of the traditionalists, however, feel anomic and uncared for by local leaders. Hogg labels this polarization of orientations in the community as schizoid.

The construction phase, typically fairly short, intensifies change in the community. Outside workers move in, rents increase, local services are strained, and bureaucratization increases. But when construction is completed and operation begins, community reaction tends to be, "Where did they all go?", and overplanning for the construction phase and overexpectation about the project become evident. Unemployment increases when the construction workers leave, and usually some of the community's youth emigrate as well. The tax base decreases. Services which expanded during construction may now decline. Lower-class and blue-collar workers feel the effects more than others.

In the postconstruction phase, social revitalization begins. In what may be the most important sociological insight presented in his paper, Hogg points out that sometimes the demoralization of the community and the ensuing disorganization is so great as to give neighboring communities, rather than the community that was the focus of the original plan, a chance to reap the benefits, especially those from recreational development. Overplanning for the construction phase may very well weaken the community if it is not supplemented and balanced with long-range planning for taking advantage of the aesthetic and recreational potential of the new reservoir. Further research into the probable, but locally unanticipated, consequences of water resource development would certainly aid planners in helping communities plan for social change.

At least one conditional limitation is placed on Hogg's generalizations by Stamm's report that the "arrival of construction men for dams affects the local people in inverse proportion to the size of the town."[40] Apparently, a larger community can absorb both the positive and negative effects of construction with less weakening of the social structure. At the other extreme, Bates found that very small towns are largely unaffected by reservoir construction since the construction workers prefer to live in nearby larger towns and commute to work.[41]

RECREATIONAL USES OF WATER

Water is being used increasingly as a recreational resource.[42] Many reservoirs built to serve other objectives have become major recreation centers. Planners learned from a series of such experiences to provide facilities for recreational visitors. Now the planners regularly include recreation benefits in determining economic feasibility. The kind and distribution of benefits that reservoir recreation facilities provide nearby communities are also very important from the viewpoint of local support for a project and are of more direct concern to sociologists.

According to Ferriss the increased popular participation in *active* water-oriented recreation is a result of growing population rather than any rise in the per capita rate of participation.[43] He says that the increase in *total* water-oriented recreation is associated more with the relatively inactive pursuits such as picnicking and sight-seeing. Ferriss's idea is in some disagreement with a 1962 study by the Outdoor Recreation Resources Review Commission.[44] This report indicated that people respond to new recreational facilities by using them; and many kinds of recreational demands dramatically outstrip population growth. James and Lee state that "every forecast indicates the use of reservoirs for recreation will expand much faster than the total population."[45] In one forecast, Cicchetti, Seneca, and Davidson estimated that before the year 2000 swimming would increase almost threefold, waterskiing would double, fishing would rise by a quarter, and demand for boating facilities would almost triple.[46]

Several studies examine the role of socioeconomic status in the choice of recreational pursuits. Burdge makes the generalization that for almost every type of leisure activity, the probability is that the participants will be mainly from the middle or upper classes.[47] Ferriss says that high income, education, occupational status, and urbanization are associated with greater participation in water-related activities. Recreation users are also nearly always white. This fits with Andrews and Geersten's finding about the emphasis urbanites put on the recreational benefits of a proposed interbasin transfer of water. Krutilla and Knetsch point out that lower-status urban people (ghetto residents) tend to use "market-oriented outdoor recreation," such as playgrounds, parks, and amusement spots in the city, whereas higher-status people tend to use the more "resource-oriented" forms of outdoor recreation.[48] A recent study of 137 rural Iowa residents found that the typical outdoor recreation participant was married, had children, and that his participation directly increased with income and education.[49] However, the last trend probably does not apply to the very rich.

The population of participants in water-oriented outdoor recreation contains several interesting relationships. For instance, the kind of water recreation desired is predictive of where and how far people will travel.[50] Sailors and waterskiiers tend to travel only short distances to lakes on the fringe of metropolitan areas, whereas fishermen and nonspecialized boaters tend to travel longer distances to more remote lakes. Pleasure-boaters travel intermediate distances. In a study that attempted to differentiate travel distance among types of boating specialists only one social variable was found to be predictive—the type of boating group (whether family or friends). Otherwise, variables like the horsepower of the boat motor were more useful indicators.[51]

Fishermen, when compared to hunters in some northeastern states, were found to be more often married, older, and more likely to be better educated and from urban centers than hunters were.[52] Also, fishing is more likely to be a family affair than hunting. Other such findings indicate that most water-based recreation is a group affair.

Data on the socioeconomic characteristics of participants in water recreation are useful for predicting demands, estimating what kinds of water recreation will be needed, and foretelling potential economic benefits. They also show severe socioeconomic and racial disparities in participation in recreation by the middle class as opposed to minorities and low-status people who get "the short end of the stick" in this area of life as well as most others. The remedy, however, probably does not lie in special programs to make outdoor recreation available to the poor, but rather in the reduction of poverty so that water recreation becomes an optional form of leisure activity for people.

COMMUNITY ORGANIZATION AND PARTICIPATION
IN WATER RESOURCE PROJECTS

As has already been noted, local participation is very important to water resource planning and development. Many studies stress the interplay among the community, the attitudes of landowners, and proposed projects. Wilkinson, in a case study of the response of two Mississippi communities to the small watershed program of the Soil Conservation Service, examined the proposition that "the greater the linkage of a watershed program to the structure of the community, the greater the likelihood of project accomplishment."[53] He also hypothesized that "community structure is highly related to the success of a watershed project, and a program which does not relate itself to this structure or does not involve the local people may be in the community, but not necessarily of the community."[54]

He found that few rural landowners in either community were aware of the project's details nor had the majority participated in any way.[55] Watershed development was carried on as a relatively isolated, special-interest activity. Generalized community leaders had to initiate the special-high interest activity for the watershed project in one community. The other community had a history of special-interest activity, and their actors in the watershed programs were more adept at securing the required local financing and legal commitments. The program was more successful, and the attitudes of rural landowners toward watershed development were more favorable.[56] In the former community, however, the population was more rural. In summary, Wilkinson concludes that "technical, special-interest projects such as watershed development operate more smoothly where community structure is less well-integrated."[57] His initial hypothesis was not correct, and the degree of integration of the community was negatively related to project success, given the presence of special-interest groups. Interpretation of this finding, however, should note that Wilkinson defined integration as local participation through local leaders. By another common meaning, integration does not necessarily exclude the separate but well-articulated actions of special-interest groups.

Several sociological studies document how local people can organize and complete a successful project. A small community in West Virginia (population 1,700) mobilized and through integrated efforts built a flood prevention project.[58] The businessmen, school teachers, and farmers were key personnel in this successful project, presumably because they were opinion leaders in some respect. In another case, three hundred residents in Utah planned, constructed, and financed a water pipeline project.[59]

One researcher argues that water resources planning will be more successful if local people, working through local organizations with the help of state governments, are willing to take and sustain the major initiative and to bear a major cost, seeking federal assistance only for what is beyond their technical and financial capabilities.[60] He also says the farmers who have participated in collective watershed projects show a remarkable increase in their usage of soil and water conservation practices. The latter statement forms an interesting and easily testable hypothesis. Wilkinson's findings seem to contradict this idea, but they may, in fact, reflect another dimension of integration, as mentioned above. Where a community has a history of special-interest groups taking the initiative in planning and carrying out projects for the general good, these groups may be the most effective agents for the job. Or it may be the case that small watershed projects require only interest group participation, whereas reservoir, sewage and community water supply systems require broader community participation. Or may it be that where there is no such history of interest groups in the community, then grass-roots participation may be a key to a project success? Further research is needed to resolve this issue.

Peterson's recent study of community organization and rural water supply system development gives further insight.[61] He cites literature to confirm that "existing community organization and participation by local leadership was strongly related to project success" and "project accomplishment in watershed programs was positively related to the degree of linkage between the program and the structure of the community." He proceeded to test the related hypothesis that "community organization is positively related to the level of effectiveness and water-system organization" in numerous Mississippi communities. He found a high level of organization in communities already having organized water systems or in the process of organizing them. Little community organization was found in those communities not participating in water system programs.

However, where there is a multicommunity water system, community organization is less important. Where the water system is to serve a single community, the process of organizing it tends to strengthen local leadership and is a sign of the continued existence of a rural community, whereas the opposite is true in multicommunity systems. In other words, community integration seems to be enhanced by a single community water system. Peterson also points out that the first communities to organize water systems were significantly better organized than those doing it later.

Peterson points out that the introduction of a water system in farming communities makes the household water consumption pattern more like that of the suburbs. Also, the residents begin to consider their land in nonagricultural terms, regarding their land as potential homesites having an increased value. Members begin to see the possibility of their community expanding in size and becoming increasingly composed of rural nonfarm workers. A contradictory influence is that water systems facilitate the extension of farming operations.

From the foregoing review, it seems clear the community involvement in water development programs needs to be studied much more extensively before any generalizations can be confirmed. The conditions under which community organization and integration are independent variables cannot yet be clearly specified. However, available data on the attitudes of people toward watershed development offer clues on conditions that generate positive attitudes, clues suggesting hypotheses that can be tested.

COMMUNITY ATTITUDES AND PARTICIPATION IN WATER RESOURCE PROJECTS

A study by Dasgupta in two Mississippi communities with watershed development programs established the importance of certain attitudes.[62] "Attitudes of the local landowners toward the watershed development program are a very important factor upon which the success of the program depends to a large extent. The way people perceive the needs which the program seeks to fulfill, the way they evaluate the effectiveness of the program in fulfilling these needs, and the way they see their own involvement in the program may all be considered to be crucial for the success of the program." Dasgupta found four status variables to be positively related to attitudes toward watershed development: organizational involvement, occupation, education, and level of living. He also found knowledge about a project to be an important intervening variable, as were the degree of technical contact and participation in planning. More information on correlates of receptivity to change is found below in a discussion of the adoption of innovations.

A recent five-year longitudinal study (Peterson and Ross) found that overall the attitudes of landowners toward land treatment for conservation on a watershed basis had improved over time.[63] Those who tended to have more favorable attitudes had experienced severe floods in the past, were able to perceive the probability of personal benefits for themselves in the program, had higher socioeconomic status, and knew more about the project than did persons opposed. Direct contact had more impact on knowledge of a particular project and attitudes toward it than on attitudes toward water conservation in general. Wilkinson and Singh concluded in a study of 114 community leaders that "the intensity of participation in a watershed project is related to generality of commitment to and participation in community action."[64]

Hogg and Smith studied acceptance of a system of two dams in the Santiam River Basin. They found it helpful to link attitudinal and community-structure factors together.[65] They offer the interesting insight that in the linkages among larger sociocultural systems, a lack of articulation and planning among the various elements of the social system restricted the full development of potential benefits from reservoir construction. They conclude that consumer values and action must be sought and used as inputs to develop the full benefits of a water project.

In summary then, willingness to participate in water development programs seems to be related primarily 1) to the presence of a water resource problem (flooding) or need (desire for irrigation); 2) to some as yet unclearly defined level of community awareness and motivation to participate as well as, possibly, the degree of community integration; 3) to knowledge on the part of potential participants about the project; 4) to expection of personal benefit from the project; and 5) to higher socioeconomic status.

Perhaps the primary impetus to community action on water resource development is the existence of a situation in which such development has come to be regarded by the community as the answer to a significant social problem. Then, as Ballweg and Ibsen note, it is practically "impossible to prevent sectors of the public and community leadership from taking action."[66] This is particularly true for communities that have been affected by disasters. Not only do individuals respond, but effective organizations develop to deal with the disaster situation.

Burdge and Ludkte's findings about people who are being forced to move because of reservoir construction may be a special case—a situation where unfavorable attitudes toward a dam are generated because of a reluctance to change one's life and where the necessity of moving creates an extremely stressful situation. Here, knowledge cannot mitigate negative attitudes. Using Smith's terms, the pre-relocation stress may be so great as to nullify any effects that knowledge of the project might have on the person. Such knowledge, for any prospective migrant, reminds him of the painful fact that he must move (which is precisely what he does not want to do) and creates an extremely stressful cognitive pattern. Provision of better information seems to be a plus factor only in gaining support from those who do not perceive personal adverse effects.

ADOPTION OF INNOVATIVE WATER PROJECTS

Water resource development requires innovative adoptions on the part of beneficiaries before they can effectively use project output. Certain generalizations from the work of Everett Rogers and associates on the process of innovation directly apply to this situation.[67] For example, the first innovations normally come from those with higher education, higher social status, greater exposure to mass media and interpersonal channels of communication, greater change-agent contact, higher social participation, and a relatively cosmopolitan orientation.[68]

Rogers and Burdge have noted that the individual adoption process is analogous to the community decision making process.[69] The outline they provide for a rural setting is as follows: farmers first become aware of an innovation by noting the experience of others, reading farm journals, or through other media. Usually, farmers then seek further information from such sources as the county extension agent or manufacturing firms. Evaluation by the farmer of the information in terms of pros and cons for his own operation is the next step. Variables which affect the decision to adopt a given innovation include its relative advantage over present practices; its complexity (whether it is easy to understand and use); and its suitability for trial by initial, limited use. Often, the most important variable is visibility of results. The farmer who evaluates most of these variables favorably is likely to adopt the innovation.

The presence and role taken by the change agent is also important.[70] The job of this person, who may be the county agricultural extension agent or a planner, follows the sequence of developing an awareness of need for change among his clients, implementing and stabilizing the change, and terminating the relationship. His probability of success in securing the adoption of an innovation is improved by 1) the extent of his effort, 2) the extent of his client-orientation, 3) the fit of the program to the client's needs, 4) the agent's empathy with his clients, 5) his similarity of background and interests with his clients, 6) the extent to which he works through opinion leaders, 7) his credibility with clients, and 8) his efforts to help his clients to evaluate innovations. All these factors should be considered by those trying to benefit people through resource development.

Rural sociologists have given descriptive categories to adopters in terms of the time of adoption.[71] Innovators adopt first and are followed in sequence by the early adopters, early majority, and the late majority. Innovators and early adopters tend to have more education, greater upward mobility, larger farms and a commercial orientation, higher incomes, and greater social status. They also have more favorable attitudes toward change, risk taking, education, and science. They tend to be less fatalistic, have higher achievement motivation, and aspirations; and they experience greater social participation.[72] "Laggards," the last adopters, tend to be suspicious of innovations, to have small farms, low incomes, and relatively little formal education. They are also tradition-directed.

The concept of laggards relates to consideration of those who are least favorable toward water resource development. Because the conservation movement is broadening the reasons for and hence the population base for opposition to resource development, the following generalizations should be regarded as tentative. It appears that age, traditional ruralism, low socioeconomic status, and lack of knowledge about water projects accompany conservatism and resistance to new projects.[73] It seems plausible, however, that if laggards were made (through the dissemination of information) to perceive personal benefits from the project, that this would be powerful enough an intervening variable to mitigate and possibly overcome their antagonism. A practical question that needs to be addressed in planning water projects is how can benefits be increased to those in the community who ordinarily gain little or nothing, the very people most likely to be laggards. This would require a special effort, since as James and Lee note, "water resource projects are not particularly efficient in redistributing income because the rich always reap part of the benefit and the poor always pay part of the cost."[74]

POSSIBLE LIMITATIONS ON THE THEORY OF DIFFUSION OF INNOVATIONS

Some of the most innovative proposals for applying new technology to water resource management relate to weather modification. Strodbeck studied attitudes toward weather modification in a small town in South Dakota.[75] In relating his findings in the light of larger and more systematic research on openness to innovation, he concluded that the "first, pervasive and undeniable concomitant of resistance to change is low education." He goes on to say that "low education is part of a complex belief system composed of fatalism and ascetic Protestantism."[76] He also suggests that where there is a change-resistant orientation, there is a "supporting selective use and mastery of relevant mass media information." He challenges Roger's formulations of the diffusion process, asserting that they do not describe the situation with regard to weather modification. Effects are less certain and more community consensus is required than Rogers implies. Strodbeck points out that weather modification is a troublesome area to understand, and Craik agrees: "Water resources engineers trained to intervene in and control environmental processes, are surprisingly reluctant to advocate large scale weather modification and heedful of possible unforeseen consequences."[77]

Strodbeck points out that opposition may well become too great before the "goodness" of weather modification can be shown. He compares the resistance and acceptance processes to those encountered in fluoridation. He observes that the average citizen who approaches a community issue is not technically well informed. When a strongly negative opinion becomes prominent, the average citizen does not seek technical information; rather, he seeks guidance from the established political leadership. If established leadership expresses itself strongly against the protest, the average voter will follow the leadership and vote for the innovation on the referendum. But if the leadership does not think the innovative issue is clear enough in its political implication to warrant a stand, the average voter will conclude that the vocal minority has the case and will vote against the measure.

York studied the controversial fluoridation issue and the effect of information on community attitudes.[78] His before-and-after attitude measures showed an improvement in attitudes after a film extolling the benefits of fluoridation was shown to students. York also studied the differential effects of using the film alone and the film followed by group discussion. The latter combination yielded the most favorable attitude change. One month later, however, the group uniformly showed a reduction in favorableness toward fluoridation. It should be noted therefore, that manipulation of attitudes cannot even guarantee the short-term acceptance of a controversial issue.

Sasaki studied the failure of a Navajo Irrigation Project, and his findings explain some of the disfunctionalities of innovative water resource planning in which human consequences are overlooked.[79] He concluded that a lack of preparedness on the part of the people in the area can cause a development project to fail. The greater the expected change from current social and cultural structure, the more intensive the study should be of methods which can be used to overcome the expected negative consequences.

In general, persons who, through knowledge or experience, are able to perceive benefits from a possible innovation are more likely to accept it. However, there does seem to be sufficient evidence to qualify the generality of this theory of perceived personal benefit as the motivating force in the diffusion of innovations. For instance, where a people's belief structure is threatened in some fundamental way (as with the South Dakota traditionalists), where the consequences of an innovation are unknown (as with fluoridation), or where the fabric of a culture is threatened (as with the sheepherding Navajos), unless the innovation can be aligned with belief systems, political goals, or cultural norms, it is not likely to be adopted. More generally, the diffusion of innovations, to be successful, must occur under the conditions specified by the theory. Whenever a sufficient (but still unspecifiable) number of the specified conditions are missing, there is a greater likelihood of project failure. Further research is needed to learn how functional innovations can be made compatible with existing social systems and how to minimize the social and cultural conflicts engendered by such innovations.

A NOTE ON METHODOLOGY

Community studies are the predominant type of water-oriented research by sociologists. Most of the researchers have used either random samples of householders or chosen samples of community leaders, depending on whether they were studying the community as a whole, or just the participation of significant leaders. By and large, the methodology has drawn on commonly used techniques, such as interview schedules and attitude scales, and most of the data are reported both in quantitative and qualitative terms. The degree of sophistication in use of data runs from simple tabulations of percentages by classification to a sophisticated experimental design leading to multivariate analyses or regression equations. However, the more complicated techniques appear to have contributed little or nothing to the findings. Although sociologists are dealing with complex subject matter, they have not acquired enough data control to achieve much capability in model building, or in quantitative prediction. The findings from most studies are tentative—only the relevant variables and the general directions of relationships between variables have been established. Most findings are hypothetically generalizable, but confirmation is going to require support from many similar studies through replications.

URBANIZATION AND WATER POLLUTION

Urbanization may be thought of as the physical process of new suburbs, industrial parks, shopping centers, and residential areas invading former fields and forests. To the sociologist, urbanization is a major process of social change and one that complicates water resources management. Even before physical urbanization began, Peterson and Ross found that bringing a water system to a small farming community changed attitudes by introducing suburban viewpoints with respect to both land and water. Spaulding's studies found that water use increases with socioeconomic status.[80] The spreading affluence of modern society can thus be expected to increase water use; and the growth of both suburbia and high-rise apartments, primarily for the middle and upper classes, will require larger water supply facilities. People will continue to gravitate toward large urban centers and compound water supply problems unless there is a shift in the locus of employment opportunity to smaller towns and cities or to rural areas.[81] Water use will continue to increase with advances in the standard of living unless rising prices or legislation can curb use and pollution.

Moreover, urban development has multiple impact: it accelerates the rapid runoff of rain water and snowmelt; it results in an increase of household as well as industrial water consumption; it increases the use of water for street washing and fire fighting.[82] Water in urban areas is diverted from normal surface and underground courses into sewage systems, drainage channels, and reservoirs, and it is polluted by both household and industrial use. The major difficulties associated with industrial use of water are the great quantities needed and the extremities of pollution introduced.

SOCIETAL VALUES AND WATER POLLUTION

The most fruitful line of inquiry whereby sociologists can contribute to solving the pollution problem is through a theoretical study of the value-bases in society that lead to wasteful water use or to water pollution; "an interpretation of the social and cultural relevance of an environmental feature also defines the rules of deportment with respect to that feature."[83] Societal values are an important key to why people pollute. Klausner says that "current problems of pollution call attention to those rules regulating behavior with respect to environment held, used, or enjoyed in common by large groups of men. These rules regulate the relationship of individuals to the collective to which they belong. Problems arise when some men change the common environment in a way that impinges on the rights of others."[84]

Some important contributions toward understanding how societal values lead to unwise resource use have already been made. The primary value orientation underlying abuse of water resources seems to be "that the common land or water or air is the responsibility of no one in particular. Each man uses the environment for his personal ends, treating it as if it were abandoned property."[85] Klausner calls man's abuse of the environment "the tragedy of the commons." Air and water and land are things all men hold in common, yet each man's orientation is "functionally specific." That is, he uses collective property for his own interests with little concern for other users. The man who damages the commons damages it not only for all others, but he hurts his own interests as well.

Belief systems include elements that have been made ecologically dysfunctional, as Caldwell has explained, "by the lag between the changing circumstances of man on earth and his assumptions, behavior patterns and institutions."[86] First on his list is the belief that "speculation in land values is a legitimate way to windfall wealth." Access to water-oriented esthetic and recreational values enhances the profitability of real estate, but development to realize that profit is often contradictory to the public interest. A second belief is that the government must help enterprise, but should not control it. The counterbelief is that private enterprise should be given a public character, to ensure greater environmental responsibility. The third belief is that growth is an absolute good. Rather, as Caldwell indicates, selective growth, nongrowth, and even retrenchment are environmentally sound values. The fourth value is that "people have a right to do as they please with their property." Here Caldwell proposes that "usufruct" (the right to enjoy the property of others so long as no damage is done) might be an appropriate concept to replace the concept of ownership, and Klausner adds that this could form a "realistic and socially acceptable basis for the regulation of relationships among men."[87] The fifth belief is that "government by judges is preferable to government by administrators," but Caldwell asserts that administrators would be better equipped than judges to deal with complicated environmental problems.

Burdge suggests that the values of freedom, practicability, pecuniary worth, science, and progress affect the attitudes of individuals toward water and its use.[88] Water has been a cheap and easily available resource for most people, and this freedom of use, reinforced by feelings about ownership, has caused many people to resent regulation of their water use. This instrumental or functional view of water is a major factor in industrial pollution. Burdge discusses the conflict of instrumental with esthetic views of water and suggests that pollution control will not be achieved until high-quality water is seen as a good thing, and a goal in itself. The use of free water for pecuniary gain is related to industrial pollution in that water is seen as something to be exploited for economic benefits. The economic or benefit-cost criterion is also used to justify the construction of many water conservation structures. Science and technology are highly valued causes as well as consequences of economic growth, and their pervasive influence—many perceive them as required for their jobs and life style—may account for some of the public disinterest and inaction in preserving esthetic values. Notions of progress and growth, cited also by Caldwell, lead falsely or at least paradoxically to the depletion of natural resources. Moreover, progress and growth go hand-in-hand with growing consumerism and concomitant problems of waste disposal. Progress and conservation are in apparent conflict at this point, and ideas of progress need to be revised to reflect ecological value in the public mind if environmental problems are to be solved.

INDUSTRY AND WATER POLLUTION

In a paper on industrial organizations and environmental quality, Roy Rickson examines the cultural assumptions that underlie the industrial use of natural resources: "Mastery over the physical and social environment has been the consistent objective and recurring theme of the industrial and scientific communities," and "extensive exploitation of natural energy and social order are basic requirements of industrial development."[89] He broadens the point to say "generally, modern industrial civilizations relate to the physical environment in terms of its utility for their institutional goals rather than for its intrinsic qualities."[90]

Burch has a related observation that "a society organized according to class rather than caste is more likely to treat nature as a commodity."[91] The argument is that with class organization one must exploit the environment to one's own benefit to fully realize the potential of upward mobility through whatever openness there is in the class system.

Noting industrial resistance to adoption of available pollution control technology, Rickson proposes that it "can be explained as a product of the value hierarchy of an industrial economy and a general value structure that is supportive of the industrial system."[92] The salient values to which he refers are that 1) industrial organizations perceive the environment as means to ends or as inputs to production; 2) the values of industrial growth and full employment overshadow esthetic and environmental values; and 3) technological innovation and progress contribute to the growth and stability of the industrial system. With specific regard to water, inadequate consideration is given to substitution possibilities, or to water's relationship to other factor inputs in the production process, or to the impact of technological change on industrial water use. Water is seen (often because of government subsidies) as free and relatively clean, and thus its use is not adequately regulated by the pricing system. The right to dump effluents without cost is also still taken for granted. Moreover, the history of industrial uses of water, until quite recently, has been one of virtually autonomous industrial determination of water-relevant decisions. As a result of the dominance of these values and practices, the economy as a whole pays considerable hidden subsidy to underwrite the use of "nominally free" resources. The result is a "huge, unintentional market incentive to pollution."[93]

The difficulties in curbing industrial pollution are manifold. For example, Rickson suggests that "extensive quality control over industrial effluents could disrupt seriously the core technology."[94] The effluent process and core industrial technology are functionally interdependent, and the requirements of current industrial systems are so overweening as to bias powerfully any research activities relating to the prevention of pollution. In a further interpretation, Rickson notes that dirty water is less important as a problem to industry than it is a problem to people. "Industrial organizations as rational systems will, therefore, attempt to influence the definition of water quality and compete and cooperate with other public and private groups so that the logic of their production process will suffer only minimal change and [so] that the social environment will remain predictable."[95]

Resistance to change in the use of water resources is thus inversely related to organizational capacity for innovation, and Rickson hypothesizes that "the less adaptive or innovative they are, the more apt are industrial organizations to use their power to define water quality and affect the general rules for water use."[96]

POSSIBLE SOLUTIONS TO WATER POLLUTION PROBLEMS

Historically, most effective social movements have originated in the middle classes; poor water quality is one problem in which the middle classes are more affected than the lower classes. Studies have shown conservationism to be an upper-middle class social movement, and this offers hope that conservationist values will follow the pattern of extending through the middle and lower-middle classes as ideas, fads, and fashions do.[97]

Spaulding found awareness of pollution in all socioeconomic status groups.[98] Even though he found more awareness among high and middle levels, respondents in all classes were more uninformed than informed about pollution. This fits with a finding by Ibsen and Ballweg (from a random sample of 500 people) that only three percent of the sample perceived water as a "major problem facing the world today."[99] Thirty-four percent indicated that they considered water a problem, and the problem mentioned most often was pollution. Seventy-five percent of the sample had read or seen something on the water problem. Television was the most common source of information. The solution most often proposed was more effective legislation. Spaulding found that the majority of the sample believed in the possibility of man's control over water pollution and water supply and that this belief was more prevalent in higher than in the middle or lower status groups.

In another study, David showed that the public has a definite image of water pollution, and the forms most often mentioned (algae, dark water, soapsuds) are visual.[100] Few people mentioned chemicals and disease germs as forms of pollution. This study, as well as that by Ibsen and Ballweg, points to the necessity of educating the public about pollution. This is a potential role for sociologists; they know from studies of response to disasters that the public can organize and respond in meaningful ways to what they have defined as a problem. The need is to change the public's posture to a motivated awareness that results in action.

Klausner would require that whoever dumps effluents into a body of water pay for the cost of water purification in the affected communities.[101] This, it is argued, would help bring the actual costs of pollution into the awareness of both industry and the general public, thus overcoming one of the main problems cited by Rickson in our wasteful use of water. This idea would "involve social arrangements under which individuals in one collective might become subject to sanctions when their acts affect another collective of which they are not members."[102] Caldwell says that we must modify our prevailing assumptions about the nature of social responsibility; we must change the rules about the relationship of the individual to the collective. "A new, ecologically valid politio-ethical ideology is needed to legitimatize the tasks of public authority and responsibility that an effective effort to cope with man's environmental problems would require."[103] Klausner suggests that American society may move toward a form of social and political organization long associated with the democratic left to deal with the environmental crisis.

Another approach is offered by Craik who suggests study of the environmental attitudes of such decision-makers as planners, engineers, architects, transportation planners, conservationists, and so on.[104] His hypothesis is that "environmental decision-makers differ in their perceptions, interpretation, and evaluation of the everyday physical environment." Pragmatically speaking, better information on these attitudes could be used to assess which practices by which occupational groups are most hazardous to the environment, and which ecologically sound practices exist. Such information would make it easier to combat ecologically dysfunctional attitudes. Craik and associates have also begun to develop valid scales to measure environmental attitudes.

In summary, then, there is considerable agreement that basic values in American society must change if our environmental problems are to be dealt with effectively. Moreover, there is some evidence that if these values and their concomitant practices change, the fabric of American life will change as well, perhaps fundamentally. As Rickson says, "Societies are open systems engaged in transactions with the physical and social milieu. When there are drastic changes in the physical environment, some change in the internal structure of social organizations will result."[105]

More scientific inquiry is needed into the attitudes of the general public toward water pollution. The consuming public may be willing to give up some things and unwilling to give up others in return for cleaner water. If we knew what kinds of pollution control would be socially feasible, within the limits of public sanction, then those processes of control could begin to be used before further research resolved the more difficult control aspects. Better information on the part of industrial polluters on public attitudes toward pollution might be an incentive for industries to curb those types of pollution where the public is well enough informed and sufficiently aroused. Another fertile ground for research by sociologists is better means for the diffusion throughout the public of accurate information about pollution and about the consequences of alternative control measures.

It may be that public sanctions are not effective enough in and of themselves, and that a legislative (or other) reordering of industrial and national priorities will be necessary. Here the task is for sociologists to find the necessary conditions to bring about basic change in the economically based values that dominate such a large segment of our lives. Particularly interesting to study would be the concepts of growth and progress and how these values might be replaced with more ecologically compatible concepts. Robin Williams points out that once a high standard of living has been enjoyed by the public, it is extremely difficult to persuade people to do with less except in times of emergency.[106] Moreover, as new desires emerge, or a product is introduced that elicits desire, it is normal for people to want to satisfy those desires and to begin to feel that they have a moral right to satisfaction. The need here is to reorient materialistic desires in order to reduce demands on our natural resources. Possible reorientations could be creative or recreational rather than strictly consummatory uses of material goods.

Balancing our environmental interests with other values and goals introduces potential conflict situations. The objectives for water resource development as presently stated by the National Water Resources Council may be incompatible. As James and Lee note, "The quality of the environment is usually only improved at a sacrifice in national and regional income and employment."[107] The outcome of the process of conflict can disrupt the social structure or, in other cases, enhance social integration.[108] One of the important conditions that keeps conflict less intense is that sufficient resources are available to gratify opposing interests. The problems of pollution, if attacked in sufficient time, offer the possibility of creative compromise that could be a powerful stimulus to constructive social change both in values and behavior. Sociologists have much to offer by the careful study of the functions of conflict as applied to the use of natural resources.

SUMMARY OF SOCIOLOGICAL FINDINGS

The first of the three questions we were invited to address concerned the contributions of sociological research to water resource development. The major research areas and their findings have been described, and their probable impact is discussed in the concluding section. It is important to note the scientific status of our findings; many are tentative or conflicting. Many may only be true in the case studied. Examples of water problems needing further study include the role of community integration in water resource development, the social consequences of solving water problems with innovative technology, the effect of knowledge about water projects on attitudes, the conservation movement and its interactions with water resources management, and the characteristics associated with resistance to change. However, some findings, such as those on diffusion of innovations, public participation in planned change and community decision making, and the role of attitudes and values in the acceptance of change derive from a much larger body of sociological research and are much more reliable and generalizable.

Some indications of problems associated with water resource development that might move toward solution with the aid of sociologists have already been given. Perhaps the most outstanding example is pollution. Almost every aspect of society is affected by pollution, and further research into almost every area of sociology with an eye to its relationship to pollution would be extremely fruitful. For example, what are the most effective forms of social control for curbing pollution? How can we stop having so many children and teach the children we do have to respect environmental necessities? How can migration patterns be changed so as to balance supply and demand of water? How do we change deviant behavior such as littering and illegal industrial pollution of water? How do we change our values and behavior to make this an ecologically viable society?

We need to study the forced resettlement of people affected by planned social change and how to ease the transition for them and their communities. Even more generally, enhancement of the general social welfare through water resource development poses a large and difficult problem. At an even more macroscopic scale, how can water resources management be used to alleviate such stubborn social problems as crime, poverty, racism, urban unrest, decay, and overcrowding? What kinds of institutions will facilitate the linkage of water resource systems to the other social institutions so that we can have a coordinated system that furthers national well-being?

The question of professional incentives and rewards for participation in water-related research is a touchy one. Belonging to a somewhat fledgling science (as compared to the natural sciences), many sociologists are reluctant to enter applied sociology. This reluctance is due partly to fear of failure—we don't know enough yet to apply anything. It is also due to a fear that pure science cannot be advanced by practical application, especially if it is diluted by an interdisciplinary effort (boundary-maintenance) or by cooperation with governmental agencies. Some sociologists fear topicality in research—that to be timely and relevant means that one cannot be objective, and a true scientist. And underlying it all, marginal pursuits outside mainline sociology have not been as well rewarded nor as admired (nor pursued as often) as traditional ones. Many of the younger or more adventurous sociologists (not necessarily the same people) are branching into nontraditional areas of study; natural resources is one of them. Sociological contributions are increasing steadily in number, and their quality is improving as well. Moreover, every new area offers the chance to confirm things we already know in yet another social context, to modify things that are no longer true or that are true only under certain conditions, to explore uncharted areas of social concern with the possibility of new insights into the complexities of social life, and with that, of contributing new knowledge to the field.

Some limitations on this optimistic statement are found in the concluding section. In order for sociological research in water resources to contribute as it should, such institutional constraints as the reward-and-status system within sociology must be altered, and the scientific status of the research must be improved. Moreover, part of the role of a professional is to inform, and we need better means of diffusing our information throughout the public and private sectors of our society.

THE IMPACT OF SOCIOLOGICAL FINDINGS

The sociological (and ecological) meaning of water resources research and the way research findings are used will depend on how the completed studies intersect with social, political, and economic action. This paraphrase of a statement by Klausner on the meaning of water provides a phenomenological reference point from which to discuss past, present, and future research in the sociological aspects of water resources. Generally, sociological contributions have so far only had impact in terms of social, political, or economic action in a very narrow way. Access to the literature is a requirement for the diffusion of knowledge, and most of the studies discussed here are not widely read by sociologists or others because they languish in mimeographed publications produced by water resource institutes and circulate mainly to relevant government agencies, other water resource institutes, and to various experts in the water field. At best, findings are published in relatively obscure journals with a small audience or are presented at professional meetings. Pollution is now a widely recognized issue by the general public and by academic institutions. Sociologists, however, cannot take much credit for whatever knowledge there is about pollution in the public mind. Relevant sociological information has not been given wide exposure.

Much of the research discussed here has been "facilitating" in nature. In other words, the goal has been to help understand and create the conditions under which water projects would be accepted by communities. Although many findings about attitudes, community participation in decision making, and diffusion of innovations are potentially generalizable and have had practical impact, this impact has been limited to a few specific communities. Moreover, the mere fact that sociologists study what is happening to an area with a water project does not guarantee that the findings will be used in other than functionally specific ways by those agencies and industries whose business it is to build and manage such structures. Another way of saying the same thing is to suggest that, on occasion, sociologists have allowed instrumental and pecuniary considerations to influence their research effort in much the same way as they have described the influence of the same values on pollution. For instance, much of the research described here was done either at institutional request, or because of the availability of governmental money for specific kinds of water resources research. Much research has ignored, by and large, the dysfunctionalities engendered by many water resource projects, such as impelled migration and what it does to people or increased urbanization around major water bodies and the concomitant pollution. Moreover, most of the information is primarily an "in-house" form of specialized knowledge. If these observations are correct, the sociological impact of this knowledge on social, political, or economic action is not at all uniform. It is *not* public, collective knowledge which could be used to promote socially or environmentally sound policies (though this is not to say that those with access to this information will not use it in an ecologically responsible manner). The probability is that dominant value-bases in this society will continue to bias the research effort in ways that enhance the status quo.

This is not to say sociologists should become revolutionaries bearing the banners of ecology, social responsibility, and antibureaucracy. Rather the research effort should be a more enlightened developmental one with respect to the potential impact of proposed water management practices on the physical and social environment, and an effort needs to be made to broaden the audience to which our findings are addressed.

This chapter was developed from a paper presented by Wade H. Andrews, professor of sociology, Utah State University, at the University of Kentucky colloquium, "The Social Sciences and Planning and Management of Water Resources," November 1969. The author also acknowledges the helpful criticism of Rabel J. Burdge, associate professor of sociology, University of Kentucky.

1. Duane D. Baumann, "Potential for Policy Change in the Recreational Use of Domestic Water Supply Reservoirs," in *Proceedings of the Fourth American Water Resources Conference,* ed. Phillip Cohen and Martha Francisco (Urbana, Ill.: American Water Resources Association, 1968), pp. 559-69. Baumann used Festinger's theory of cognitive dissonance to explain how managers of reservoirs try to reduce dissonance about the demand for recreational use of their reservoirs. However, Baumann predicts that when the demand becomes great enough, the water managers will change their cognitions and therefore have no dissonance about recreational use of their reservoirs. An abstract of this article can be found in *Water Resources Abstract 3,* 18 (15 September 1970): 58.

2. See Fred L. Strodbeck, "Weather Modification as an Uncertain Innovation," in *Social Sciences and the Environment,* ed. Morris E. Garnsey and James R. Hibbs (Boulder: University of Colorado Press, 1967), pp. 103-24; Phillip Selznick, *TVA and the Grass Roots: A Study in the Sociology of Formal Organization* (New York: Harper and Row, 1966); and Roy E. Rickson, "Industrial Organizations and Environmental Quality: Some Questions for Sociologists" (Paper presented at the Southern Sociological Association Meetings, Miami, Florida, 1971).

3. A useful summary and review of sociologically slanted water resources literature up to 1968 may be found in R. N. Singh and Kenneth P. Wilkinson, *Social Science Studies of Water Resource Problems: Review of Literature and Annotated Bibliography* (State College: Water Resources Research Institute, Mississippi State University, 1968).

4. Samuel Z. Klausner, "Thinking Social-Scientifically about Environmental Quality," *Society and Its Physical Environment, Annals of the American Academy of Political and Social Science* 389 (May 1970): 5.

5. Ibid., p. 6.

6. U.S. Water Resources Council, "Procedures for Evaluation of Water and Related Land Resource Projects" (Washington, D.C.: Government Printing Office, 92nd Congress, 1st Session, Committee Print, no. 92-20, September 1971).

7. Singh and Wilkinson, *Social Science Studies of Water Resource Problems,* especially pp. 7-10.

8. Ibid. The author assumes full responsibility for the use of the generalizations presented here.

9. Ibid., p. 8.

10. The following discussion is based on Ibid., and Selznick, *TVA and the Grass Roots.*

11. Singh and Wilkinson, *Social Science Studies of Water Resources Problems,* p. 1.

12. Selznick, *TVA and the Grass Roots.*

13. Discussion based on Ibid.

14. William E. Folz, "The Economic Dynamics of River Basin Development," *Law and Contemporary Social Problems* 22 (1957): 205-20. Cited in Singh and Wilkinson, *Social Science Studies of Water Resources Problems,* p. 24.

15. The following generalizations are taken from Ibid., pp. 7-10. The author is responsible for their interpretation.

16. Carl F. Kraenzel, "The Social Consequences of River Basin Development," *Law and Contemporary Social Problems* 22 (1957): 221-36. Discussed in Ibid., p. 12.

17. Ibid., p. 35.

18. Ibid.

19. Wade H. Andrews and Dennis C. Geersten, *The Function of Social Behavior in Water Resource Development,* Research Report no. 1 (Logan: Institute for Social Science Research on Natural Resources and Center for Water Resources Research, Utah State University, 1970).

20. Rabel J. Burdge, John H. Sitterly, and Frank So, *Outdoor Recreation Research* (Columbus: Natural Resources Institute, Ohio State University, 1962), p. 17.

21. Wade H. Andrews and James L. Gillings, "Some Factors Affecting Social Change in Water Resources" (Paper presented at the Rural Sociological Society Meeting, San Francisco, 1967). Cited in Singh and Wilkinson, *Social Sciences Studies of Water Resource Problems,* pp. 37-38.

22. Paul M. Felton, "Citizen Action in Water—Asset or Liability?" in *Proceedings of the Fourth American Water Resources Conference,* Cohen and Francisco, pp. 304-9. Cited in *Water Resources Abstract 3,* 18 (15 September 1970): 58.

23. Discussed in Rabel J. Burdge, "Comments on Sociology and Water Resource Management" (Unpublished Manuscript, Department of Sociology, University of Kentucky, 1970), p. 7; Desmond M. Connor and Keith T. Bradley, *Public Participation in the St. John River Basin* (Washington, D.C.: Preprint of Conference Proceedings scheduled for publication by the American Society of Civil Engineers, 1972).

24. Thomas E. Barton, Katherine P. Warner, and J. William Wenrick, "The Susquehanna Communication-Participation Study: Selected Approaches to Public Involvement in Water Resources Planning" (Alexandria, Va. and Michigan University: Institute for Water Resources, 1970). Cited in *Water Resource Abstracts 7,* 1 (1 September 1970): 54.

25. Norman Wengart, "Public Participation in Water Planning. A Critique of Theory, Doctrine and Practice," *Water Resources Bulletin 7,* 1 (February 1971): 26-32.

26. David Brune, "Citizen Action in Water," in *Proceedings of the Fourth American Water Resources Conference,* Cohen and Francisco, pp. 296-303.

27. Connor and Bradley, *Public Participation in St. John River Basin*, p. 2.

28. Ibid., p. 5.

29. Henry Hart, cited in Singh and Wilkinson, *Social Science Studies of Water Resources Problems*, p. 38.

30. Donald F. Smith, "Changing Public Opinion: Problems and Prospects," in *Proceedings of a Conference on Water Resources Planning and Public Opinion* (Lincoln: University of Nebraska, 1971), pp. 45-49. Cited in *Water Resource Abstracts 4*, 16 (15 August 1971): 52; Everett M. Rogers and Rabel J. Burdge, *Social Change in Rural Societies* (New York: Appleton-Century-Crofts, 1972), pp. 273-78.

31. The following discussion illustrates the utility of using well-substantiated findings from other areas of sociology in the study of water resource problems. Everett Rogers and his associates are probably the best-known representative of diffusion research in the field. See especially Rogers and Burdge, *Social Change in Rural Societies* and Everett Rogers and F. Floyd Shoemaker, *Communication of Innovations* (New York: The Free Press, 1971).

32. Harry M. Satterfield, "The Removal of Family from Tennessee Valley Authority Reservoir Areas," *Social Forces* 16, no. 2 (December 1937): 258-61.

33. Charles R. Smith, "Economic Institutions as Social Indicators" (Paper presented at the Symposium of American Society for Ethnohistory, Ithaca, N.Y., 1969). Cited in *Water Resource Abstracts 4*, 8 (April 1971): 58.

34. Charles R. Smith, *Anticipation of Change, A Socioeconomic Description of a Kentucky County Before Reservoir Construction*, Research Report no. 28 (Lexington: Kentucky Water Resources Institute, 1970).

35. Rabel Burdge and Richard L. Ludtke, *Factors Affecting Relocation in Response to Reservoir Development*, Research Report no. 39 (Lexington: Kentucky Water Resources Institute, 1970). Richard L. Ludtke and Rabel Burdge, *Evaluation of the Social Impact of Reservoir Construction on the Residential Plans of Displaced Persons in Kentucky and Ohio*, Research Report no. 26 (Lexington: Kentucky Water Resources Institute, 1970).

36. Catherine J. Becker and Rabel J. Burdge, "The Effects of Familism, Traditionalism, and Socio-Economic Status on Attitudes Toward Reservoir Construction in an Eastern Kentucky County" (Paper presented at the Rural Sociological Society Meetings, Denver, Colorado, 1971).

37. Vince Webb and Gordon L. Bultena, "Attitudinal Change Toward Reservoir Construction: A Test of Reference Group Theory" (Paper presented at the Rural Sociological Society Meetings, Denver, Colorado, 1971).

38. Thomas C. Hogg, "Social and Cultural Impacts of Water Development," in *People and Water*, Director, Emery N. Castle (Corvallis: Seminar Conducted at the Oregon State University Water Resources Research Institute, 1968), pp. 11-23.

39. Ibid., p. 14.

40. Gilbert G. Stamm, "Water Development and Society," in *Sociological Aspects of Water Resources Research*, ed. Wade H. Andrews, Report no. 1 (Logan: Social Science Institute Series, Utah State University, 1968): 82.

41. Clyde T. Bates, *The Effects of a Large Reservoir on Local Government Revenue and Expenditure*. Research Report no. 23 (Lexington: Kentucky Water Resources Institute, 1970).

42. Aside from pollution and the effects of water systems in the nation, many significant sociological studies appear in this area, though I have not given it representative attention, because these studies are well-represented by such publications as the *Journal of Leisure Research*.

43. Abbott E. Ferriss, "The Social and Personality Correlates of Outdoor Recreation," in *Society and Its Physical Environment*, pp. 63-70.

44. *Outdoor Recreation for America*, A Report to the President and the Congress by the Outdoor Recreation Resources Review Commission (Washington, D.C.: Government Printing Office, 1962), p. 42.

45. L. Douglas James and Robert R. Lee, *Economics of Water Resources Planning* (New York: McGraw-Hill, 1971), p. 395.

46. Charles J. Cicchetti, Joseph J. Seneca, and Paul Davidson, *The Demand and Supply of Outdoor Recreation*, (New Brunswick: Bureau of Economics Research, Rutgers, The State University of New Jersey, 1969), p. 207.

47. Rabel J. Burdge, "Levels of Occupational Prestige and Leisure Activity," *Journal of Leisure Research* 1, no.3 (Summer 1969), pp. 262-74.

48. John V. Krutilla and Jack L. Knetsch, "Outdoor Recreation Economics," in *Society and Its Physical Environment*, pp. 63-70.

49. Dean R. Yoesting and Don L. Burkhead, *Sociological Aspects of Water-Based Recreation in Iowa*, Sociology Report no. 94 (Ames: Sociological Studies in Leisure and Environmental Resources, Iowa State University, 1971).

50. Barry Lentnek, Carlton S. Van Doren and James R. Trail, "Spatial Behavior in Recreational Boating," *Journal of Leisure Research* 1, no. 2 (Spring 1969): 103-24.

51. Carlton S. Van Doren and Barry Lentnek, "Activity Specialization Among Ohio's Recreation Boaters," *Journal of Leisure Research* 1, no. 4 (Autumn 1969: 296-315.

52. Malcolm I. Bevins et al., *Characteristics of Hunters and Fishermen in Six Northeastern States*, Bulletin no. 656 (Burlington: Northeastern Regional Research Publication, Agricultural Experiment Station, University of Vermont, 1968).

53. Kenneth P. Wilkinson, *Local Action and Acceptance of Watershed Development*, (State College: Water Resources Research Institute, Mississippi State University, 1966), p. 19.

54. Ibid.

55. This is also discussed in Singh and Wilkinson, *Social Science Studies of Water Resource Problems*, pp. 29-30.

56. Wilkinson, *Local Action and Acceptance of Watershed Development*.

57. Singh and Wilkinson, *Social Science Studies of Water Resource Problems*, p. 30.

58. Ibid.

59. Ibid.

60. Carl B. Brown, "Developments on the Small Watershed Approach to Flood Prevention and Conservation," *Journal of Soil and Water Conservation* 10 (1955): 13-18. Cited in Ibid.

61. John H. Peterson, Jr., *Community Organization and Rural Water System Development* (State College: Water Resources Research Institute, Mississippi State University, 1971).

62. Satadal Dasgupta, *Attitudes of Local Residents Toward Watershed Development*, Preliminary Report no. 18 (State College: Social Science Research Center, Mississippi State University, 1967) cited in Singh and Wilkinson, *Social Science Studies of Water Resource Problems*, pp. 36-37.

63. John H. Peterson, Jr. and Peggy J. Ross, *Changing Attitudes Toward Watershed Development* (State College: Water Resource Research Institute, Mississippi State College, 1971).

64. Kenneth P. Wilkinson and R. N. Singh, *Community Leadership and Watershed Development* (State College: Water Resources Research Institute, Mississippi State College, 1970).

65. Thomas C. Hogg and Courtland L. Smith, *Socio-Cultural Impacts of Water Resource Development in Santiam River Basin* (Oregon Water Resources Institute Report WRRI-5, 1970). Cited in *Water Resources Abstracts 4*, 12 (15 June 1971): 65.

66. John A. Ballweg and Charles A. Ibsen, "Water Resources as Social Problems," *Water Resources Bulletin* 7, 5 (October 1971): 935-40.

67. Rogers and Burdge, *Social Change in Rural Societies;* and Rogers and Shoemaker, *Communication of Innovations*.

68. Rogers and Shoemaker, *Communication of Innovations*, pp. 347-49.

69. Rogers and Burdge, *Social Change in Rural Societies*.

70. Rogers and Shoemaker, *Communication of Innovations*, pp. 365-68.

71. This is based on a discussion of their work by Burdge, "Comments on Sociology and Water Resource Management."

72. Rogers and Burdge, *Social Change in Rural Societies*, p. 347.

73. These generalizations are culled from Rogers and Shoemaker, *Communication of Innovations;* Rogers and Burdge, *Social Change in Rural Societies;* and Strodbeck in *Social Sciences and the Environment*.

74. James and Lee, *Economics of Water Resources Planning*, p. 114.

75. Strodbeck in *Social Sciences and the Environment*.

76. Ibid., pp. 108-9.

77. Kenneth H. Craik, "The Environmental Dispositions of Environmental Decision-Makers," in *Society and Its Physical Environment*, p. 90.

78. C. Michael York, *Attitudes and Attitude Change in Relation to Water Resources* (OWRR Completion Report, 1970), cited in *Water Resources Abstracts 3*, 20 (15 July 1970):59. Also, "A Feasibility Study in Communications Effectiveness Evaluating a Persuasive Film Relating to a Water Issue" (Atlanta: Addendum to Report WRC no. 569, Water Resources Center, Georgia Institute of Technology, 1969), cited in 15 July 1970 *Water Resources Abstracts*.

79. Tom T. Sasaki, "Socio-Cultural Problems in Introducing New Technology on a Navaho Irrigation Project," *Rural Sociology* 21: 307-10. Cited in Singh and Wilkinson, *Social Science Studies of Water Resource Problems*, pp. 32-33.

80. Irving A. Spaulding, *Household Water Use and Social Status*, Bulletin no. 392 (Kingston: Agricultural Experiment Station, University of Rhode Island, 1967).

81. Bernard Berelson and Gary A. Steiner, *Human Behavior* (New York: Harcourt, Brace, and World, Inc., 1964), p. 593.

82. Singh and Wilkinson, *Social Science Studies of Water Resource Problems*, p. 23.

83. Klausner, *Society and Its Physical Environment*, p. 5.

84. Ibid.

85. Lynton K. Caldwell, "Authority and Responsibility for Environmental Administration," in *Society and Its Physical Environment*, p. 107.

86. Ibid., p. 110.

87. Klausner, *Society and Its Physical Environment*, p. 9.

88. Burdge, "Comments on Sociology and Water Resource Management," pp. 10-12.

89. Rickson, "Industrial Organizations and Environmental Quality," p. 5.

90. Ibid., p. 3.

91. William R. Burch, "Resources and Social Structure: Some Conditions of Stability and Change," in *Society and Its Physical Environment*, pp. 27-40. Quoted by Klausner, *Society and Its Physical Environment*, p. 7.

92. Rickson, "Industrial Organizations and Environmental Quality," p. 7.

93. Ibid., p. 8.

94. Ibid., p. 9.

95. Ibid.

96. Ibid.

97. There appears to be some uncertainty surrounding this particular finding. Cf. Joseph Harry, Richard P. Gale, and John Hendee, "Conservation: An Upper-Middle Class Social Movement," *Journal of Leisure Research* 1, no. 3 (Summer 1969), pp. 246-54; and William B. Devall, "Conservation: An Upper-Middle Class Social Movement: A Replication," *Journal of Leisure Research* 2, no. 2 (Spring 1970), pp. 123-26.

98. Irving A. Spaulding, *Social Class Variation in Attitudes and Conceptualizations*

Pertaining to Water Pollution and Supply (Rhode Island: Rhode Island Water Resources Center, n.d.). Also, Irving A. Spaulding, "Public Knowledge of Water Pollution and Supply" in *Concerns in Water Supply and Pollution Control: Legal, Social and Economic,* Bulletin no. 1 (Kingston, University of Rhode Island Community Planning and Area Development, 1971): 14-19.

99. Charles A. Ibsen and John A. Ballweg, "Public Perception of Water Resource Problems," in *Water Resources Research Bulletin* 29 (September 1969). Cited in *Water Resources Abstracts 3,* no. 6 (15 March 1970), p. 49.

100. Elizabeth L. David, "Public Perception of Water Quality," *Water Resources Research 7,* no. 3 (June 1971), pp. 453-57.

101. Klausner, *Society and Its Physical Environment,* p. 7.

102. Ibid.

103. Caldwell, in *Society and Its Physical Environment,* p. 107.

104. Craik, in *Society and Its Physical Environment,* p. 89.

105. Rickson, "Industrial Organizations and Environmental Quality," p. 10.

106. Robin Williams, *American Society* (New York: Alfred A. Knopf: 1970), pp. 592-609.

107. James and Lee, *Economics of Water Resources Planning,* p. 116.

108. Williams, *American Society,* p. 592-609.

7 Reviews and Observations

L. Douglas James

This book began with a challenge to the social sciences. Many social choices are made in almost complete ignorance of their consequences, and the social sciences possess an expertise that can make it possible for decisions to be based on better information. By using their expertise, social scientists can increase the probability that the choices made, by individuals or by society as a whole, will be in mankind's best interest in the long run.

Some of the most important social choices are those that influence or direct the development and adoption of innovative technology. The technology used in this book as the data source for a case study is that of water resources management. The specific guidance water resources planners want from the social sciences is help in focusing attention on new alternatives, more reliable forecasting of the consequences of those alternatives under consideration, determining what people really want, implementing selected choices, and monitoring the social consequences of selected policy. Representatives of five social sciences—anthropology, economics, geography, political science, and sociology—addressed the contributions made by their discipline, the problems their discipline could help solve, and the incentives for scientists in their discipline to work on these problems. The purpose of this final section is to assess the response of the social scientists.

The assessment is in three parts. The first part examines reactions obtained from colleagues of each author in order to gauge the readiness of each discipline to contribute to practical problem solving. The second part examines the reactions to the set of five papers by individuals knowledgeable and experienced in the practical problems of water resources management in order to see what kind of constructive suggestions they have for more fruitful interaction between planners, engineers, and social scientists. The third part is an analysis of the challenge, the papers, and the reactions first from my viewpoint, as a water resources engineer, and second from the viewpoint of a social scientist more familiar with his discipline than with practical water management problems.

This organization is deliberately chosen to focus attention on the importance to water management policy of increasing the contribution of the social sciences, on the kind of contribution needed, and on ways to increase that contribution. A chapter organization placing all comments relating to a given discipline under a separate heading would make it easy for a reader from a given discipline to concentrate on his narrow interests; however, water management problems do not neatly classify by social science disciplines. Many comments apply to the social sciences as a whole, and no one readily distinguishes among the roles the various social sciences should take. Interdisciplinary problem solving requires a concept of the total problem before any expertise can find its own role, and it is the total problem that is addressed in this section.

DISCIPLINE REVIEWS

Each paper from the social sciences in this book is the work of a specific author. Because viewpoints on contributions, problems, and incentives vary in any discipline, each paper was sent out for review by others within the same discipline known to have professional interest and experience with water management problems. One objective was to use the resulting comments to strengthen the papers; but, as it turned out, the variation among the disciplines in review content gave some valuable insights into the readiness of a given discipline to contribute to solving practical management problems.

Generally speaking, the disciplines displaying greater agreement between the author and his reviewers showed a clearer understanding of water management problems, had accomplished more toward solving them, and had expanded their theoretical base by doing so. The disciplines displaying greater controversy showed uncertainty as to what the problems were and had fewer substantive contributions to mention. While social scientists like to delay applications while they debate how much theory must be acquired in order to solve practical problems, the empirical evidence is that those social scientists who understand the problems are able to demonstrate progress toward solving them even though they have minimal theory to apply. Furthermore, they find that their work contributes to developing their discipline's theoretical base as well. The ability to grasp the problems and the reasons that they are not being solved seem to be a key to producing research results that will contribute to solving real world problems.

Anthropology

Anthropology differs from the other social sciences in its approach to water resources management. Whereas the other four disciplines emphasize a data base directly reflecting current problems and sometimes cite the same studies, anthropology has developed a literature from a historical data base. Other social scientists and water planners are almost totally unfamiliar with that literature, even though it provides many valuable insights. Bennett's work is a pioneer attempt to review an extensive series of important studies pertaining to water management.

The other social sciences display a greater tendency to seek universal solutions expressed in purely qualitative terms. Societies, modern ones more than ever, contain a diversity of cultures; small groups vary widely in consensus viewpoints. A social science that tries to prescribe for all situations from the same criteria is suffering from the naive oversimplification that society can have a commonality of goals. Anthropology has avoided this trap in studying a diversity of societies without trying to force their value systems and physical and social settings into a common mold, that is, specify a universal water management policy. One review pointed out the need for a strong statement that no *single* set of goals should be developed to guide water management decision making. Anthropology can make its greatest contribution by developing ways for examining any group or culture to determine the water management goals that best meet its needs. The question is what properties of a group of people should be measured and how should those measurements be used to establish the best policy for a given situation.

Economics

Of all the social sciences, economics has the most extensive literature and has made the most impact on water resources management. Where the other authors could review our present state of knowledge and future research needs by listing papers on topics of interest, the extent of the economics literature required instead a thoughtful review of what the profession has done and should be doing. An exhaustive literature review would fill several volumes. The need was to concentrate on major contributions in order to clarify the role of economics in water management.

One consequence of this approach was the frequent mention of literature that the reviewer felt the author should not have omitted.

Economics has avoided the trap of universal solutions by concentrating on decision rules. The economist has a systematic procedure for collecting and analyzing information in order to determine whether or not a given proposal is wise. He will often support one dam while opposing another based on how the two rate according to his test. The political scientist, as a contrasting example, is more likely to favor the reduction of the number of small governmental jurisdictions as a general rule without seeking hard information on specific merits in a given situation.

Geography

While geography does not have the massive literature that economics does, both literature and contributions are extensive; and the same approach of thoughtful review was used by the author. Again, the reviewers expressed general agreement with the author but pressed for a fuller explanation or the mention of some additional item in the literature.

Geography rejects universal solutions and seeks recognition of a fuller range of management alternatives. The discipline strives to broaden awareness of the many possible human adjustments to water management problems. It seeks a fuller understanding of the individual perception of alternatives and the characteristics of the perceptions that favor certain choices. Water planners are provided with a greater variety of approaches in their search for the best choice.

Political Science

The initial version of the political science paper displayed considerable difficulty in integrating a variety of studies by political scientists into a central theme. Its reviews revealed considerable disagreement among political scientists over what the theme should be and over the extent to which their discipline should be concerned with water management problems. The final version of the paper was then structured around a search for some ordering to the political science of water management decisions.

The discipline as a whole has not been able to change focus from universal to specific solutions. One reviewer noted that the approach to administration most widely held by political scientists is based upon a simple hierarchical model which presumes a unity of purpose and a linear chain of control reaching from the top to the bottom of the administrative establishment. An example is the traditional concern over administrative fragmentation accompanied by expressions of need for integrated, metropolitan government. The opposing viewpoint within the discipline is that a polycentric political system may be more efficient and responsive.[1] Research is needed to establish whether this view is correct. The fact that this kind of question is now being asked within political science is a very good sign that the discipline is on the verge of making a more substantive contribution to better water management.

The new objective involves searching for an analytical theory that can portray institutional capabilities and anticipate institutional failures and thus prove useful to decision makers concerned with preventing rather than curing water management problems. The failure of the water practitioners to respond to the unifying models of the 1950s and the failure of the discipline to respond more quickly to prototype diversity may well account for the recent period of decline of interest of political scientists in water.

One value of studying polycentric decision making is the insight it gives into the various centers or levels in which decisions are made. Political scientists have for some time studied the roles of interest groups and other influences on legislative behavior. More recently, they have shown increased interest in decision making at the local level within structured local government, as well as informally among people interacting in small groups. One reviewer noted how different groups work in different ways to influence decisions. Some provide publicity. Some influence votes. Some use money to promote causes. Some work on bureaucrats in office with various types of persuasion. Some approaches are effective in situations where others are at a disadvantage. Some groups are advantaged and others are disadvantaged by any given organizational arrangement. Political science can contribute greatly to better water resource management by providing better means for predicting the consequences of alternative organizational arrangements for decision making.

Sociology

The involvement of sociologists in water resources management is more recent than that of the other social sciences. The typical reviewer mentioned areas that sociologists have studied, largely in contexts having very little to do with water resources but which might be applicable to the solution of water resources management problems. The consensus both inside and outside the discipline seems to be that sociologists have made a very small contribution to date, but that they have potential to make a very meaningful one because they have expertise of the sort needed to advise on major water resources management issues.

The fact that the contribution of sociology is in an earlier stage of development than that of the other social sciences is seen in the propensity of the discipline to prescribe general solutions rather than procedures for generating specific ones. Sociologists are prone to do empirical studies that are poorly linked to social theory or to be uncritical in applying the theory they use. They need to concentrate on defining the sociological elements of problems, on finding better ways to collect data, and on integrating their findings with theory. Sociologists have much to contribute in developing problem-solving approaches as well as to resolving the larger questions of population control, environmental quality, and social values.

The Holistic Viewpoint

All five papers (and this chapter as well) reveal a propensity to take a holistic viewpoint. Everyone wants to provide a general critique of the overall situation from a detached perspective. No one can deny that holistic analysis is valuable. Many water development projects have been poorly planned because they applied a narrowly conceived approach. Yet, it is also true that each discipline has a unique set of theory, empirical data, data-gathering methods, and viewpoint; planning is likely to suffer even more if any discipline fails to develop and apply its own expertise. Social scientists must be careful not to spend so much time looking at the forest that they do not see the trees, even as they object correctly to engineer planners doing the reverse.

VIEWPOINT REVIEWS

In the 1950s, water resources development was widely supported by the American public. Most people wanted more dams, channelized waterways, swamp drainage, and other projects. The few who objected mentioned such grounds as a preference for development of revenue-producing facilities by private enterprise or a belief that expenditures should be minimized to reduce deficit spending or taxes. Others supported the overall program and limited their objections to particular projects that they believed were not economically justified. Nevertheless, the people who perceived that they and the country as a whole would benefit from continued water development were in a strong majority and strong enough politically to build projects that were economically marginal at best. Thoughtful analysts expressed the opinion that development schemes had suffered because they were not planned as carefully as they would have been had the opposition been stronger.

The leadership of the agencies charged with water resources development were convinced of the social importance of their programs and wanted the help of the social scientist in expediting plans and selling them to the public. Even in the social sciences, the prevailing mood seemed to be that continued expansion of the public sector through resource development was in the public interest and that opposition to the program was largely from special interest groups who would undermine the public welfare for selfish reasons.

Engineer planners recognized that some development proposals were undesirable and that every project requires sacrifice by some so that others can gain. They did not want to be involved in projects that could in the long run threaten their ability to serve the public. Engineer planners knew that by building undesirable or undesired projects, they could create an adverse climate. The role they saw for social scientists was to help in the review of the many projects proposed by the public in order to choose the most worthy and to improve the designs and presentation to the public of the projects accepted for implementation. The emphasis, however, often seemed to be on how to sell the program rather than on how to reach better decisions.

The years since have brought a growing opposition to continued water resource development. Many now perceive an environmental loss each time anything in nature is modified by man. Empirical evidence is accumulating that losses to the "naturalness" of man's surroundings may in the long run be detrimental to his psychological well-being. Others are concerned over the ability of ecological systems essential to man's life support to withstand the pressures of intensified competition for space. The pollution problem is particularly critical. The collective effect is a growing support for the viewpoint that further water resources development as well as other manifestations of economic growth must be sacrificed in order to maintain the quality of life. A growing group of social scientists now see the promoters of resource development as the ones who would undermine the public welfare for selfish reasons.

As the conflicts between project promoters and environmental preservers become more clearly defined, it becomes evident that most people support both sides. Individuals who oppose the environmental consequences of building a new power plant would also object if they could no longer have electric power whenever they wanted it. Professionals see a situation where it is increasingly critical to find new ways to minimize the conflict between resource development and social and environmental factors, ways to maximize power production within the constraint of acceptable environmental disruption, for example. Agency administrators are seeking professional help to effect this same type of compromise.

One can picture a continuum with individuals at one extreme favoring reconciliation of all conflicts in favor of economic growth and with those at the other extreme favoring reconciliation in favor of preserving the environment. The attitude a person takes toward the role of the social sciences in water resources management is influenced by his position between these extremes. An individual tends to believe that the social sciences have a responsibility to substantiate the type of reconciliation that he believes to be right. It is a bias of the type discussed at length in the economics paper.

The set of five discipline papers in the body of this book were reviewed by representatives of seven different viewpoints: 1) agriculture, 2) conservation, 3) engineering, 4) law, 5) state water planning, 6) federal water resources implementation, and 7) federal water resources policy. The representative from agriculture defended the necessity of continued water resources development to meet man's need for food and fiber. The views of the representative from a leading conservationist group fell toward the environmental end of the continuum. The representatives from engineering and law saw the need to develop sound and effective means for compromising diverse viewpoints. The representatives from government seemed more committed to getting help from the disciplines in deciding what to do than in getting reinforcement for any preconceived policy.

Each of the seven reviewers was asked: 1) to assess the usefulness of the papers from the five social sciences from his viewpoint, 2) to discuss the practical water management problems for which help from the social sciences is needed for effective resolution, and 3) to suggest ways whereby the social sciences might become more effective in solving major management problems. The balance of this section presents and discusses their comments. In some cases (particularly political science and sociology), the authors of the five social science papers have revised their original drafts to the point where it will be difficult for the readers to pinpoint specific passage mentioned by the reviewer, but these instances, too, add insight to the total situation.

First Viewpoint: Agriculture

Substance of the Comments: Allen Grant, president, California Farm Bureau, observed that agriculturists do not consider themselves students of the sciences relating to water resources management. Their interest is in the better management the sciences makes possible or, more precisely, the more efficient water service careful management can provide for agriculture. The reviewer felt that each social scientist submitted ideas which could contribute to fuller resource utilization. He did not feel it appropriate for conservationists to condemn agriculture for pushing for fuller resource development. Technologically, the industry is highly dependent on water. Greater populations and higher standards of living require more food and fiber, and more food and fiber can only be grown with more water. If agriculture does not press for more water, it will not be able to deliver more food. Such a failure would be contrary to the moral responsibility of the industry.

Those who want water don't care who takes the initiative or who does the job nearly as much as they want to see the job done. They have a hard time understanding the difficulties of the social scientists in defining the role of their discipline. For example, why should an economist be troubled professionally by being "used" to justify a project that provides water to people who need it? They have difficulty understanding the need for complicated constructs to improve decision making in government when they see failures to use common sense in daily decisions. They see the social sciences as making "simple" things unduly complicated.

Observations: The propensity of social scientists to classify, define, and protect professional territories is not contributing to the image of the disciplines held by laymen. Those seeking a solution to a specific problem are not impressed by discussions of boundaries among disciplines, by efforts to enhance professional status, or by reasons social scientists give for confining efforts to intellectually satisfying subjects. Those pushing for water resources development and hearing numerous complaints that such development is ignoring important social factors are particularly disgruntled when the "experts" cannot tell them how to do a better job. No matter what reasons social scientists can give for not providing practical advice for decision making, those who feel the impact of poor management are judging the social sciences by their lack of contribution. Disciplines that cannot help the public are going to lose popular support in the long run—financial support as well as top-quality students.

Social scientists have studied the reasons individuals fail to work together to solve common problems and have found and tried to explain the reasons behind time series of erroneous perceptions, misunderstandings, incomplete information, biased communications, and resistance to change. It seems to the lay reviewer that similar patterns occur in papers by social scientists. This criticism of social science does not deny that rigidity in the thinking of agriculturists can also be an obstacle to efficient water resources management. Farmers want more water for their farms, but they are not maximizing crop yield from the water they have. The point is that from the viewpoint of agriculture, social scientists are not behaving rationally either. The situation suggests a polarization between the academic social sciences and people with practical problems; social scientists need to consider this situation carefully.

The social sciences cannot afford to overlook the need to study the sociological structure of their own disciplines and how that organization affects their capacity to practical problem solving. As noted by Bugliarello, important factors include the sociological characteristics of professional societies, publication policies of prestige journals, viewpoints of academic leaders, communication systems within a discipline, educational systems, reward systems, and other relationships among professionals.[2] He goes on to state that the educational "system boosts skills, but at the same time, it can exclude some that would be innovators, who fail to meet the standards set by those who are within the system."[3] Much the same statement could be made for the communication and reward systems individually or for all three systems collectively. It is a topic that the academic community needs to consider carefully.

Second Viewpoint: Conservation

Substance of the Comments: Roland C. Clement, vice president, National Audubon Society, found the papers on the role of the social sciences in water management both helpful and timely. They are helpful because they sketch in a missing perspective for those who specialize in other areas but want to take a look at the socioeconomic and ecological implications of water use in the context of national land-use policy and nonpolicy. The papers are timely because this broadening of horizons is now a national phenomenon.

The introduction could have been much more insistent on new assessments, given the general consensus that we face a crisis of confidence in existing water-use approaches. The emphasis on the aggregate consequences of many thoughtless little choices that need to be brought into the conscious realm is worthwhile. Certainly the tyranny of small decisions is a psychosocial fact and a major human problem that the sociologist and the economist can help resolve.

The task of the scientist is to close the gap between theory and practice, to build models that respond well under field conditions. But since planners and engineers have made their share of blunders—more than they have admitted—the only cause for meekness in the social scientists is their failure to get involved in these problems much earlier, when they could have helped to prevent many rueful blunders.

This, of course, is hindsight, and this demand for forcefulness might have seemed inappropriate when the symposium was in progress and the participants were uncertain of the staying power of the wave of environmental awareness. Even so, the papers fail to assess the role of the Congress in perverting so many "public" issues and in preventing application of as high a level of technical and socioeconomic rationality as the practitioners could provide. The task of science is not merely to engage in dialogue but to provide critical assessments of both alternatives and performance.

The overview of the anthropologist's contributions is provocative and sweeping in its inclusiveness. It is good to be reminded that man in all parts of the world and in all climatic regions has evolved a multitude of techniques for making water do his bidding. The big dam, so popular today, is only one of these, and not always the wisest investment. Nowhere are the failures to anticipate the full social costs of large water projects more tragic than in the dislocations visited upon the primitive peoples of tropical regions by the ecologically untested development of large man-made lakes.

It would indeed be helpful if anthropologists articulated a more functional theory relating the growth and decline of civilizations to water policy. The relationship stems from the universal importance of water resources and the heavy financial burden that water management imposes in the early stages of economic development. The historical evidence that ancient irrigation systems, as their modern counterparts, often did not have sufficient capital reserves assigned to maintenance is an important reminder. Even when such projects were not premature, the failure to capitalize them fully may often have been a piece of legerdemain designed to ease sale to the public; the reaction to such deception may be one of several reasons why the public's willingness to be taxed varies so much with time.

The emphasis on the difference between disguising predetermined decisions with economic language, and active use of economic concepts to guide management decisions is a heartening acknowledgment of a specialist's divorcement from living reality that the intellectual must face. This substitution of the form for the substance of economics is surely at the heart of the public distrust of economists. This frank statement illustrates the importance of specialist insights, just as one must often use a thief to catch a thief. One hopes that other economists will hereafter join in clarifying this confusion by speaking out on the issues.

The geography contribution is thoughtful. It is heartening to compare the changes in the public valuation of environmental effects to the Oklahoma Land Rush, this time an intellectual and moral stake-out rather than one of land. But it is disappointing that the author's sixth element of decision making, the "social guide," which helps constrain or advance the other elements by drawing lessons from past activities, is not better supported by examples. The reason, of course, is that we have hardly ever assessed postproject conditions and thus have not been able to provide a satisfactory measure of attainment of socioeconomic goals through structural solutions to water problems.

The contribution from political science emphasizes Arthur Maass's novel thesis that the community at large reaches agreement upon collective purposes and that the state merely provides the means for focusing on issues and for translating agreement into action. It would have been helpful to have a more critical assessment of Maass's idealized view; the literature does contain several rejoinders. Here, the role of the Congress is a crucial interface, and the behavior of agencies like the Corps of Engineers has certainly complicated the decision process. The Corps, for example, though it is an executive agency, has over the years been much more responsive to members of Congress than to the Chief Executive. The Corps has shown willingness to change, but this is a slow, uncomfortable process. Exposing the constraints to change would facilitate the evolution of more independently responsible governmental agencies.

Observations: The theme from the conservation movement is that the social sciences should concentrate on understanding and rectifying the decision processes that have fostered management mistakes. The theme is negative in its emphasis on ways to prevent future failure rather than to enhance future successes. Neither does it squarely face the issues which must be resolved in reconciling differences of opinion. One man may praise the very decision another calls a mistake, and the role of the social sciences is much broader than selling the public on the value of either development or conservation.

One of the most timely suggestions from this review is in its expression of the need for a series of case studies of the choice processes that have led to what later came to be widely recognized as unwise, or disastrous, management policy. The results could be very helpful in establishing mechanisms to guide future decision making. Past choice processes should also be explored for forces or processes (within academic circles, professional societies, government agencies, and others) that restrict employment of all the know-how at the social scientist's command in formulating improved management policy. Congress has indeed restrained, if not perverted as some have alleged, the planning process by forcing the adoption of policies and projects later proven to be unwise and by preventing the adoption of those later found to be sound. Lower-level political bodies and all levels of administrative agencies have done the same.

The social sciences need to work for a better understanding of the biases within existing choice processes. What kinds of bias are inherent in the various forms of institutionalized decision making and what can be done to minimize them? The suggested functional theory of how resource use relates to the rise and fall of civilizations may well lead to interesting discoveries about how institutional biases change over the history of a society. The primary issue may not be one of controlling the misuse of resources to prevent subsequent suffering. It may be one of preventing institutions from becoming so inflexible that they refuse to adjust resource management policy with changing conditions and thereby cause suffering when pressures for resource reallocation bring the system to the point of collapse. Social breakdown caused by inflexible institutions is a much more frequent historical phenomenon than that caused by the collapse of technological systems.

The factors that make processes irreversible are more social than physical because the physical world is more easily changed back into a former state than are people. A dam can be removed. With nominal expenditure for restoration and with the passage of time, the countryside will approach its original form. It would, that is, if it were not for social processes such as the patterns of settlement, industrial development, and transportation that the dam stimulated, and the influences these processes had through secondary and tertiary linkage to still other processes. The social sciences need to determine the aspects of social processes that are reversible and those that are irreversible and to assess the kinds and relative effectiveness of strategies available for achieving reversal.

Third Viewpoint: Engineering

Substance of the Comments: Harvey O. Banks, consulting engineer, commented that the engineering practitioner perceives many issues that the social sciences possess the expertise to help resolve, but he has experienced little success in incorporating that expertise into planning, developing, or managing water resource systems. In the planning process, the engineer-planner is required to address a specific need or to solve a defined problem. He rarely has the option of waiting for all the information he would like and is forced to draw upon his judgment and skill in dealing with uncertainty while comparing available alternatives. The social factors that he considers while operating in this context are those imposed by the community for which he is working or those he has learned during his past exposures to the social sciences.

The engineer simply does not know how to make social scientists active and effective in the planning process with which he is familiar. Furthermore, the five papers are not much help in overcoming this practical problem. He asks: How and when in the time stream of planning, study, and decision making can the expertise of social scientists be effectively introduced? How can their contribution to the examination of the water resource problem be made in such a way, and at such a time, as to make the social scientists active participants in the decision making and to share the responsibility for the effects of the decisions reached?

It is a willingness to accept responsibility that is required before social scientists can assume their proper role in water resource management. The engineer-planner must live with the solution he recommends. Too frequently in the past (to some degree this attitude is reflected in the five papers) the social scientist has confined himself to critical review on an after-the-fact basis. When his critiques affected subsequent policy, he remained comfortably shielded in the academic community from the consequences of his recommendations.

The question addressed by the papers of the symposium may be the wrong questions for eliciting affirmative appraisal of the potential roles of social scientists in water resource development and management. Key questions not asked are what is the *responsibility* of the social scientist, as a professional with a valuable contribution to make, to seek active participation in water resource management decisions and implementation, and how can active participation be achieved? The question of incentives and rewards is largely irrelevant.

The five papers repeatedly discussed water resource development and management in terms of the construction of dams and reservoirs. A major reservoir project may be the most dramatic water resource development; however, such a project is generally only a part of the total system the engineer-planner uses to serve the community. With or without the before-the-fact participation of an interdisciplinary team of social scientists, the engineer-planner—if he is doing his job properly— must to the best of his ability and knowledge consider the range of social, environmental, and economic factors which relate to proper design. The social scientist needs to supplement the ability and knowledge of the planner.

The opening challenge makes a very clear statement of the many small choices through which, in the final analysis, society is selecting its course of resource development. Too frequently, the factors which enter into these small choices and the consequences of the choices are poorly understood by decision makers within the public sector. The social scientist could effectively begin his involvement by assuming the initiative for aggressively analyzing and publicizing his analysis of these small choices. The social scientist can best assist in formulating public policy and defining public goals by entering the process of public debate instead of waiting to comment upon the results of choices after they are made through political process. Decision making by small-scale choice processes is an area where the social scientist has particular training.

The design of workable mechanisms through which the contributions of social scientists can enter an early state of decision making is a problem that the academic community should assign a high priority. Too frequently, the clamor of the social scientist for consideration of values he believes were overlooked in resource development has been heard only after extensive investment of public funds in development and implementation of a resource plan, even though the fact that the project was under study was public knowledge and implementation was undertaken as the result of widespread public demand.

The anthropologist makes a very strong case for the involvement of the social anthropologist in planning water resource development by stating the benefits to be achieved through such involvement. His careful expression of the anthropologist's perspective of the relationship of water controls, conservation, water use, and environmental quality is both timely and constructive. His review of historic water systems is interesting and valuable, and it confirms the value of the anthropological and archeological method in studying and analyzing the past for lessons that can be applied to the solution of current problems.

However, his conclusion that large-scale water development may contribute both to rapid social and economic development and to ultimate longer-range sociopolitical disintegration appears to confuse cause and effect. Not all large-scale water resource development can be equated with "overdevelopment" because some situations are not amenable to small-scale solutions. Such situations must seek the full expertise of all disciplines to find solutions commensurate with the scale and complexity of the problem. Where a large-scale solution matches the problem in all its ramifications, it would appear likely that to implement it would enhance the social and political stability of the community on both the short- and the long- term bases.

The pressure that the political and economic imperatives for water resources development exerts against any delay in project implementation forces a degree of trial-and-error experimentation in social and ecological change. Certainly, many water resource development projects have not been fully pre-examined for the social and ecological changes that might result; however, the social scientist must share the responsibility. He has failed to analyze past developments for the purpose of drawing conclusions that can be translated into guidelines for the design of projects proposed for the future. Resource development projects have produced social and ecological consequences for thousands of years.

Perhaps the past experience could be most effectively used in assisting societies of the present to establish value systems within which resource development decisions can be made rationally. Unfortunately, values held by one segment of the community may be partially or totally in conflict with the values of another segment. Without a clear definition of these conflicts, to which the anthropologist should be able to make a valuable contribution, it is unlikely that the community can make objective choices.

The paper properly emphasizes the urgent need for anthropologists to concern themselves with contemporary practical problems of resource development. The author also points out, with commendable candor, the reasons why anthropologists are reluctant to become involved with such problems. It is to be hoped that the discipline will "discipline" itself and take a more constructive role in seeking the proper solutions to the increasingly complex problems of resource control, conservation, development, and utilization to satisfy human needs, both short and long range. Their contribution will be more than welcome.

The paper from economics properly emphasizes the need for economists to be involved in water resource planning decisions from the inception of a project through its formulation and final implementation. Most water resource planning agencies would concur in the value of the economist's contribution to the identification of alternative courses of action and to the selection among resource development alternatives. The author rightly protests the use of economists to justify decisions already reached, rather than as participants in the examination of the available alternatives. This has happened either as a result of a fundamentally poor approach to the planning process or from limitations in the planning agency's authority.

The paper makes an interesting point in setting forth the need to distinguish between economic concepts and economic language. From time to time, engineers and planners have felt that economists have retreated behind a wall of incomprehensible linguistic manipulation. The extent to which this has resulted from pressure from planning agencies to force economists into positions of justifying decisions dictated by other considerations, as opposed to an unconscious defense mechanism on the part of some economists to avoid accepting the responsibility for decisions taken, is problematical.

One problem engineers have had in using the expertise of economists is the wide range of recommendations with which they respond to a given problem. The engineer has learned that a group of economists will arrive at a wide diversity of answers when starting from a common problem and data base. The decision maker, therefore, tends to select that answer which best fits his preconceived views. If the results of economic analyses were more consistent, decision would be less biased.

The economics paper presents a constructive evaluation of the potential for interaction of economics with the other social sciences. This evaluation demonstrates again, however, the lack of clear distinctions among the social science disciplines. The social sciences could profitably interact to aggregate their approach in the early stages of planning for the manipulation of the environment to achieve social goals.

Measurement of nonmarket consequences of resource development programs may very well be outside the scope of economic evaluation. Current economic methodology provides no means by which nonmarket values may be balanced to set priorities on projects; and, here again, the engineer-planner is left with judgment based on qualitative evaluations. This does not in any way detract from the validity of the recommendation that nonmarket values should be a subject for continued economic research.

The geography paper notes several major recent changes in the approach the public desires to water resources management. These include an increased emphasis on considering more alternatives, an increased desire for research to answer complex issues, and a more resistant attitude in society toward manipulation of the environment. The paper clearly expresses the need for truly objective and interdisciplinary examination of the consequences of water resource development projects and for developing techniques for predicting the consequences of projects and programs under consideration. It recognizes the limitations in the achievements to date of the social scientists, either individually or as interdisciplinary teams, and then carefully considers the adjustments within and among the various disciplines that will be required to resolve the major issues.

The emphasis in geography of building a strong relationship among the social sciences in order to address the overlap in the various disciplines will certainly broaden the scope of analysis of water resource alternatives. The contributions of the social science team, however, will be affected by the questions asked by water planning agencies. Social scientists must assume the initiative in defining the help they can provide in the time framework in which the water resource planner and developer must reach decisions. The fact is that planners, as a whole, have a very poor concept of the types of questions the social scientist feels best qualified to answer.

The statement in the political science paper that political analysis of water resources development is relatively inactive but potentially fruitful raises a serious question as to the cause for the decline in interest by political scientists in public-works issues. All public-works investments must proceed from planning to implementation through the political arena. Why then, would political scientists have lost interest in this arena at this point in history when resource management decisions are so important to the public welfare? Is it because they have emphasized how the theory of political science can be enhanced by involvement in water resources? An emphasis on the contribution political science can make to the effective management of water resources would be much more productive to both groups. This preoccupation of the social sciences with building their own image may be creating major social problems by default.

Much of the paper deals with the appropriate level of government, and of geographic unit, for the various types of decision making required by water resource programs. The critical factor in moving any public-works project through the political process is involvement of the affected levels of government and the citizens participating in those levels of government. Keys to involvement are the intensity and the commonness of the public interest and the potential for engagement of the established political units in decisions. Probably no problem has more consistently plagued water resource development than poor decisions made because of limited public involvement.

The paper recognizes that the effectiveness of water resources decisions must be measured in terms of the full range of social and economic goals. The present concern with environmental quality may very well pose new questions to which the political scientists must give their attention and join with other social scientists in order to achieve effective yardsticks by which the consequence of various alternatives for water resources management can be measured.

The marketing of water project output is a question on which widely divergent opinions are held and vocalized. Charges for water use and for discharge of effluents into public waters are management tools whose end results are not clearly predictable. Whether effluent charges would achieve the desired enhancement of environmental quality or whether they would be regarded by the public as a continuing license to pollute, as many of us directly involved in environmental planning believe, is a subject for research by political scientists as well as economists. The problems confronting a regulatory agency are a fruitful field for the political scientist as he measures the effectiveness of regulatory practices in achieving the environmental goals that are becoming increasingly well defined both locally and nationally.

One must disagree with assertions that political science is less capable than geography and economics to help calculate water plans and that the political scientist's primary function is not to help design plans but to conduct "postaudits" to determine how decisions have been made in the past and what consequences follow. If the political scientist confines his study of water resource management to postaudits, the value of his contribution will be greatly reduced. The varying governmental requirements of different alternatives must be weighted as an integral part of formulating a sound plan. "Postaudits" yield much useful information, but a greater effort should be directed to solving current and foreseeable problems using information already available.

The sociologist recognized the potential use of water resource development programs as a tool in shaping the social and environmental climate of the community. She did not take the succeeding step, vital to the maximum realization of this potential, of setting forth a means for predictive comparison of the consequences of the alternatives for shaping the quality of life of a community. The paper notes the need for the ecologist and sociologist to work together to solve the problems of environmental impact; however, the compartmentalization of discipines may be a stumbling block among the social scientists. Perhaps some consideration should be given to an aggregation of interacting disciplines into a new group called *environmentalists.* Such an aggregation could accept the contributions of all social scientists—and hopefully natural scientists—to increase the probability that any manipulation of a resource, either social or natural, would contribute to the achievement of value goals commonly held by the society served.

Perhaps the true problem is that no aspect of water resource development is limited to the expertise of any one discipline. Recorded history— and probably unrecorded history—involves a long, broken sequence of conflicts involving water holes. These were not simply sociological conflicts—they have involved the geographers, the political scientists, the anthropologists, the economists, as well as warriors, demographers, geologists, engineers, politicians, and laymen. In retrospect, more sensitive channels for communication among the disciplines must be developed in order to achieve the constructive interaction of information from all fields of human knowledge relevant to water resources development. All the disciplines must dedicate some of their energy to breaking out of their own compartmentalized, self-justifying world into the more truly intellectual world of shared judgment and skill. They must become involved in actual water resource management.

A principal shortcoming of some of the papers is the almost complete preoccupation with academic research, largely of theoretical interest. Too little interest is demonstrated in active resolution of the day-by-day problems of management. Substantive involvement of the social science disciplines will come only at the time and to the degree that these disciplines participate in the solution of "gut" issues. Is water development an appropriate tool for shaping social structure? If so, what are the effective interrelationships and how can they be applied? Can—and how can—immediate and identifiable economic consequences of choices between water resource development alternatives be integrated with broader social consequences? What legal and institutional arrangements must be created to assure the appropriate impact of the social science considerations on the political process directing water development?

As the subjects covered by the papers so clearly indicate, the social scientists have much to contribute to sound water resource management. It is the earnest hope of those actively engaged in the field that the social scientists will step forward to undertake their proper role in full collaboration with all other disciplines, including engineers.

Observations: The engineer perceives a water resources problem as a pressing need. He works for a client, either the group with the need or an agency of government representing them. Often his client tells him that every day's delay costs so much money or needlessly extends some other kind of hardship. The bias of his training gives the engineer the greatest confidence in his ability to achieve successful performance in problem solving from structural measures. He can promise his client that a completed facility will immediately physically perform its design function. After he completes his job, the engineer can impress his client with a beholdable facility and show him how to operate it to meet his need. From the engineer's perspective, structural measures perform quickly in solving immediate needs where nonstructural approaches are better suited for long-term efforts to avoid future problems.

Maybe even more important, an operating physical system is attractive to the layman, and the nature and implications of this attraction are themselves subjects worthy of research by the social sciences. A man in danger from flooding prefers a dam to a zoning ordinance. A man suffering from drought prefers having the water brought to him over going where the water is; are engineers monument builders or are the people monument wanters? What bias does this fascination with physical solutions introduce into water management systems? Are people so beset by short-term problems that they have no time to look for long-term solutions?

The engineer considers a wide range of alternatives. He wants quantitative information differentiating the consequences of one alternative from those of another. The information he gets from the social sciences when he is trying to decide is at best (except for certain economic data) a general qualitative description of the kinds of consequences of a given alternative. The engineer has only his judgment to balance this information against all the pros and cons that he hears from other groups. He doesn't want general statements of principles, he wants day-to-day help in balancing the good against the bad in achieving the best possible compromise.

When the engineer-planner fails to get such help, his bias toward physical solution is increased. If he must be alone when it comes to defending a design, he wants to defend one he understands. If something goes wrong during implementation, he wants a design that he knows how to adjust to correct the malfunction. He is prepared to accept responsibility if a design fails structurally and even if *his* design fails socially. If he is going to depart from a design he understands, he wants those who talked him into the departure to accept responsibility and to be readily available for consultation as problems arise during implementation and through the years of subsequent operation. His clients will not be happy with a solution that does not function.

The engineer, who feels a responsibility for meeting social needs, is amazed when social scientists mention the incentives required for people in their disciplines to become active in meeting human needs. He feels that the social scientist who knows how to meet a human need and does not because it will bring him no recognition from his peers is failing in his responsibility. Such an argument makes a strong appeal, but despite what one may say about the right thing for social scientists to do, there is a practical need to find what will do the most to make the contribution from the social sciences more effective. For example, social scientists may not think of themselves as capable of helping people by promoting wise resource use.

A more fundamental question is whether people perceive themselves as being helped by the solutions social scientists offer. Maybe people want structural solutions and reward those who provide them. If so, the engineer enjoys the reward. The social scientist, upon being rejected, may feel that people are doing the wrong thing, may want no part in aggravating the situation, and thus, by his aloofness, may demonstrate a higher order of responsibility. If this interpretation is correct, the social sciences need to do a better job of selling the public on long-term approaches. They also need to commit themselves to substantive talks on problems and solutions with engineers rather than expect laymen to choose between two groups of experts.

Further analysis reveals a major difference between engineers who are responding to water management problems and the social scientists who are not. The engineers are working professionals whose success depends on solving the problems of their clients while the social scientists are members of the academic community interested in teaching and research. Engineering professors are often not much more responsive than social science professors in resolving water management problems. The answer to the problems of incentives and responsibility may well lie in the establishment of a working group of social scientists at a level comparable to that of the practicing engineer. Water resource management agencies are trying to hire such people, and they are looking to academic social scientists to train them.

Fourth Viewpoint: Law

Substance of the Comments: Frank J. Trelease, dean of the School of Law, University of Wyoming, commented that the request to review the five manuscripts from a practical perspective runs into the difficulty that a professor almost by definition is supposed to be impractical. A law professor has the function to learn, to teach, to do research which leads to better understanding, and only possibly to reform. On occasions, he gives clients advice, acts as a negotiator, formulates arrangements, and even forays into the adversary process as an advocate. These operations enhance the claim to practicality; but even as a teacher in a professional school, a law professor is supposed to turn out competent practitioners, and should have some notions of practicality.

The role of law has been defined in a quite theoretical manner. The function of law is to regulate the relations between men or groups of men. In playing this role the law serves essentially a dual purpose. It provides a mechanism, the law suit, for the solution of conflicts after they have arisen, and it furnishes a guide, the rule of law, for the ordering of future conduct. The general goal of all law has been stated by John Dewey, the philosopher, who describes the law as "a plan for organizing otherwise independent and potentially conflicting energies into a scheme which avoids waste, a scheme allowing a maximum utilization of energy." Roscoe Pound, the great student of jurisprudence, expressed much the same thought in this way: "What we are seeking to do and must do in a civilized society is to adjust relations and order conduct in a world in which the goods of existence, the scope for free activity, and the objects on which to exercise free activity are limited, and the demands on these goods and these objects are infinite. To order the activities of men in their endeavor to satisfy their demands so as to enable satisfaction of as much of the whole scheme of demands with the least friction and waste has . . . been what law makers and tribunals and jurists have been striving for . . . . By and large, the law at any particular time and place represents the will of the majority for encouraging action deemed desirable by them and for discouraging or forbidding action thought to be in conflict with the public interest. By encouraging some actions, but discouraging others, a state may use the actions of individuals to reach its own desired goal. There are few laws that are self-executing in the sense that they control all conduct and leave no choice of action to the individual. Much law does not literally regulate conduct in the sense of requiring or forbidding certain action, it instead provides an area of free choice, setting outside limits within which a person may act as he chooses. Many of these laws, such as those relating to property and contracts, unobtrusively form the basic framework of our society. Western water law follows this pattern. The goal of the state, in adopting the law governing the use of water, is to obtain the maximum benefits, both social and economic, from the use of the resource. The law is designed to permit people to do some things that will advance this aim, and to prevent people from doing things that would be contrary to the maximization ideal."[4]

This quite obviously describes a social science. Professors in law schools have in recent years tried very hard to be accepted as such scientists, even as humanists, and not solely for the prestige but sometimes to grasp for government and foundation money available to more respectable academics. Thus, this review may not accomplish the same function as do those from representatives of government, the consulting professions, and user and conservation groups. Those will give views from the outside, while this view is from an outsider only to the extent he is excluded from the group.

A lawyer is a cultural anthropologist with a somewhat limited outlook. After all, the rules under which a hunter divides his kill among his kin are not too different from the rules under which a corporation divides its profit into dividends, accumulations of capital, and payments to the Internal Revenue Service. Perhaps for this reason I found the anthropology paper enormously interesting. Its gathering of archeological studies of the works of ancient and primitive man may have little practical bearing for a lawyer, but it was fascinating reading. The paper shows the typical bias of the anthropologist toward the ancient and the primitive, in its contrast of "delicate small-scale adjustments to local conditions" to modern large projects "of stereotyped design." Still, it reluctantly recognizes the difference between the Hohakam and the residents of metropolitan Phoenix, and moves into the more difficult problems of fitting modern man into the "natural" setting.

The paper did one of the best jobs of describing the substance of the contributions from its discipine. The studies of "tropical river development" provide valuable lessons for planners and have some relevance to lawyers. Americans may generally feel that a property owner displaced by a water project can be paid a cash equivalent for the value of his land and that he will take his condemnation award and invest it in a similar or perhaps even more attractive enterprise. The problems of the Tonga people of Zambia show that this is not a universal truth, and some of the studies of the Tennessee Valley (cited by the sociologist) show that relocation may mean dislocation even in America. Comparative law teaches similar lessons. The law of the market place may not be as suitable in South America as in the United States for assuring that water moves to its highest and best use. An American farmer who sells his water rights may have wide opportunities for reinvestment, while South American Indians may have literally none. Further study of the comparative law of water shows that other nations, with different climates, economic conditions, and backgrounds, have chosen water law as a tool to solve nonwater problems: strengthening national security, correcting underdevelopment, improving the lot of native peoples, and remedying long-standing social and economic maladjustments. These differences in social objectives make it easier to understand why different people have chosen different laws and demonstrate the folly of trying to impose upon the people of one country a water law system designed for another.

The anthropologist's concluding analysis of competition and cooperation is almost a legal study in itself. It gives lawyers some idea of the variety of legal solutions that may be found for common problems and of the conditions which may make some suitable and others unacceptable.

Law and economics have formed a particularly fertile interdisciplinary partnership. Procedures and policies for project analysis suggested by economists have had an important effect upon law, and institutional arrangements made by lawyers have leaned heavily upon economics. Even the regulatory functions of law take on an economic cast. The law has integrated many rules of behavior in an economic mold, such as the laws of water rights, pollution control, and environmental protection.

This interdependence did not always exist. Today one rarely finds the economist who is unmindful of the fact that the legal framework is the very basis of his work. Nor does one often find the type of economist who regards the law as a constant, an immutable Medes-and-Persians set of unchangeable rules. Economists are now aware that the law, like other human institutions, is constantly changing and that one of the major forces for change can be a demonstration of the economic undesirability of current law.

The trend toward interdependence is also true of today's lawyers. Not too many years ago any economic foundations or implications of law were purely subliminal. Today, the economist is a frequent expert witness, often giving the crucial argument for the client. At a recent meeting of the American Law Institute, discussion focused on a restatement of the common law principles of nuisance and riparian rights and on a proposed model land-use code. In each session lawyers, law professors, and judges bandied about the concepts of benefit-cost analysis and externalities in a way that might have surprised, and probably would have horrified, many economists.

The modern geographer is a mysterious person to one with little formal training in that subject. Geographers seem to be economists, sociologists, or anthropologists wearing false moustaches. At least a reading of this paper helps form a definition of a geographer: some other kind of social scientist—almost any kind—who deals with a particular area. In other words, geography is social science in a spatial context.

Of greatest interest to the lawyer is the contribution of inducing resource developers to think in terms of multiple aims and to consider multiple means. The examples are occasionally fascinating, although the description of the literature sometimes assumes that the reader knows about it or will eventually read it. Again, the impact of the geographer, like those of other social scientists, seems to fall mainly in helping the developer and planner. However, a slight shift in emphasis can make the concept of "perception" extremely interesting to the lawyer seeking legal improvement and reform. If, as is often the case, people living under a system of law are not exposed with some frequency to its disadvantages, the person advocating badly needed and extremely useful reforms is too often dismissed as a do-gooder.

The political science paper starts out with an excellent analysis of the soft spots in institutional arrangements, law-making bodies and law-making processes. Yet strangely, this is not too useful to the "water lawyer." The discussion is oriented too much toward projects and plans, toward actions by governments. This is not to say that the approach is not very good for others, including some other lawyers. In particular, legal counsel attempting to negotiate and influence water development decisions and to provide the legal framework for the agreed-upon solutions will find the work very valuable. Political science has a common blind spot in that it deals almost exclusively with the legislative and executive branches of government. The third branch, the judiciary,·is all too often completely ignored.

Sociology similarly seems to have little for the lawyer or law maker, though undoubtedly much for the project planner. The presentation does contain a warning that behavior patterns change and that the laws of yesterday or even of today may not fit tomorrow's society. Perhaps the subjects are too close and the connection too obvious. The thought may be obscured because the law reflects societal needs and changes very closely. Yet these must precede a change in law, and the sociologists have not made the impact of which they are capable. The cited literature contains only a few studies whose titles would attract a lawyer seeking improvement or change of the law.

As a whole, the social science papers are too oriented toward government development and government projects to suit the tastes of the lawyer. Extremely important factors in water development are private development and the processes and mechanisms for day-to-day operations. The law, in directing and ordering the affairs of men, accomplishes many goals through the cumulative affects of many individual private actions. The introductory paper does not overlook "the aggregate effect of little decisions" in water management, but some of the others do.

Many social scientists are concerned with the processes of decision making. Some seem to lean heavily on consensus, but I believe that conflict is the more normal human reaction. Conflicts may be decided by the power structure or by a majority vote, but very often they are decided by the judicial process. The law of property rights protects those who act; the laws of public regulation protect those who may be harmed by action. The function of the law suit as a decision-making process is coming into special prominence today with the rise of the modern "public-interest law suit" for the protection of public (diffused) rights and environmental values.

But the law has something to learn from the other social sciences, and lawyers can learn how to be better social scientists. The law too must be holistic, and the lawyer, law reformer, legal draftsman, and craftsman must take into consideration the other branches of human relations. Yet it must not be left unsaid that the holism of the other social scientists should take the law into consideration and should understand its function better.

Observations: The thrust of the five papers is directed toward achieving more meaningful and effective contributions from the social sciences to water resources management policy. The policy may be expressed in terms of broad goals or objectives, but its operational expression is some combination of structural and nonstructural measures passing through phases of design, implementation, and operation. No matter how carefully a set of measures is formulated and applied, conflicts between supporters and opponents are going to arise. Some objectives can only be achieved through sacrificing realization of other objectives, and individuals forced to make sacrifices will be in conflict with those who gain. Some effort in policy formulation is appropriately devoted to establishing administrative arrangements for resolving conflicts. For example, water quality control agencies establish rules for resolving conflicts between upstream polluters and downstream water users. The lawyer as a social scientist has a function to perform in the design of optimum administrative procedures.

Even the most carefully formulated administrative procedures will, however, encounter unforeseen conflicts. The lawyer sees his primary mission as maintaining judicial procedures that can resolve conflicts that administrative systems are not equipped to handle. He wants help from the social sciences in evaluating the merits of the positions taken by conflict adversaries so that he is in a better position to achieve an equitable compromise. Like the engineer, he feels that he has received more concrete help from economics than from the other social sciences; but also like the engineer, he feels that the information base and expertise of the other social sciences surely contain useful concepts for reaching better decisions. He further recognizes that the cumulative effect of many individual judicial decisions is to change the social system. Without some coordination between the resolution of individual conflicts and social goals, the legal system may work against the goals established through political processes. The lawyers want help from the social sciences on how to adjust the rules of equity used in court decisions to maximize conformity of judicial decisions with the public interest.

Fifth Viewpoint: State Water Planning

Viewpoint Background: Few states in the United States have undertaken major water resource development projects. Their traditional role has been to represent the interest of the people of the state as a whole in reviewing the federal water development program and in regulating development by local government or by private enterprise. The state is not so much interested in formulating a water resources development program for implementation as it is in knowing how to interact in program formulation by others in order to achieve modifications beneficial to its people. To some extent, this traditional role is being changed by recent emphasis on nonstructural measures because planning and zoning functions are implemented either directly by the states or by local bodies as authorized by state law. For example, a state that never had a program for flood control by structural measures may be active in floodplain regulation. States are looking for help from the social sciences for both reviewing structural programs and designing nonstructural ones.

Substance of the Comments: William C. Ackerman, chief, Illinois State Water Survey, noted that the papers deal with an important question because water resources management badly needs the active involvement of the social sciences. The physical scientists, engineers, planners, and decision makers want this active participation, but they are not generally getting it, even though there are notable exceptions. The practical question is what this book might contribute to the motivations and rewards necessary to 1) advance the level of the social sciences and to 2) bring their expertise to bear upon problems of water resources management.

The physical scientist and the engineer have made spectacular changes to the natural environment. The considerations weighed in designing these changes have not regularly included consequences to biological systems and have often had a rather narrow concept of benefits to mankind. Therefore, the social scientist is needed to consider the needs and wants of society, and to communicate these to the decision makers, and to provide practical help and consultation as the decision makers weigh the consequences of alternatives.

The excellent chapter on anthropology should be required reading for all those concerned with planning water resource management projects. The author himself sums up the relevance of the subject by saying that he is "impressed with the great potential contribution of anthropological research to practical applications of resources management and development theory." In a time of environmental crises, anthropological studies of resource management contain considerable data on human ecology with direct relevance to problems of conservation and environmental quality. The frequent failure to use such data on the part of those making practical planning decisions is part of the general failure of our society to develop a sense of environmental values. The anthropologist has an impressive opportunity now that public awareness of the problem has become acute.

It is clear that the study of ancient "hydraulic" civilizations contains important lessons, particularly in the effect of their extensive water development systems upon sociopolitical institutional arrangements and in the factors that eventually led to system failure. Other lessons are found in the failures of recent African lake developments which seem to have been implemented after exhaustive studies for technical feasibility, but with no more than inadequate, last-minute programs to resolve human problems. All water management schemes are physical, economic, and social systems, and all three kinds of feasibility studies are needed if economic profitability and social usability are to be attained.

Despite the great potential value to better water management from listening to what anthropologists have to say about the lessons of ancient and modern water management, the failures to listen are not all with the planners and decision makers. The anthropology profession often awards greater prestige to research topics remote from these practical concerns, and the most able people in the field usually cannot be induced to participate in resource management decision making. The paper gives some hope that anthropologists may become more interested in the water problems of contemporary society, but the author has no instant formula for more extensive involvement.

The economics chapter accurately reflects the discomfort of leading economists who are asked to prove the economic justification of pre-ordained development. Economists prefer to consider the full range of development alternatives (including that of no development at all) in a context wider than that permitted by an agency mission.[5] They feel that the agencies have often bought a favorable benefit-cost ratio couched in unsupportable assumptions and misused economic language when they really need a scholarly application of economic concepts to select a course of action.

Economists have made a substantial contribution to water resources management over the past thirty-five years. The concept that benefits must exceed costs if a project is to contribute to national income has been influential in eliminating the worst projects. The concept has become a major factor influencing project design, and economists have been industrious at working out the details needed for specific applications.

Economists have had some difficulty in dealing with water since it is neither a free economic good nor does it behave as private property in a free market. Water is a human necessity; it may be publicly owned; services tend to be monopolies; and it has significant esthetic and other nonmarket values. Because of these peculiar properties, the economist has found, as have we all, that he only contributes to, rather than controls, water management decisions.

The author sees for economists in the future planning of water development the important and major role of integrating consideration of alternative approaches, relationships to other resources, economic efficiency, ecological restraints, and new technology. For example, in studies of the economics of the environment, the economist can provide analyses of costs of decision alternatives. Operations research and systems analysis are a current and popular wave which largely builds on the analytical techniques of the economists. Full utilization of the more sophisticated new analytic techniques is frustrated by important gaps in information and by the fact that such studies can supply only part of the total information needed to guide decisions. Economists can contribute a great deal to remedying these deficiencies.

The economist states with much more conviction than do the other social scientists that his discipline will play an increasing role in the future of water resources. Economists are attracted by an interest in people and their economic problems and by the importance of resources issues. The broader opportunities in the future will appeal to today's youth. The importance of challenging courses in resource economics in universities is rightly emphasized.

The statement that the contributions of geographers have been modest, future responses are more encouraging, but present incentives are weak sets a theme for the book; This is about what each of the social scientists, in turn, said. However, geography has made substantial contributions toward planning based on practical multiple aims and multiple means and toward recognition of the possibility of more than one public aim in water resources. The paper points out with good credibility that to bring a geographer into an interdisciplinary study increases the likelihood of a comprehensive view and of a full assessment of alternatives.

The paper rightfully stresses the large number of sophisticated analyses of proposed projects as contrasted to the handful of studies which examine the results of such plans once executed. Interdisciplinary research is widely recognized as needed to resolve certain complex problems, but there are few experiences to demonstrate that such efforts are really fruitful.

The paper contains an indirect answer to the question that gave rise to this book by saying that the response of the social sciences will be linked to the kinds of questions asked by water planning agencies. A sincere desire on the part of agencies for study of alternative aims and means will increase the supply of social research.

The political science paper summarizes the status of political analysis of water resources as relatively inactive, but potentially fruitful. The assessment is somewhere between accurate and optimistic, and the major problem of how scholarly analysis in political science is translated into practice is not really answered by the chapter. The situation is quite different from the relationship between the physical sciences and engineering practice where despite moaning about the time lag between research and application, the probability of eventual adoption of research findings is high.

The author is dead right in speaking of declining involvement of political scientists during the 1950s and 1960s. The most successful activity during that period was the U.S. Senate Select Committee on National Water Resources led by a practical politician, Senator Robert Kerr, with an engineer, Theodore Schad, as his staff director. The report of this Committee had tremendous influence and led to the Water Resources Planning Act, the Water Resources Research Act, the Water Resources Council, the river basin commissions, and subsequent activities in the office of the President. This report issued in January 1961, dominated water resources politics and institutional arrangements in the 1960s, modified primarily by the environmental movement and by eager politicians running for office. It would have been useful for the author to have recounted this chain of events, but in all seriousness, he may not have considered it political science.

Otherwise, the author has accurately described the evolution of events. For example, there has been the shift in views from favoring the basin as a decision arena for water resources management and possibly for other activities of government to the present cooling toward the basin concept. He brings out well the problems of metropolitan areas with their proliferation of special-purpose districts, and the loss of economies of scale. But the hand of the political scientist does not seem to be reversing or influencing these phenomena except, as the author points out, indirectly through the metropolitan planning and federal granting agencies.

The weakness of the states and local areas in their ability to plan or manage their water resources deserves attention. The author suggests other useful and productive areas for political science research and indicates that the climate *may* be right for a new period of such study to illumine man's political behavior. He seems less than sure that more such studies will take place or that, if they do, they will reform our politics of water.

The sociology paper points out that increasing population, growing concern with the environment, and changing values are augmenting the interest of sociologists in water resources development and management because these trends are creating problems for which the understanding of human behavior is basic to the derivation of solutions. A key point is that the physical sciences and their engineering applications may have unique solutions, but the social sciences encounter many different cultural and behavioral patterns. Natural phenomena do indeed have few variables but many manipulations, while social phenomena have many variables and relatively few manipulations.[6]

The number of items of published work by sociologists on water management problems is amazingly small. Reports have dealt with the community, patterns and attitudes, impacts and constraints, decision making, perceptions and the role of institutions, but the profession has not yet really recognized the implications of replacing the traditional device of measuring the merit of a plan by dollars with a more broadly based index of human value. Sociologists are only beginning to team with ecologists to consider the role of such factors affecting how man treats his environment as power, prestige, altruism, esthetics, and idealistic achievement. The challenge in the future for the sociologist is to provide for considering these factors means that are just as credible as the means engineers and economists have for considering other factors.

Observations: The main strength of this review was that it demonstrated the perceptiveness with which an experienced water resources engineer can abstract helpful advice from the works of social scientists and in turn can focus on key practical issues for the social scientists to study. Social scientists, as do members of other disciplines, have difficulty, or maybe more accurately, reluctance in communicating with those who have differing vocabularies and viewpoints on issues of substance in their professional work. This review should be of value in showing the level at which meaningful interdisciplinary interaction is possible. Individuals with practical experience in dealing with situations in which social science theory can be applied may not have impeccable credentials from an academic viewpoint, but they can often see major flaws in the constructs social scientists propose. Social scientists need interdisciplinary participation in building better theories in the same way engineers need public participation in devising better plans.

Sixth Viewpoint: Federal Water Resources Implementation

Viewpoint Background: Five agencies in the United States government are involved in a major way in implementing water resources management programs. The U.S. Army Corps of Engineers has been involved in an inland waterway program for 150 years and in a nationwide flood-control program for 35 years. The Bureau of Reclamation began its program of bringing irrigation to the desert seventy years ago. The Soil Conservation Service has been working in small rural watersheds for over thirty-five years, and the Tennessee Valley Authority has been seeking to build the economy of an impoverished region through resource development for about the same length of time. The evolution of the Environmental Protection Agency as the agency responsible for pollution control and environmental enhancement has come about through a number of name changes and program redefinitions over the last twenty years. Each one of these agencies is administering a water resources management program to which the comments of the five social scientists apply. For reasons of conserving space, however, the viewpoint from a man with long-time experiences with only one of those agencies is included here, and, of course, that view is unofficial.

Substance of the Comments: Eugene Weber, U.S. Army Corps of Engineers, retired, said that from 1945 to 1965, he spent much of his time trying to involve social scientists in planning and helping formulate the action recommendations his agency made to the President and to

Congress. The discussion by the social scientists of their past accomplishments and their presentation of the issues that the social sciences can help resolve are helpful in inducing greater involvement because social scientists who are not excited professionally (often through inexperience and limited information) by the opportunity to work on specific applications are provided a better background of the broader issues. On the negative side, neither the question nor the coverage in the papers on incentives and rewards were very useful.

The introductory paper hits the nail squarely on the head by stressing that the responsibility for better choices rests with the social sciences and that their inputs must be expressed in a language understandable to planners. Social scientists have the responsibility to initiate needed research and to provide practical help to planners (usually engineers) and to decision makers (usually politicians or political appointees) in formulating management policy. Social scientists, who have in the past felt discouraged when planners did not respond to their suggestions, will find engineers becoming more receptive. The American Society of Civil Engineers has adopted a statement of "Principles for a Sound National Water Policy."[7] The National Society of Professional Engineers subsequently adopted and distributed to its members essentially the same policy. Implementation of these principles requires active participation by social scientists in the planning and management process. Such active participation is being achieved in the current Susquehanna and North Atlantic Regional studies.

Social scientists need to contribute to the formulation of local, state, regional, and national goals for better water management. For example, the goal of flood control as expressed by legislation is to use structural measures to prevent flood damages whenever the benefits to whomsoever they may accrue exceed the costs. This goal is self-defeating to the degree that it actually increases flood damages by inducing overdevelopment in the floodplain. Engineers are not adverse to redefinition of the goal, but social scientists must lead the way.

Social scientists can also help establish guidelines for achieving formulated goals and objectives. For example, rules for paying for water services are fixed by the type of service (flood control, irrigation, power, and others) and are largely independent of the circumstances of a particular project. Yet these rules may profoundly affect which of many alternatives decision makers select for achieving a particular goal. Until social scientists devise and lead the way in implementing sound pricing policies, plans will be biased toward arrangements whose financing is more easily achieved. Furthermore, social scientists need to devise ways to display nonmonetary considerations and to show all of the advantages and disadvantages of each course of action. With such information, decision makers may be better able to select courses that will result in wise resources use. The recognition that economic efficiency should not be the sole criterion in plan evaluation needs to be followed with operational procedures for planning on the basis of multiple objectives.

Water planning has, in recent years, faced up to the problem of externalities better than other types of planning; however, better integration with planning for other purposes is needed. The air, the use of land, urban development, transportation, and, in fact, practically everything affecting the earth as an ecosystem are related to water and to each other. If ways could be found to achieve comprehensive planning for the best possible use of the earth's resources for all the needs and goals of man, water planning, land-use planning, and the others could proceed under a common umbrella. The social sciences hold the key to integrating planning of all human activity through a better understanding of effects on people. Short of this ideal, analysis by social scientists of the effects of past decisions and actions in water and related resource management may help. Systems are needed for 1) routine monitoring of the social effects of water projects; 2) analysis of what could have been done in planning to avoid adverse social effects; and 3) communication of the results to planners in language they can understand sufficiently to prevent repeated mistakes.

Many top level decisions are based on information provided by professional planners. Planning agencies require qualified personnel, effective organization, sufficient funds, and adequate time to do a good job of compiling and analyzing the needed information. To be effective, the organization must provide methods for achieving routine understandings within the planning group and must develop ways to get pertinent information before the decision maker. The planning system needs to respond quickly to day-to-day problems in ways that will not aggravate the adverse, long-range effects of actions which seem advisable to solve current needs. Political scientists need to work toward such a feedback system and need support from other social scientists in devising ways for monitoring system performance.

Attempts to apply new planning theory and new technology for examining alternatives (such as the approaches that have grown out of the Harvard studies) are stymied by practical difficulties in implementation.[8] One difficulty is in achieving a balance among multiple goals that all the people affected will *accept* as equitable. A second difficulty is in forecasting such social effects of projects as the losses suffered by people forced to move from lands taken for project right-of-way. The third difficulty is that the institutions available for plan implementation are not responsive to what the people really want.

When the Bureau of the Budget asked the federal agencies to apply a Planning, Programming, Budgeting System (PPBS) to their activities, the promise was to build through the system the continuous comprehensive data bank needed for accurate comparison of the consequences of alternative plans for immediate action and of the long-run consequences of changes in goals, objectives, policies, and tradeoffs. Whatever drawbacks PPBS may have had, social scientists can and should contribute to formulation of some such system that will display to decision makers the many alternatives for use of resources and for achievement of various goals.

Observations: The theme of this review is that engineer-planners have no quarrel with the vision social scientists have of the need to make water resources management policy more responsive to the public welfare. Planners looking for practical advice on how to do better next time, however, are little helped by inventories of past mistakes. They feel lost in trying to apply the social science information they are getting. The physical sciences had to provide more than Newton's laws before engineers could design physical facilities for resource development, and the social scientists will have to do much more than they have so far in order to provide planners with sufficient guidance on how to apply the basic principles of their disciplines.

Seventh Viewpoint: Federal Water Resources Policy

Viewpoint Background: The agencies in the United States government that are involved in implementing water resources management programs historically have used diverse planning methodologies in project formulation. A long series of efforts have been instigated by Congress or by the President in order to coordinate agency activities and to establish more uniform design criteria and project evaluation procedures. One aspect of this effort has been to sponsor research and thereby establish an improved information base for reconciling differences. Another aspect has been to survey water-related needs in order to establish a planning framework through which agency activities could be better coordinated. A third aspect has involved promoting interaction among the agencies by requiring the officials to reconcile conflicting policies and to review each other's projects. The last viewpoint review was by an economist active in these efforts.

Substance of the Comments: Gary Taylor, National Water Commission, commented that the papers reflect the analytic standards of the disciplines more than the principles of effective communication to the intelligent layman. They reveal much more about the controversies within and among the disciplines than is really needed to address the purposes of the series.

The question on the contributions made by members of the respective disciplines to solving water management problems was answered reasonably well by all the participants. Each paper communicates a useful image of what those in the discipline have done and with what kinds of questions the members are concerned. The impact of the research on policy makers is, however, not sufficiently discussed. The economics paper is the most responsive. It is probable that there is more evidence of impact in economics than in the other disciplines, but it is unfortunate that the other papers do not say more on this point.

The responses on water resources management problems that researchers in the discipline might help solve are uneven and not very convincing. This may have resulted in part from an ignorance of critical water-related problems or from lack of interest in such issues within the disciplines. Probably, it also reflects an uncertainty over the research performance expected by those presenting problems for solution or awarding research contracts. Finally, it may be a recognition of the complex nature of critical management problems and the inherent difficulty in conducting the interdisciplinary research required to resolve them.

The responses on professional incentives and rewards are short, candid, and pessimistic. The possibility of government research employment for members of the disciplines was not seen as particularly appealing, and the authors did not think in terms of those trained in the disciplines at the bachelors or masters level working in the agencies on resolving day-to-day problems. The academic rewards for working on water problems were not felt to be too encouraging. The papers also seem to suggest little interest in interdisciplinary academic research, but the question is not really addressed.

The book is probably not of much interest to top-level water resource policy makers. The major reason is that books are generally not usable sources of information for busy men faced with day-to-day "panics." The book will be of more interest to professionals on policy staffs and to lower-level administrators. The policy makers will be indirectly influenced if these lower-echelon people have their minds stretched by the variety of interesting principles and concepts in these papers.

It is fairly easy to build a convincing case of the need for a more comprehensive social perspective in planning and policy making. However, this situation does not automatically require more social scientists or more social science research. Peter Drucker has cynically asserted that the post-World War II performance of Western economies has been inversely

correlated with the number and prominence of economists in their governments, and he gives Japan and Great Britain as extreme examples.[9] This is
not to say that Japan has acted in economic ignorance, but rather that
Japanese leaders and institutions have followed the best economic principles in spite of a relative shortage of influential economists. The point is
that the presence of social problems, in and of itself, does not necessarily
mean that more social science research is needed or that social scientists
should necessarily be interested in trying to solve these problems.

Hard thought needs to be given in order to define more precisely the
role of social science. The influence of the social sciences is advanced
through research, teaching, and professional involvement in water resources policy formulation and planning processes. Some individual social
scientists make notable contributions in all three areas, but examples are
rare. Furthermore, it is doubtful that academic and governmental incentive
systems are going to be changed to produce relatively more "triple threat"
individuals. If this assessment is correct, the need is to improve the
performance of each social scientist in his chosen role as a researcher,
teacher, government staff person, consultant, or planner. One could look
at the role of the researcher as a scientific role and the others as professional roles.

The engineer (professional physical scientist) often has great difficulty
relating to the social sciences in spite of many sincere attempts to interest
social scientists in his problems. Generally, he either expects far too much
or nothing at all from the social scientists. This situation relates to the fact
that character and present state of knowledge in the social sciences have
resulted in a research emphasis on building up the basic theoretical
structure of the disciplines. This emphasis on theory is reflected in the
academic incentive structure. It results in a low priority for problem-
oriented research and, in turn, the lack of direct influence on the policy
makers reflected in the discipline papers.

The nature of social phenomena, the tools available for promoting
social objects, and the state of the art of measuring social accomplishment
do not permit process specifications of the precision and accuracy possible
in the physical sciences. Furthermore, the multidimensional characteristics
of social progress do not permit the use of a "safety factor" in the same
way as is possible to insure against physical failure. Social answers can go
wrong along a number of dimensions. Rare, but recurring, incidents of
dam break and bridge failures should remind the social scientist, in a
pessimistic way perhaps, that natural phenomena also involve stochastic
surprises even when appropriate safety factors are employed. This situation should encourage him to try even with his "crude" tools.

The problems that must be overcome in formulating water resources management policy can only be resolved through interdisciplinary effort. However, severe time constraints often force critical decisions based on handy and specialized information. Furthermore, our policy makers and their supporting staffs often have a bias against the social sciences, stemming from a lack of breadth in their academic education. The information base can be broadened and the bias reduced by developing a greater variety of institutional sources of research output including universities, private foundations, consulting firms, and government organizations. As a country, we are now relatively rich in these institutional research resources, but each institution needs to establish priorities that emphasize its own unique competitive advantages. For example, the government has a strong advantage in data collection but is in a relatively weak position to study suitable organization for a bureaucracy.

One way for the universities to increase the influence of the social sciences would be to provide a broader education for the engineers and lawyers who dominate water resources management. Course offerings can be expanded to help the new generation of students, and interdisciplinary seminars, short courses, and workshops of various kinds can help water resources professionals. Professionals exposed to some of the basic principles of the social sciences would at least then ask the "right" questions more often. Such inquiries would promote an atmosphere of interest and communication that would encourage the graduate social scientist to devote his career to government service.

Professors from the various social sciences working to broaden the education of the water establishment would be more likely to generate interdisciplinary research on water problems. The interdisciplinary personal relationship thus developed could also result in a more enlightened specification of suitable issues to be pursued through interdisciplinary research. Such activities would also increase the value of the academic person for effective consulting work with water-related agencies.

Such a strategy for the increasing involvement of the social sciences in water resources management is pragmatic and not too exciting. It may, however, be more fruitful than the usual exhortations for the social scientist to face his responsibilities and for the policy maker to sponsor interdisciplinary research for better answers.

Observations: The above comments are central to the hiatus between the water planner's sense of pressure to solve immediate problems and the social scientist's objections to solutions that aggravate the situation in the long run. The recommended strategy for increasing interaction between the two groups is constructive in that it gives each individual reader from both sides something that he personally can do.

The engineer can (by reading, by taking additional courses, and by inviting presentations from social scientists to engineering meetings) foster his own comprehension of and appreciation for the social science viewpoint. He can encourage young engineers to interact in the same ways. The engineer and his clients will gain as he discusses his problems with social scientists.

The social scientist can (by reading reports on research into the social science aspects of water resources management, by making some effort to familiarize himself with the relevant technology, and by inviting engineers and others with practical problems requiring social science inputs to his meetings) foster his comprehension of and appreciation for technical viewpoints. He can encourage young social scientists to gain some familiarity with applied technology. This need was observed by an anthropologist during one of the colloquia when he noted that his students had difficulty studying a primitive culture because they had no idea of how its basic tools functioned. The social scientists, his students, and his profession will gain from discussions on relevant research topics with engineers.

The engineers who step out to increase their exposure to the social sciences are going to encounter social scientists who have no concern for resource management problems. Similarly, the social scientists who step out into the worlds of technology and resource management are going to encounter engineers who have no appreciation for social concerns. Frustration can be reduced if better ways can be found to get those interested from both sides together. An educational institution provides one of the most efficient settings for stimulating people to take fresh approaches. A university administration that commits itself to building and maintaining a water management program that can apply the expertise of the soil sciences to promote better resource use provides an important contribution. When such commitments are made, they should be strongly supported by water management agencies. These agencies should send their employees to such schools for further training, use the contacts established to express their management and research needs to the faculty, and seek ways to use the research capability of the university to mutual advantage. This last step implies financial support for research, but it also implies agency-university interaction during the research to keep the study impartial, conceptually sound, and useful.

Such a strong water-oriented program should not be rushed into by every university, but good programs should be nurtured at a few universities with a strong faculty understanding of and commitment to solving water problems. There is simply no need for every university to specialize in water resources management; certainly society has enough other problems to keep everyone busy.

Some of the advances in the theory and methodology of the social sciences that will be required to deal with the many water management problems referenced in the previous pages must come in quantum jumps. A few social scientists are going to have to be willing as to take major professional risks as they join efforts such as that described above. Some will need to develop quantitative prediction models from what colleagues will call an inadequate theoretical base. Others are going to have to work on such professionally unrewarding topics as designing, filling, and maintaining data banks of necessary information. Such people will radically reorder their careers and the rewards they receive. The fact remains that individuals who take personal risks are the most likely to accomplish substantial social improvements.

1. Vincent Ostrom and Elinor Ostrom, "Public Choice: A Different Approach to the Study of Public Administration," *Public Administration Review*, March 1971.

2. George Buglierello, "Technological Innovation and Hydraulic Engineering," *Journal of the Hydraulics Division (ASCE)*, 98 (May 1972): 759.

3. Ibid., p. 761.

4. Frank J. Trelease, *Law, Water and People* 18, *Wyoming Law Journal* 3 (1963).

5. The typical water development agency has its mission specified by laws stating the kinds of management practices that it can and cannot employ.

6. The points referenced in this paragraph were made by Wade Andrews in the University of Kentucky colloquium series.

7. American Society of Civil Engineers, "Principles for a Sound National Water Policy," *Civil Engineering* 36 (December 1966): 38-40.

8. Arthur Maass et al., *Design of Water-Resource Systems*, (Cambridge, Mass.: Harvard University Press, 1962).

9. Peter Drucker, *The Age of Discontinuity: Guidelines to our Changing Society* (New York: Harper and Row, 1968), p. 139.

8 Recommendations from a Water Resources Planning Viewpoint

L. Douglas James

Both thoughtful social scientists and people knowledgeable in the practical problems of water resources management recognize the importance of incorporating the expertise of the social sciences in formulating policies to meet long-term human needs. Each of a group of leading social scientists has in chapters two through six discussed the potential contribution his discipline can make and has provided constructive suggestions for its involvement. Each of a group of people knowledgeable in practical management problems has in chapter seven assessed the papers and provided supplemental constructive suggestions, and the editor has supplemented these suggestions with his own observations. The purpose of these last two chapters is to summarize key points and consolidate specific suggestions. The first set of recommendations is from the viewpoint of a water resources planner, and the second set is from the viewpoint of a social scientist.

RECOMMENDATIONS FROM AN ENGINEERING VIEWPOINT

Assessment Instruments

The engineer tends to approach water resources management by seeing an immediate problem and formulating a physical approach that will solve it.

He has established a sequence of steps for determining which factors are critical to success, gathering data measuring each factor, analyzing the implications of the information to the performance efficiency of each alternative, supplementing uncertain conclusions with judgment, recommending a design, implementing it, and then being on call to remedy any malfunction. These instruments for assessing the situation have been highly successful in eliminating those alternatives not able to pass the test of physical performance and thereby in establishing a public confidence that what is built will work.

The social sciences often make observations on management issues and get a favorable reaction from engineers and the public, but find that no one really knows how to convert their ideas from a proposal to a working reality. Furthermore, the public has developed a highly skeptical, if not cynical, attitude toward recommendations it gets from social scientists (zoning welfare programs and price regulations, for example) because these programs are not perceived as accomplishing their intended objectives. The way for the social scientist to increase this credibility is through better performance—creating programs people will perceive as successful.

The social scientist needs to pinpoint those factors critical to social performance, to determine what data is relevant to measuring these factors in the context of a particular management alternative, to develop routine and effective means for gathering this information, to establish appropriate techniques for analysis, to develop an information base for making appropriate judgments, to formulate a specific policy recommendation for a specific situation, and to stand ready to correct unanticipated consequences. The need is best conceptualized in the context of considering the steps required to formulate a successful approach to water resources management. The concept of adjusting patterns of human use, as opposed to patterns of resource availability, opens a multitude of management possibilities. Examples include adjustments in use of floodplains, use of watercourses for the discharge of pollutants, uses by type and by time pattern made of water or electric power, patterns of use of recreation areas and the resulting effects on the quality of the facilities, and many others. Nonstructural programs include campaigns to change public use by providing information and appealing to some combination of self-interest and public spirit, establishment of economic incentives involving fees and charges, and use of various types of regulatory systems involving police enforcement and court-determined penalties.

All such nonstructural measures need to be as carefully conceived as structural measures are. A plan needs to be designed so as to function in a satisfactory manner. It needs to be delineated in a way that those responsible for implementation will be able to follow. It needs to be presented in a manner that will lead the public to accept it as making good common sense. With his plans and specifications at hand the social scientist needs to watch the implementation process much as engineering inspectors have traditionally watched the construction process in order to ensure compliance and to catch unforeseen contigencies that appear and are likely to affect performance. On-the-spot design changes will sometimes be necessary. After implementation, routine operation will have to be watched (to make sure nonconforming uses do not creep into the floodplain) and routine maintenance will be required to keep the system current (to make sure the management policy reflects such current economic and social conditions as technology, economic demand, and public goals change).

A nonstructural approach must achieve widespread, if not universal, compliance in order to be effective. One major polluter or one floodplain developer can compromise a plan into ineffectiveness. All affected individuals will not react to a given approach in the same way. The social scientist needs to explore how the way a person reacts to various nonstructural measures varies with his personal characteristics and his patterns of communication with others. The social scientist needs to develop instruments for examining a specific situation (settlement in Floodplain A or littering in Park B) in order to determine individuals whose actions will have to be changed. He must then develop other instruments for predicting how those individuals will react to the nonstructural alternatives. Such instruments can then be used to examine social situations for the purpose of formulating the policy (for example, floodplain management or litter control programs) that will have the greatest probability of success with a known group of people in a known physical setting.

The success of economists in contributing to water resources management is at least in part associated with their ability to give planners exactly the information they need to test for economic feasibility. Too often, the other social sciences give only general prescriptions that are hard to apply to specific problems (for example, pleas for coordinating activities among governments or calls not to move native peoples from tribal areas). The planner has no quantitative information, only his own judgment for working such general prescriptions into his analysis of tradeoffs among alternatives.

The design of assessment instruments that can be used to formulate successful nonstructural programs is still largely unresearched. Some relationships between human response and personal characteristics can no doubt develop to predict responses from census data or other readily available sources. Some response predictions will require public hearings, systematic interviews, or in-depth interactions with citizen panels. The procedures for assessing nonstructural alternatives need to be tied to policy needs and social situations.

Social Indicators

The engineer monitors completed water developments for signs of any tendency toward physical failure. Gages are incorporated into large dams to spot settlement or seepage problems before they become severe. Maintenance inspections are routine. Flows are monitored and performances are observed. If water resources management is in fact a means to promote multiple *social criteria,* monitoring is necessary to assess progress toward these goals and to have advanced warning in time to instigate preventive action against impending social failures.

The concept is to use assessment instruments to predict the most probable course of events for the purpose of initial design and implementation, and then watch social indicators so that corrective action can be taken before an unlikely or unforeseen event sequence causes needless trouble. Social scientists will need to establish indices for measuring the welfare of people by small groups and of the public at large, procedures for routine collection of relevant data, and analytical approaches for interpreting the results. Example indicators might detect trends toward disregard of pollution-control laws, growing dissatisfaction with park and recreation facilities, or increased concentration of income in the hands of the few. A great deal of work has been done to map the physical environment and to keep the maps current as new development occurs; the role of social indicators is to provide a data base for mapping and keeping aware of the current status of the social environment.

Institutional Flexibility

The good that can be accomplished by maintaining an awareness of the social environment is only fully realized when institutions respond to monitored signs of an intensifying problem by taking quick and effective corrective action. As institutions grow, they lose flexibility. In part, this comes from the inertia of larger institutional size, but commitments (sometimes legally binding) to causes and to past positions often make shifts in policy more difficult as the institution ages. Institutions need to be more committed to *rules* for deciding policies and less committed to specific developments or even management programs. One can only speculate how its flood control program might have been affected if the Corps of Engineers had had authority to implement any structural or nonstructural measure from the start. This is the kind of issue the social sciences should explore seriously. The long history of water management provides many opportunities for comparative case studies of situations where some institutions failed to respond to manifest social needs while others responded efficiently.

Bias for Structural Measures

While the first three recommendations are to develop better management tools, it would be a mistake to interpret this as advocating a narrowly based analysis. For example, the anthropology paper describes a number of problems associated with construction of Aswan Dam. Eugene Black describes how the dam acted as a force for nonviolence having a "deterrent quality understood very well in both Tel Aviv and Cairo."[1] If construction of the dam did in fact prevent (or even delay) a major war in the Middle East, the project had a benefit that could well make all the ills described in the paper worthwhile. The social sciences need to develop methods for testing hypotheses on the role water management programs have had and can have in channeling human energy toward productive contributions rather than destructive activities.

Social scientists can help determine which kinds of management problems make the best foci for efficiently converting human effort from destructive to constructive channels and which approaches to a given problem are most efficient in this regard. A related question is whether nonstructural measures can be presented to the public in a way that will generate the public enthusiasm that popular structural projects have had in the past. If they cannot, the bias for structural programs will be very difficult to overcome. The depth of the problem is best illustrated by visualizing what it would take to make a community as proud of its zoning ordinance as some now are of their dams and reservoirs.

Interdisciplinary Organization

Execution of the first four recommendations will necessarily include people from all the disciplines within the social sciences as well as many other kinds of experts. Some disciplines have been built on methods of analysis (statistics) while others have concentrated on problem areas (structural engineering). Most disciplines have achieved expertise in a mixture of mutually associated problem areas and have developed tools appropriate to studying those areas. Current discipline boundaries have a long evolutionary history; and since they are not likely to change soon, approaches to help interdisciplinary teams become more productive are needed. Practical techniques for interactive exchange are likely to be more helpful than suggestions for massive reorganization of discipline structure.

The problems of interdisciplinary organization are most intense at the university level because the whole formal structure of the university is based on discipline divisions. Activities to build the discipline within the university are often viewed as helping build the institution as a whole. One interdisciplinary team that studied a water management problem in a university setting recommended that team members who are problem oriented be recruited, that members have sufficient discipline focus to be able to constructively apply discipline tools, that each member be given a viable assignment and clearly defined responsibility, that the team as a whole have access to administrative services and support not subject to any particular discipline, and that informal support be cultivated throughout the university hierarchy and community.[2] A great deal more work needs to be done in order to make interdisciplinary work groups productive.

Professional Staff

Social scientists working on water resources management problems have heretofore largely been concentrated in universities and research institutions. The agencies responsible for management programs have employed a number of economists and some people from the other social sciences, but the growing relative importance of the skills of social scientists to sound water management policy will necessitate cultivation of a much larger body of working social scientists. Such people might typically have a master's degree and the training needed to apply the tools of their discipline to resolving practical problems. They would have a level of expertise in the social sciences roughly equivalent to what most engineers now have in the physical sciences. The concept, however, is not so much to develop social engineers who are able to design social programs as it is to develop professionals who can competently apply the expertise of the social sciences to resolve the full range of management issues.

Academic social scientists must take the responsibility for training such people. Responsible resource management agencies must hire them. Interdisciplinary interactions within the training program will be essential if the academic social scientists are to train well. Short-term job experiences (during a leave of absence or on a consulting basis) helping resource management agencies solve practical problems, will also help academic social scientists stay more relevant.

Academic Support

The training of professional social scientists to work on key water resources management issues must involve the university. One way to strengthen communication lines among interested academic social scientists and between academic groups and the management agencies would be to establish lists of experts (by area of expertise and proven performance) that the agencies could contact on a consulting basis as particular problems arise. The benefits would accrue to the agencies using the social scientists, to the people served by better plans, to the social scientists who build practical experience, and to the students who receive better training. The societies in the social science disciplines can perform a real service and strengthen themselves by developing facilities for recommending expert consultants.

1. Eugene R. Black, *Alternative in Southeast Asia* (New York: Praeger, 1969), p. 129.

2. L. Douglas James, "Remedial Flood Plain Management as the Focus for an Experiment in Interdisciplinary Team Research" (Atlanta: Georgia Institute of Technology, Environmental Resources Center, ERC-0771, October 1971).

9 Epilogue: Recommendations from a Social Science Viewpoint

Thomas Maher

The preceding pages contain an almost bewildering variety of approaches, results, and insights into the social dimensions of water development. Embedded both explicitly and implicitly in this broad overview, however, are a number of key issues which provide foci for further thinking about the role of the social sciences in water development.

IMPLEMENTATION OF RESEARCH FINDINGS

The issue which seems most crucial involves the manner in which knowledge gained through social research comes to be applied by policy makers and practitioners. Even as the contributors to this volume provide much insight into the social consequences of water management, one might legitimately ask how much of the research cited has found its way into policy discussions. It is Gilbert White, in fact, who provocatively raised the issue of applicability, and in doing so, cuts to the heart of the basic problem. In most of the pages of this work (excepting the economics chapter), there is little indication that any effective application has been made of any one study or set of studies. In fact, an overview of the literature across the social sciences hints at fragmentation, incompatability and rapid obsolescence (as a glance at the dates of publication of citations will show).

A register detailing the specific studies which have had direct and visible impact upon policy decisions would be worth compiling.[1] To be most helpful, the register should include an analysis of the social circumstances surrounding successful translation of the data and theory into practice. This gap in our understanding of the employment of scientific information in the context of social institutions signals the availability of a potentially fruitful area of social research. In the evolution of water policy, for example, all concerned could benefit from a better understanding of the set of institutional arrangements which have been successful in seeking, filtering, digesting, and applying the products of social research. Perhaps we may learn by first studying the utilization of *technical* information by water agencies, a process which seems to proceed in a rather effective fashion. Despite the fact that this focus of concern might seem secondary to field studies of water problems, it is in the overall picture a key to effective participation of social scientists in resource development.

The problem of research dissemination and application, of course, transcends the problems of water development. It is appropriate everywhere that institutional structures are involved in the solution of social problems which transcend jurisdictions of the disciplines and professions. City planning, law enforcement, poverty, conservation, and education are examples of multidimensional problems which have taken on a new order of complexity in our increasingly interdependent modern society. Successful attack upon these problems requires a continuing flow of new configurations of knowledge. For a number of reasons, responsible agencies have not developed the capacity for adequate conceptualization of the challenges which are rapidly emerging from these new and comprehensive problem areas. At the same time, information-generating organizations often fail to produce the kinds of knowledge that are most appropriate to this new order of social-technical-environmental problem. In turning more intense attention to the production and application of the results of social research, the behavioral sciences would not only be confronting a problem integral to successful resource development, but also would be analyzing an issue critical to their own maturity and to the determination of the quality of life in the nation.

PUBLIC PERCEPTION OF PROBLEM IMPORTANCE

Several of our authors, notably John Bennett, have shown that throughout history, strategies of water use have been intimately related to the developmental patterns of all cultures. As he surveys the several contributions to the volume, the reader is continually reminded of the importance of effective water development. There is, however, a real question as to public perception of the urgency of the matter. Most intense public controversy over water projects seems to be localized and of relatively short-term duration. One might suspect that to the general American public, water development is an interesting, but not a critical, issue. Other concerns such as crime, consumer abuse, air pollution, mass transit, and inner-city decay are more visible and possibly more glamorous. After all, most Americans have clean, clear water delivered to their homes at what is really infinitesimal cost. Most citizens falling into higher socioeconomic strata have ready access to aquatic recreational areas. Despite politics and bureaucracy, it must seem to many "men on the street" that things do get done in the water area in a reasonably effective manner. Water development, when viewed in the context of the stream of images and concerns encountered daily, is obscured in the public eye by what seem to be more immediate and critical issues.

The nature of public concern over water development is of great consequence for the future of local, state, and federal policy. It should be stressed once more that the question of evolving public opinion and its impact (or lack of impact) on water policy is immediately researchable territory for the behavioral sciences. Intensity and impact of the concern of public-interest groups over time deserves more attention than it appears to have been given by most of the social sciences represented in this volume.

ASSESSMENT OF DECISION-MAKING PROCESSES

Assessment of the consequences of water projects is an issue which has drawn much attention in the past decade. The advent of Planned Program Budgeting Systems (PPBS), for example, has necessitated a focus of attention upon benefit-cost ratios and other economic tools. While we can be encouraged by these advances, the fact is that the evolution of the noneconomic qualitative social indicators remains in an embryonic stage. Although they have received much theoretical attention in the past decade, they have yet to be used widely and effectively in actual decision making. Much more intensive and well-integrated research is needed to design social indicators that will encompass many more dimensions of human activity.

The relatively primitive level of development of social indicators is only one of the obstacles encountered by those interested in comprehensive and systematic assessment of social outcomes. Our institutions have long ago evolved informal modes of evaluating social progress, and of applying this information to gain better mastery of the environment. Although this "indigenous" assessment often proceeds in the absence of needed information and through unexamined frames of reference, it has provided most institutions with at least enough adaptive potential to ensure survival. In contemporary society characterized by information overload and complexity of function, however, neither "indigenous" assessment nor conventional wisdom by themselves can fully alert an organization to oncoming difficulties and/or numerous possibilities for the creative advancement of its purposes.

As the inadequacy of "conventional wisdom" has become more apparent, increasing attention has been devoted to the idea of formal assessment, particularly as it is seen as an integral part of the planning process. Neither organizational theorists nor managers, however, have yet succeeded in developing an effective social guidance function in which elaboration of objectives, assessment, projection, generation of alternatives, decision and implementation are linked in a cyclical process. Perhaps this rational and somewhat theoretical function is yet too fragile to survive in the rough-and-tumble world of power politics. In any event, behavioral scientists interested in planning in any form and especially those concerned with resource development should attempt both to critique current modes of assessment and planning and to invent new approaches. The days of organizational "muddling-through" have outlived their usefulness, for although "muddlers" might master the environment of the moment, the strategic consequences of poor choices and missed opportunities can place the future of the organization in real jeopardy. To be adaptive requires an anticipatory capacity growing out of an ability to assess periodically and to imagine new possibilities continually—a competence which seems poorly developed in many modern bureaucracies.

PLANNING AND GUIDANCE SYSTEMS

The lack of ability of an organization to utilize research findings is a malfunction of its adaptive capacity. So, too, the failure of most organizations to evolve and to integrate planning or guidance subsystems can be seen as a flaw in their overall effectiveness. The dearth of adaptive potential in agencies dealing with water development can be demonstrated time and again. For example, some of the most polluted streams in the nation flow past the university offices and laboratories of the best minds in the field of water resources. Since both local agency and university bureaucracies are locked into their own ineffectiveness, the talents of these individuals are rendered useless in the context of a physically immediate problem.

In this volume, several of the authors have voiced similar concerns. Geographer Gilbert White feels "deep anxiety about the capacity of man's ponderous bureaucracies to deal with the social and physical aspects" of water development. Economist Stephen Smith argues for the creation of adaptive organizations to respond to shifts in demands for water resources. It is well to speak of these concerns, but now is the time to move to a greater level of behavioral analysis. The literature of organizational development should be brought to bear in the context of water or other resource institutions through which man imposes his wishes upon the environment. Suffice to say that a major and perhaps primary role for behavioral scientists in water resources development is penetrating study into the institutional and organizational mechanisms which both inhibit and enhance realization of the best possibilities.

FUTURISTIC STUDIES

Another casualty attributable to our bureaucracies, with their many boundaries and lines of demarcation, is the evolution of integrative theories, such as general systems, which could be of help in forecasting for the formulation and design of water resources projects. Neither are "speculative" methodologies, such as general futuristics, employed in a serious manner. Although a number of our authors mentioned prediction, little attention was given to technique and certainly no attempts were made in the papers to develop images of future water demands and alternative routes to meeting them. The problem seems to be that the techniques of futuristics studies (with the exception of technological forecasting) by their nature are "soft" and speculative, not rigorous enough and too nebulous to be included (at this stage of their development) under the wing of any discipline. Nevertheless, the collected articles suffer from the lack of this future context, and its absence compels us to call for more serious behavioral study of means of projecting social futures, especially as they relate technological interventions into biological and social systems.

Let it be said, however, that technological forecasting (as an element in the cluster of approaches which constitute futuristics) has matured greatly over the past two decades. Practitioners aid in planning water development projects. Indeed, our society with its tendency to specialize and analyze seems most effective in developing and applying technology to immediate, short-term solutions. Yet, effectiveness in prediction declines when we integrate technological and biological systems; and our control and anticipatory capacities literally dissipate when we intervene to link technological, biological, and social systems in dynamic inter-relationship. It appears that the behavior of the social system injects the maximum quantity of unpredictability into our framework, for it is usually the least well understood.

BARRIERS AMONG DISCIPLINES

In many respects, the growing bureaucracy of the American multiversity, has hindered interaction among water-oriented specialists and thus the growth of potentially integrative ideas. Coincidently, the job structure of most governmental water agencies has grown in accordance with the varied disciplines and professions represented in the universities and adds further obstacles. The hegemony of the disciplines in the evolution of research tactics is evidenced first by the organization of this book by disciplines (rather than by problematic divisions) and next by the range of sources utilized by each author. A brief study of citation patterns suggests that there is little relationship among the specialized interests of the authors who have contributed to this volume. Contributors cited a total of 287 primary authors. But only between geography and anthropology were there as many as three cross-citations between disciplines. It is fair to note, however, that if this group of social scientists had been asked to write on a specific water management problem rather than on their own discipline, the overlap would have probably been much greater. Each discipline appears to be in the process of establishing its own social space vis-a-vis water or general resource development. At first glance there seem to be few bridges, actual or theoretical, which could begin to serve as the matrix for building even a rudimentary common language.

On the other hand, there is sympathy for a transcending view. In his essay, Smith argues that "each of the issues (in water development) should be approached in macrocontext." He contends that a holistic approach must become more than a methodology, that it should become essentially an attitude or Weltanschauung. Of course, environmental philosophers have for years been telling us to study natural environments as webs of interconnected processes. General systems theorists, especially, have argued that their perspective is a key element in the repertoire of the successful resource manager. In many respects, systems theory appears to have the potential for becoming the holistic approach which Smith alludes to. Yet, it is discouraging to note that none of the participants in this symposium dealt in-depth with this subject. Perhaps this is an index of how far we have to go.

Here we face a dilemma. In defense of the specialist, it must be recognized that given the limited roles in which most water resource professionals operate, systems theory quickly loses its utility. Specific skills are the coin of the contemporary realm. At the present, then, systems theory and other holistic approaches remain at best an attitude, a perspective, a way of seeing things. They can allow us recovery of wholeness at any point in an investigation and are probably best utilized in an integrated fashion with specialized skills and methodologies. Hopefully, more attention will be given by the behavioral sciences to the conditions under which this integration might be brought about and how it might indeed be amplified.

MAJOR SOCIAL CHANGE

Throughout this work, the various authors implicitly take the position that American society will continue to function much as it has during the past half century. In many respects, this is called for by the format and relates to the current inadequacy of the behavioral sciences to provide meaningful alternative images of society and to project possible futures. While continuation of current societal trends may indeed be the most probable future for the United States, it is certainly conceivable that major elements of surprise await us. Throughout the recent popular-ecology boom, we have heard much shallow speculation about steady-state or no-growth economics. At a more complex level, Forrester and his colleagues at the Massachusetts Institute of Technology have recently advanced novel, controversial but provocative views on the future limits of growth.[2] Realization of any of these images of a social order would dramatically affect the water-society interface. Unfortunately, the disciplines seem to shy from the engagement with these larger or first-order questions.

Much criticism has been leveled at the conservatism of the behavioral sciences. Our small contingent of radical social scientists tend to labor in other vineyards, so that resource policy makers do not often have the opportunity to be nudged into thinking through dramatically varying potential states of society and consequent pattern of resource use. A disciplined though radical critique of contemporary water policy is overdue and could provide an entirely new dimension to the direction of thought in this area. And it can easily be argued that the behavioral sciences can be the best agency to conduct such a critique.

CONCLUDING REMARKS

In retrospect, it can be said that the chapters of this volume touch literally all of the key issues, survey the literature, provide penetrating insights, and sometimes underscore areas of import by conscious or unconscious omission. As seen from these readings, many new avenues and ventures in resource planning appear to be opening for further study by the social sciences. I have, of course, decried what I see as an overemphasis on specialization and analysis and have offered tentative quantitative evidence of the lack of interaction and integration among the social sciences. Bureaucracies in both the university and the agencies appear destined to retard the emergence of interaction and theoretical integration.

Yet, as we attempt to use our knowledge at the technological, biological, and social interface to assume some control over the consequences of our interventions, all hope of attaining real interdisciplinary cooperation and holistic, working overview is not lost. Despite the divergence of citation patterns, the authors introduce a number of potentially integrative questions in embryonic form.

In summary, I would re-emphasize that investigations into the use of research data in applied contexts could well engage the attention of a variety of social scientists. The whole notion of adaptability of organizations and institutions is a critical question which should engage the attention of most social disciplines. The linkage of the question of adaptive organization to water development is thus potentially integrative. Public choice and public opinion and their potential impact on resource development is another area which could benefit by an integrated analysis on the part of several disciplines.

The development of a holistic methodology is not now central to the concerns of most social scientists concerned with water resources. The real utility of systems theory and other integrative strategies has yet to be realized by practitioners. On the other hand, some practitioners and theoreticians in the various social science disciplines are using general systems theory in a wide variety of ways. Perhaps it is this network which may at some future point coalesce and convince a larger audience of both the operational utility and esthetic value of these approaches.

There is a final avenue of study which might provide even more opportunity for integrative endeavor. Our most perceptive observers have for years been calling for the development of an ecological ethic. Despite the recent wave of popular ecology, it is still too early to know whether the ecological movement is a fad or whether it is a harbinger of a new global consciousness. Since the prevailing value system will ultimately affect the nature of the water policy, it might be somewhat interesting and important to learn more about the nature of environmental values from a behavioral point of view.

In effect, I am calling for the expansion of the biological-technological-social interface to include the humanities or at least humanistic concerns. We should know the characteristics of these value systems and their behavior in a public-opinion context. Perhaps more importantly we should understand how to foster appropriate ecological values. It seems essential that the most fundamental human values be considered in the development of public policy.

1. This is not to depreciate the idea of a long-term building of a body of scientific knowledge in this area. More than likely, this is of a top priority for the social sciences. Yet, in order to keep attention focused and to achieve research support, there must be some payoff in terms of applicability. (This, of course, is to say nothing about the immediate needs of social planning in concert with water development.)

2. See especially Donella H. Meadows et al., *The Limits to Growth* (New York: Universe Books, 1972).

NOTES ON CONTRIBUTORS

L. Douglas James is a professor in water resources planning and management in the Environmental Resources Center at the Georgia Institute of Technology, Atlanta, Georgia. His research has emphasized the formulation of flood-control programs through the integration of economics, hydrology, social factors, and considerations relating to the value of open space to urban communities. He is a Ph.D. in civil engineering from the Engineering-Economic Planning Program at Stanford University and has had experience in water planning within California state agencies and in teaching at the University of Kentucky. He is the author of numerous technical publications relating to water resources management and of a textbook, *Economics of Water Resources Planning*.

John W. Bennett is professor of anthropology and senior fellow, Center for the Biology of Natural Systems, Washington University, St. Louis, Missouri. He has specialized recently in research on cultural aspects of economic development, agricultural management, and resource use in various countries. His chosen fields of concentration are economic and ecological anthropology. His most recent long-term research project has been a study of social and economic development, from ecological perspectives, of the human population of a 5,000-square mile region of western Canada. An important by-product of this project has been his work on Hutterian Brethren and Israeli kibbutzim, as examples of communal-collective socioeconomic organization. He is the author of many articles and books on all these subjects. He holds a Ph.D. in anthropology from the University of Chicago.

Stephen C. Smith is associate dean of the School of Natural Resources, College of Agricultural and Life Sciences, and professor of agricultural economics at the University of Wisconsin-Madison. His major interests have focused upon problems of resource economics, institutions, manage-ment organizations, and resource policy with a special emphasis upon water resources issues. After receiving his Ph.D. at the University of Wisconsin-Madison, he has been with the Tennessee Valley Authority, the University of California-Berkeley, and Colorado State University. Also he served as a consultant to the Secretary of the Army in water resources planning, the Water Resources Council, and the states of California, Wisconsin, and Texas. He participated in the initial organization of the Universities Council on Water Resources and served as its board chairman and is on the editorial board for *Water Resources Research* and *Land Economics.* He has published numerous professional articles, edited two books, and authored a number of research monographs.

Gilbert F. White is a professor of geography at the University of Colorado, and director of its Institute of Behavioral Science. His research has cen-tered upon geographic aspects of natural resources management and has involved studies of floodplains in the United States, domestic water use in East Africa, the impacts of large reservoirs, and river basin planning in the Lower Mekong. He is the author of numerous articles and books, including *Strategies of American Water Management.*

Henry C. Hart, professor of political science at the University of Wis-consin-Madison, is returning to the study of political aspects of water resources development and management after twelve years spent on the politics of India. He worked for the Tennessee Valley Authority in the 1930s and 1940s, then received a Ph.D. in political science and regional planning under John Gaus. His dissertation considered the ecological setting and institutional potentialities of the Missouri River basin as indicating the governmental arrangements best suited to developing the basin's water uses. It was published as *The Dark Missouri.* He has published two books on water resource development in India. With Arno Lenz, he started the seminar on river basin planning at the University of Wisconsin.

Sue Johnson is a sociologist currently employed as the program assistant, Center for Developmental Change, at the University of Kentucky, Lex-ington, Kentucky. At present, her major research effort is devoted to studying (with Rabel Burdge) the effect of forced migration from reservoir construction areas on migrants and their community. Data from four reservoir construction sites are being integrated into a model of forced migration. She is also finishing her doctoral dissertation, a demographic study of single, never-married people in the United States from 1900 to the present, for the sociology department at the University of Texas at Austin. Her other research interests include the social aspects of environmental pollution and the role of sociologists in natural resource development.

Thomas Maher is director of research and planning, Ottawa University, Ottawa, Kansas. He holds an M.S. (environmental health sciences) and a Ph.D. (higher education) from the University of Michigan. Prior to coming to Ottawa, he served as associate academic dean of Thomas More College and as director of program analysis and evaluation at the University of Kentucky. His interests center upon "institutional futures."